Key

how to
teach listening

PEARSON
Longman

series editor:
Jeremy Harmer

Pearson Education Limited
Edinburgh Gate
Harlow
Essex
CM20 2JE
England
and Associated Companies throughout the world.

www.longman.com

Printed in Malaysia (CTP-VVP)

Produced for the publishers by Stenton Associates, Saffron Walden, Essex, UK. Text design by Keith Rigley.

Illustration on page 62 by Phillip Burrows.

ISBN 978-1-4058-4775-9

Acknowledgements
We are grateful to the following for permission to reproduce copyright material:

Macmillan Education for an extract from *American Inside Out Pre-Intermediate Student's Book* by Sue Kay, Vaughan Jones and Philip Kerr copyright © Sue Kay, Vaughan Jones and Philip Kerr 2002; and *Inside Out Elementary Student's Book* by Sue Kay and Vaughan Jones copyright © Sue Kay and Vaughan Jones 2002. Reproduced with permission; Oxford University Press for extracts from *Headway Activity Book Elementary* level by Tim Falla, John Soars & Liz Soars, 1994; *Clockwise Classbook Advanced level* by Amanda Jeffries 2001; and *Natural English Intermediate Students Book* by Ruth Gairns & Stuart Redman, 2002 copyright © Oxford University Press; Pearson Education for pages and extracts from the following *Advanced Matters: Student's Book* by Bell & Gower, 1999; *Cutting Edge: A Practical Approach to Task Based Learning: Advanced Student Book* by Sarah Cunningham & Peter Moor, 2003; *Market Leader Upper Intermediate: Coursebook NE* by David Cotton, David Falvey and Simon Kent, 2005; *New Cutting Edge Intermediate: Student's Book* by Sarah Cunningham & Peter Moor, 2005; *Sky 2 Students Book* by Brian Abbs and Ingrid Freebairn, 2005; *Intelligent Business Pre-Intermediate: Course Book* by Christine Johnson, 2006; *Total English Intermediate: Student's Book and DVD Pack* by Antonia Clare and JJ Wilson, 2006; *New Opportunities Pre Intermediate* by Harris and Mower, 2007 and *Total English Advanced: Student's Book and Advanced Workbook* by Antonia Clare and JJ Wilson, 2007 copyright © Pearson Education Limited; PFD for the poem 'Smithereens' by Roger McGough from *In the Glassroom* by Roger McGough copyright © 1976 Roger McGough, reproduced by permission of PFD on behalf of Roger McGough; Thomson Learning for extracts from *Innovations Elementary* 1st edition by Dellar and Walkey 2006, reprinted with permission of Heinle/ELT a division of Thomson Learning www.thomsonrights.com Fax 800 730-2215; and Warner/Chappell Music Ltd for the lyric reproduction of 'Wonderful Tonight' Words & Music by Eric Patrick Clapton © 1977 EC Music Ltd. All rights administered by Warner/Chappell Music Ltd, London W6 8BS, Reproduced by permission.

For my parents, David and Elizabeth, with love and thanks.

Contents

Acknowledgements

How to Teach Listening benefited enormously from the input of a wonderful team of colleagues, friends and family. I am extremely grateful to the following people, who read early drafts of the manuscript: my father, David Henry Wilson, who has read pretty much everything I've written of consequence since I was three, and always found brilliant ways to improve it; my sister, Jenny Wilson, a superb editor with an eagle eye; Nick Dawson, my friend and colleague, for his ideas, injections of humour and dedication (while sitting up in a hospital bed in the summer of 2007, he insisted on reading a chapter of the unfinished manuscript); and my wife and best friend, Alexandra Neves, for her perceptive comments and her support. Thanks also to the anonymous readers for their excellent suggestions, many of which found their way into the final draft of the book.

I'd like to thank the Pearson team, particularly Jeremy Harmer and Katy Wright for their invaluable help in shaping the book, and also my outstanding editor, Helena Gomm, whose expertise, patience and good humour were much appreciated. Thanks are also due to Kate Goldrick for keeping the whole project on track, and for the behind-the-scenes work of Sharon Buss, Jane Reeve, David Briscoe and Eddi Edwards. I would finally like to thank my long-time collaborator on other projects, Antonia Clare, for her encouragement.

J. J. Wilson
New Mexico, USA

Introduction

Listening should be impossible. Fluent speech is a motorway pile-up. One word crashes into the next, and the individual sounds – just like the rear and front ends of cars – are 'concertinaed' out of shape. This is why children love saying, 'I scream for ice cream', and why one learner once misheard 'the stuffy nose can lead to problems' as 'the stuff he knows can lead to problems'. Indeed, when individual words are extracted digitally from recording tape, thereby taken out of their context of connected speech, they are mainly unrecognisable, even to native speakers.

Furthermore, the things listeners do – pick up acoustic signals, re-imagine them into words, turn the words into meaningful sentences, organise the sentences into propositions using linguistic and non-linguistic contexts – are bewilderingly complex cognitive processes. When the acoustic signal is in a foreign language, the processes become more complex still. And yet many language students manage to listen successfully, to maintain conversations, chat with strangers, follow directions to Harrods and listen to radio soap operas and lectures on astrophysics.

How to Teach Listening will answer several questions about the skill: Why do we do it? How do we do it? And the core of the book: How can we (teachers) help others (students) to get better at it?

The book opens with a general discussion of listening, and the main principles behind listening in the ELT classroom. This first chapter, 'Listening in the world and in language learning', also gives the reader the background to some of the debates (bottom-up versus top-down theories, for example) and the research findings that have influenced the way we conceptualise and speak about listening.

In Chapter 2, 'Listening texts and listening strategies', we look at what makes good listening texts and how students can deal with them. There is also a discussion of the merits of authentic versus inauthentic listening texts – a topic much in debate in recent years. In Chapter 3, 'Listening sources, listening tasks', we discuss where to find listening material and what our students might do with it. This chapter also assesses different types of listening text (from television, coursebooks, the Internet, etc).

We then move on to the very practical core of the book. Chapters 4, 5 and 6 provide a number of pre-, while- and post-listening skills and activities, plus discussion of the principles behind them. These chapters should give any teacher, of however limited experience, the tools to teach a listening lesson competently. Here we deal with a number of activities and skills, ranging from the long-established – activating schema and listening for gist – to more innovative ideas stemming from recent developments in ELT.

Chapter 7 covers a number of areas that will concern teachers, such as adapting materials, anticipating problems and planning the listening component of specialised courses like business English or English for young learners.

Finally, Chapter 8, 'Listening in the wider context', discusses long-term development for both the teacher and the student. In many ways this is the most important chapter in the book as it looks at how students can continue to improve their listening outside the classroom and beyond the duration of any formal course. It also deals with professional development for teachers. The chapter considers issues such as assessing listening, using the language laboratory and action research.

How to Teach Listening has been written for teachers, teacher trainers, directors of studies and materials writers involved in teaching English as a foreign language. While the book caters for teachers with little or no experience in the EFL classroom, more experienced teachers will find fresh ideas and perspectives on the teaching of listening. In general, *How to Teach Listening* assumes that the classroom has some form of equipment to expedite the use of recorded material, but the book also provides ideas for the many teaching situations in which power cuts are common, technology is unavailable or untrustworthy, and the teacher's voice is the only reliable form of listening input.

Suggested classroom activities are signalled by this icon.

J. J. Wilson
New Mexico, USA

1 | Listening in the world and in language learning

We have two ears and one mouth so that we can listen twice as much as we speak. (Epictetus)

- **The why and how of listening – motivation and mechanics**
- **The characteristics of spoken English**
- **Why listening is difficult**
- **Bottom-up versus top-down approaches to listening**
- **Why students should listen to English**
- **The place of listening in language teaching**
- **Communicative Language Teaching (CLT)**
- **Hearing English in context**
- **Listening and language learning – six myths?**

The why and how of listening – motivation and mechanics

Animals listen either to stay safe or to get food. Frogs can hear predators and other frogs but nothing else. Kangaroos can hear the scales of a rattlesnake scraping on sand. Bats find their dinner by squeaking and listening to the echoes bouncing off nearby insects. Humans, on the other hand, listen not only for the sound of lions growling in the night and babies crying for food, but also to lectures, grand speeches of all lengths (Fidel Castro's used to go on for hours, apparently), idle chit-chat, radio broadcasts, instructions and, of course, foreign languages. From the small child listening out for the melodious bell of the ice cream van to the adult tuning in to airport announcements, we listen primarily because there are things we need to know. We learn to listen and we listen to learn. But humans also listen to Beethoven and The Beatles, bedtime stories and bad jokes. Why? Because, unlike animals, humans have another reason to listen: sounds can stimulate the imagination and enrich our lives.

The primary purposes of human listening, then, are information-gathering and pleasure, though there are other reasons, such as empathy, assessment and criticism. The types of listening we engage in on a day-to-day basis can be categorised as follows:

Listening for **gist**	This refers to the occasions when we want to know the general idea of what is being said, as well as who is speaking to whom and why, and how successful they are in communicating their point.
Listening for specific information	This refers to the occasions when we don't need to understand everything, but only a very specific part. For example, while listening to a list of delayed trains, we are only interested in hearing news about one particular train – the one we want to catch – and so we listen selectively for this specific information. We ignore everything else.
Listening in detail	This refers to the type of listening we do when, for example, we need to find errors or determine differences between one passage and another. We cannot afford to ignore anything because, unlike listening to a list of delayed trains, we don't know exactly what information will help us to achieve our task.
Inferential listening	This refers to the type of listening we do when we wish to know how the speaker feels. It may involve inferring, which is dealt with in more detail in Chapter 5.

As for the 'how' of listening, nothing can happen without sound waves. These are caused by movement – the whirr of a bat's wings, the tremor of a violin string, the vibrations of the vocal chords, all of which move the air around them. Sound waves need conductors through which to travel, such as air or water (the tagline from the film *Alien* – 'In space no one can hear you scream' – is literally true because there is no air, water or other conductor of sound in space). The sound waves are then 'received'. Unlike spiders, which detect sound through the hair on their bodies, or grasshoppers, which 'hear' with their legs, we have ears, specially formed for receiving sound waves. The outer ear catches these vibrations, which then pass through the middle ear, consisting of the ear drum, bones and membranes, and then through the cochlea (named after the Latin for a shell, because of its snail-like shape), which is part of the inner ear. Finally, the sound waves are interpreted by the brain, and if we are really listening (that is, concentrating on the message) as opposed to merely hearing (when the same process takes place but without a sustained focus on the part of the recipient), we may then laugh, cry or slouch off to do our homework.

The characteristics of spoken English

In recent years, with the advent of text-messaging and chat rooms, writing has begun to assume some of the features of speaking: informality, lack of attention to punctuation, transience, real-time interaction. As Jeremy Harmer writes, 'on the Internet, live sessions are not called *chats* by accident'. Indeed, the word 'chat', for many teenagers and children, is associated more now with reading and writing than speaking and listening.

common

Listening and reading both involve the decoding of messages, but there are, of course, significant differences between the two. Firstly, reading takes place over space – pages, signs, the backs of envelopes – whereas listening takes place over time. Most oral data is not recorded and has no permanent record. It is based on spontaneous performance, an invisible ink that usually disappears from the memory within seconds.

Because listening takes place over time, not space, the gaps between words that exist in writing do not exist in speech, so the listener imagines them into being. This segmentation of words from the flow of speech (recognising word boundaries) is often problematic for listeners and occasionally amusing. Rock guitarist Jimi Hendrix didn't sing, *'scuse me while I kiss this guy*, but *'scuse me while I kiss the sky*, and, if you believe one well-known linguist, the words of the hymn, 'Gladly my cross I'd bear' are routinely thought to be about a cross-eyed bear. In fact, to listeners, speech sometimes comes across like this:

Wheretherearenonaturalpausescausedbythespeaker'sbreathingtheflowofspeechisonelongsound.

Another key difference between listening and reading is that listening involves getting to grips with features of pronunciation such as **elision**, **assimilation** and **intrusion**.

Elision is when sounds are omitted, usually from the beginning or end of a word, in order to make pronunciation of the utterance easier for the speaker. For example:

She sat next to the wall.

The *t* of *next* is elided into the *t* of *to* so that it becomes /nekstə/, but we know that she did not sit *necks to* the wall (we can safely assume that she only has one neck).

Assimilation takes place when the first of a series of sounds changes to accommodate subsequent sounds. This often happens because the tongue cannot get into place quickly enough during connected speech to articulate the next sound. For example:

Tony's a heart breaker.

The *t* sound in *heart* changes to either a glottal stop or a *p* in this context: (/hɑːpbreɪkə/), though Tony breaks girls' hearts, not harps.

Intrusion is when a sound is added in order to allow the speaker to link two words more easily. For example:

He doesn't have an original idea in his head.

Speakers of British English often add an intrusive *r* sound between *idea* and *in* (/aɪdɪərɪn/); it sounds as though he doesn't have an original 'eye-deer' in his head, whatever that may be.

Another feature of pronunciation is that formulaic phrases are often chunked; this means the phrases are said rapidly as if they are one word. For example:

/nəʊwɒdaɪmiːn/ for *know what I mean?*
/gɪmiːəbreɪk/ for *give me a break*

All of these are potentially problematic for listeners, though not for readers. For a more detailed analysis of pronunciation, see *How to Teach Pronunciation.*

A further difference between listening and reading is that listening is often interactive: two or more people in face-to-face contact. This means that non-verbal communication – for example, body language – plays a role, and of course listeners are often able to ask questions, signal lack of understanding, interrupt, etc, which readers cannot do. This is why **emoticons** – those smiley faces in email correspondence such as ;) (a winking face, denoting irony) – were invented for writers (not all writers are fans; Geoffrey Nunberg wrote that the word *emoticon* 'deserves to die horribly in a head-on collision with *infotainment*'). When reading, we have to rely far more on our **inner voice**, words that we form in the mind but do not say aloud, whereas the spoken word always contains an element of performance. Pitch, **intonation**, tone, volume and patterns of **stress** can all make words come alive. Conversely, great speeches and riveting court cases, when later read as transcriptions, often come across as mind-numbingly dull simply because the drama of live interaction is missing.

Other features of this interactivity include forms for signalling attention, such as *Hey!* and **vocatives**, which are ways of addressing someone (*Mum, honey, Jim, mate*). These features are seen infrequently in writing. Question tags (e.g. *haven't you? didn't she?*) appear in approximately a quarter of all questions uttered in conversation, while in academic prose they form less than 1 per cent. Other ways of eliciting a response in conversation include greetings, farewells and **response elicitors** such as *Okay?* and *See?*

The spontaneity involved in most speech (lectures are an exception, and these often contain many of the features of writing) means that false starts, hesitation, redundancy and ungrammatical sentences are extremely common, whereas writing usually involves well-formed sentences and careful advance planning. In most formal or semi-formal writing, deviations from standard grammar are rare – at least among proficient writers.

Finally, we should mention the status of listening in relation to reading. Storytelling is an ancient art, while writing, as done by the general public, is a relatively modern phenomenon. In the past, literacy was solely for the ruling classes and the clergy. But written documents have status because they have permanence. They are also associated with vital encoded information such as the law, national constitutions, contracts, gas bills. Back in 1923, the London Stock Exchange adopted its motto 'My word is my bond', but these days an oral agreement doesn't count for much in the eyes of the law. As Mark Twain once said, 'Oral contracts – they ain't worth the paper they're written on'. A boss wanting something guaranteed will say 'Give it to me in writing'.

Because literacy is so closely bound to information and vice versa, and because literacy has to be taught (whereas listening to L1, a person's first language, comes naturally), most modern educational systems, and therefore societies at large, emphasise reading above listening.

Why listening is difficult

Many of the differences between reading and listening illustrate just why listening is considered a difficult skill. The difficulties can be grouped into four general categories: characteristics of the message, the delivery, the listener and the environment.

Characteristics of the message

Some time during the 1980s a software company was demonstrating its latest product: speech recognition technology. A member of the audience was invited to say a sentence which would then be 'recognised' by a computer and displayed in written form for all to see. The participant, deciding to stay on topic, said, 'It's hard to recognise speech'. The computer promptly, and to much laughter, flashed up, 'It's hard to wreck a nice beach'.

This story may be apocryphal – although Bill Gates admits that Microsoft's speech recognition group calls itself the Wreck a Nice Beach group – but it is a small illustration of the problems (for computers and people!) involved in listening to connected speech. As Rick Altman wrote, 'For us [teachers], listening is like reading speech. For students it is more like finding the objects hidden in the drawings of trees'. Knowing the written form of a word is no guarantee that students will recognise the spoken form. As already mentioned, recognising word boundaries is problematical, but also the irregular spelling system of English does not help matters. A sentence (however unlikely) such as:

Mr Clough from Slough bought enough dough.

would probably cause problems for students to pronounce even if they 'knew' the words, because of the variety of ways in which one combination of letters (*ough*) can be pronounced.

There are also, of course, 'slips of the ear' – simple mishearing – as when the anti-hero of Bret Easton Ellis's novel *American Psycho* hears 'murders and executions' instead of 'mergers and acquisitions' (although some would call this a Freudian slip, bearing in mind the character's murderous habits).

Other linguistic difficulties include unknown words, lexical density (short spaces of time between content words, forcing the listener to concentrate harder), and complex grammatical structures. Non-linguistic characteristics of the message include familiarity of the topic, text type and cultural accessibility. We will deal with all of these in more detail in Chapter 2.

Characteristics of the delivery

Mode of delivery is a vital factor. It may be helpful here to distinguish between **reciprocal** and **nonreciprocal** listening. Reciprocal listening involves interaction between two or more people; in other words, there is a conversation. Reciprocal listening allows the use of **repair strategies**: speakers can react to looks of confusion by backtracking and starting again; listeners can ask for clarification, ask the speaker to slow down, etc.

Nonreciprocal listening describes a situation in which the listener has no opportunity to contribute to a dialogue, for example while watching television or listening to the radio. In these situations, the listener's lack of control over the input is a crucial issue. The listener has no influence over factors such as the speed at which the speaker talks, the vocabulary and grammar used, and no recourse to asking for repetition of a word if the speaker's pronunciation renders it incomprehensible. It seems surprising to us now, but when American 'talkies' were first shown in the cinema in Britain, audiences had great difficulty in understanding the American accent.

For all of the above reasons, nonreciprocal listening is usually regarded as more difficult than reciprocal listening.

Other characteristics of delivery include organisation (do the speakers ramble on, jumping from topic to topic, or are they concise?), duration, number of speakers (the more speakers, the more difficult it is to follow the conversation) and accent. We will look at these more closely in Chapter 2.

Characteristics of the listener

As any teacher can testify, some students get sidetracked easily and simply lack the ability to sustain concentration. Other students have problems motivating themselves to listen. These are often long-term issues.

Yet other students learn better using modes that are different from listening. According to **Multiple Intelligences theory**, people possess different 'intelligences', such as linguistic, logical-mathematical, spatial, bodily-kinaesthetic, musical, interpersonal, intrapersonal and naturalist. These can be related to preferred modes of learning. Most people, at some unconscious level, realise they are more predisposed to one way of learning than to another. Someone with musical intelligence may choose to learn a language through listening to songs; someone with bodily-kinaesthetic intelligence might prefer to learn by acting, moving to sounds or physically piecing together words on wooden blocks.

Besides the students' individual dispositions, there is the age factor. Young learners can be loosely categorised as anything from the age of seven or eight (younger than this may be considered very young learners) up to those in their mid to late teens. Students at this age differ from adults considerably in their needs as listeners. Some of these differences may include shorter attention spans, fewer cognitive abilities, difficulties concentrating on disembodied voices and the importance of visual stimuli and music. Another consideration is children's familiarity and confidence with multimedia material, particularly when they reach their teenage years, which often surpasses that of older generations. We will look at the challenges of planning lessons for young learners in Chapter 7.

At the other end of the scale, older learners – those above the age of seventy, for example – sometimes have difficulties with listening due primarily to physiological factors. These might include declining abilities in hearing in general or problems with short-term memory. Teachers of older learners may need to proceed more slowly with instructions and they may also find that their students' ability to cope with fast connected speech lags behind the students' cognitive abilities. The ideas contained in Chapter 7 for adapting materials are applicable for such students.

Some temporary characteristics that affect listening might include anxiety (for example, in test conditions), tiredness, boredom or the listener having a cold (blocked sinuses affect the aural system).

Characteristics of the environment

Environmental conditions which may affect listening performance include the temperature of the room (hot rooms induce sleep), background noise (heavy traffic, for example) or defective equipment which affects the clarity of a recording.

Another problem which does not fit neatly into any of our other categories is the role of memory in listening. As we process one word, another word is 'incoming'. The mind gets flooded with words. Unless we are well attuned to the rhythm and flow of the language, and the way in which a piece of discourse is likely to continue, this can lead to **overload**, which is one of the main reasons why students 'switch off'. The idea may be heresy to poets, but the mind isn't really concerned with individual words. We tend not to remember these with any exactitude, but rather the general meanings that they convey. Jack Richards states that 'memory works with propositions, not with sentences'. Many of our students are faced with badly-conceived tasks that test their memory instead of guiding them towards comprehension, an issue that will be dealt with in Chapter 3.

Related to memory is the process of activating the listener's prior knowledge, a technique that can help to reduce the memory load. We describe this process as activating **schemata**. What is a schema? Imagine I say that I am going to the bank. Your mental model of this activity probably goes something like this: a person walks towards a brick building, pushes open a door made of wood and glass, and stands in a queue for half an hour. This is your schema for 'going to the bank'. Supposing, instead, I walk up to the bank, put on my ski mask, pull out my shotgun and shout, 'Everybody hit the floor! This is a stick-up!', your schema for 'going to the bank' is temporarily short-circuited. You revert, instead, to your schema for 'robbing a bank'. You probably imagine that I will now say something like, 'Hand over the money!' to the cashier, as this is a part of the mental model for bank robberies. If I then pause, put my shotgun down, turn to the man in the director's chair and say, 'I forgot my line. Can we do that again?', you need to 'retune' your schema once more in order to understand the situation. A schema, then, is a mental model based on a typical situation.

Activating the students' schemata allows them to tune in to the topic and helps them to develop their expectations of the input, a crucial factor in getting them to predict content. There are many ways of activating our students' schemata (showing pictures and asking questions are among the most common), as we will see in Chapter 4.

Bottom-up versus top-down approaches to listening

Listening, then, is difficult for many reasons. While examining the difficulties, researchers have tended to use two models to describe the listening process. These are the **bottom-up** model and the **top-down** model. The bottom-up model emphasises the decoding of the smallest units – phonemes and syllables – to lead us towards meaning. The approach is based on discrete units of language in the text.

The top-down model emphasises the use of background knowledge to predict content. This may refer to world knowledge, knowledge of the speaker or context, or analogy (if the situation is familiar, listeners can guess what they're going to hear next). The top-down model is based, at least in part, on the listener; much of the comprehension relies on what happens in the mind before the listening has even begun, whereas the bottom-up approach depends more on the sounds heard.

There has been much debate in recent years about which model is most salient when we listen to foreign languages. Until fairly recently it was assumed that most errors in listening comprehension were caused by students mishearing individual words – a failure of the bottom-up process. Celce-Murcia and Olshtain, quoting a study of academic listening, report one student hearing 'communist' when the lecturer said 'commonest', and another student hearing 'plastic bullets' instead of 'postal ballots'. Michael Rost reports that a lecturer said, 'another factor [promoting bilingualism] is migration' and one student later wrote a summary stating that 'one factor is vibration'.

Recent research, however, suggests that it is often top-down approaches that cause mistakes in listening tasks, a typical occurrence being that the students know the topic, hear some familiar vocabulary and make wild guesses about the content. It is an area of ongoing research, but what we can say with some certainty is that we use both processes simultaneously when we listen, something that is known as the **interactive model**.

We have so far dealt with the characteristics and difficulties of listening, and a model commonly used to describe the process. These sections are the 'how' of listening. Now we turn to the 'why'. Why do students need to listen to the language?

Why students should listen to English

On 19 August 1991, Mikhail Gorbachev, then the President of the Soviet Union, was placed under house arrest in his dacha – a holiday home – in the Crimea, while eight of his hard-line colleagues attempted a coup. The plotters announced that Gorbachev 'was unable to perform his presidential duty for health reasons'. When Gorbachev emerged three days later to be restored to power, he surprised the world by announcing that in order to find out what was going on in his country he had listened to the BBC World Service – a bad coup for the plotters (seven were arrested, the eighth killed himself) but a good one for the BBC.

Earlier in the chapter we stated that people listen primarily for information and pleasure. Here we will look at the reasons for listening specifically to English. There are actually two questions subsumed in the title of this section: 1) Why English (as opposed to Finnish, German or Xhosa)?; and 2) Why listen (as opposed to read, write or speak)? The first answer to the first question, as Gorbachev's experiences testify, is access to the world.

Access to the world

Ever since Paul Julius Reuter started sending news by carrier pigeon in 1850, to be followed shortly afterwards by the founding of Reuter's news agency in London (its growth was based on journalistic scoops such as the assassination of President Lincoln), the spread of international news has been dominated by Britain and the US. Today, although there are a number of large media organisations growing rapidly in other countries, most foreign news on the world's television screens comes from either Reuters (UK) or APTN (a US company). Besides these media giants, the BBC was founded in 1922 to broadcast over the radio, and its first Director General, John Reith, announced that the company should 'inform, educate and entertain'. These are also three very good reasons for listening to English.

Pleasure

Perhaps even more than through news and information-sharing, the English language has spread through entertainment, primarily Hollywood and pop music. For many students, music is the first contact point with English and it can be a great motivator, especially for teenagers who want to understand just what it is that well-known singers like Coldplay, Eminem or Britney Spears are really singing. For young learners, who have a shorter concentration span than older students and little experience of the world to apply, enjoyment is one of the main criteria for any activity.

Travel/tourism

Music crosses borders easily, and so do people. It is often the case that the common language between the traveller and the host, wherever he or she may be, is English. For this reason English is sometimes called a **lingua franca**. It is a tool for international communication.

Work purposes and academic requirements

English is the international language of the seas (sailors have their own dialect called Seaspeak, based on a simplified version of English), of medicine, science and technology. All over the world, conferences serving almost any modern field of inquiry – biotechnology, quantum physics – often take place in English. This also means that as an academic requirement in a number of fields, the ability to comprehend spoken English becomes mandatory.

Business, too, in the age of globalisation, has come to rely on English as the common language for people from disparate nations. For many individuals, job prospects, status, financial reward and opportunity for travel all depend partly on their English. Furthermore, companies seeking to expand beyond their own borders realise they will often need to operate in what is sometimes called **international English**, a variety that some regard as simplified.

These are all valid reasons for listening to English, but it must be conceded that no one knows how long the language will retain its predominant position. While the dominance of English is, of course, connected with historical and political factors such as colonisation, which are beyond the scope of this book, it must also be mentioned that Spanish, Mandarin Chinese and Arabic are also spreading rapidly.

So far in this section we have mainly focused on the question 'Why English?', and looked at 'real world' reasons for listening to the language. We will now move on to 'Why listen?' and examine some of the methodological reasons for listening.

The place of listening in language teaching

Of the four skills (reading, writing, listening and speaking) that are generally recognised as the keys to 'knowing' a language, listening is probably the least understood, the least researched and, historically, the least valued. David Nunan describes it as 'the Cinderella skill', overshadowed by its big sister, speaking. *but listening is a complex process*

In the past, foreign languages were learnt mainly by reading and translating rather than listening. In the second half of the twentieth century, increased research into how people learn both first and second languages, as well as developments in linguistics, sociology and anthropology, led to an understanding that listening is probably the key initial skill. After all, we cannot talk without listening first.

Another factor that led to changes in foreign language education was spying. During the Second World War the US's Army Specialized Training Program trained a number of soldiers to learn foreign languages. These soldiers spent years studying grammar and vocabulary from books, but when it came to actually speaking the language in order to infiltrate a country or to listen in on enemy conversations over the radio waves, their language skills were inadequate. The authorities realised that a new methodology was required, and this is how **Audiolingualism** came into being.

Audiolingualism, which uses recorded drills (the development of technology, including the widespread use of recording equipment in classrooms, was significant), put listening at the forefront of language teaching pedagogy. The idea was based on a premise from psychology called **behaviourism**, in which the subject responds to a prompt in order to gain a reward. In the context of language learning, students were to hear passages – mainly dialogues – which contained the target grammatical patterns, and then the students would repeat the pattern, thereby 'learning' it. The reward, in this case, consisted of a better understanding of the language. The syllabus would include structures of gradually increasing complexity.

Whole generations studied English by sitting at a console in a language laboratory, endlessly repeating 'The book is on the table', and thousands of them succeeded, even if the listening passages that they used were neither natural nor contextualised.

Then Noam Chomsky famously disputed the idea that people could learn languages through habit-formation. He put forward the idea of generative grammar, arguing that language could not be delimited to a fixed number of sentences, but that people were capable of expressing an infinite number of thoughts, and that pedagogy should reflect this. With the growing popularity of Chomsky's ideas, Audiolingualism's days were numbered, to be replaced in the 1970s by more humanistic methods. The centrality of listening, however, remained, and was reinforced by the work of Stephen Krashen.

Listening was at the forefront of Krashen's **input hypothesis**. According to Krashen, languages are acquired when people understand messages (he called these messages **comprehensible input**). The input hypothesis is consistent with what we know about children's L1 acquisition. A parent says to a toddler, 'Pass me the paper, please' or 'Put your hat on'. Although the child may not say anything, he or she is taking in the language during this **silent period** and the brain is storing it all up, categorising words, parsing verbs, examining meaning. A few months later the child begins to speak.

Although Krashen produced little empirical evidence, the theory appealed to common sense and became extremely influential in the field of second language acquisition (SLA) studies. The methodology that Krashen designed in order to put this and other theories into practice was called The Natural Approach, which places listening at its centre, with the teacher speaking to the students (telling stories, etc), but not necessitating an oral response from them. The language was to be graded according to the natural order in which people acquire L2 (for example, the present perfect is 'late acquired' and so would not feature on the syllabus until the students were fairly proficient).

The input hypothesis and the silent period also formed the basis for James Asher's methodology called Total Physical Response (TPR). The principles behind it were: learning L1 and learning L2 are similar processes; listening comes before speaking; delaying the need to speak alleviates stress on the learner; children and adults respond well if asked to react physically to speech. In practice, students were to hear instructions given by the teacher and act upon them; for example, the teacher would say 'Stand up' and the student would do so. There was no pressure on students to speak.

Some practitioners would argue that the techniques of TPR are to be used sparingly (after all, a linguistic diet of commands is probably only useful for future drill sergeants), and mainly with beginners, elementary levels and children. However, the activities in TPR can provide a pleasant change of pace in language classes, and are good for the type of learners who enjoy learning by moving around. Another benefit is that TPR activities require little preparation. Besides giving orders, a number of variations can be useful for a sagging class (these will be dealt with in Chapter 5), and the technique has been incorporated into many game-like activities that can serve as a non-threatening way to get, and react to, input.

Input

The idea of input has been central in the elevation of listening to its recent status in language learning. But what does aural input consist of? A short answer is: any aspect of the language. A carefully scripted piece of input for the language class will contain target grammar and/or target vocabulary. More natural input will probably also contain

discourse markers, examples of pragmatic use of language, features of intonation, etc. Input gives opportunities for **incidental vocabulary learning** – when students pick up on words/phrases by chance and circumstance rather than by the design of a materials writer or teacher. Incidental vocabulary learning often comes about because the topic, and the vocabulary learnt, may be of personal interest to the listener. Perhaps he or she really needs the words to accomplish a personal goal. This type of vocabulary learning – achieved because of personal interest or necessity rather than, say, the demands of a coursebook – is often more memorable for students so they are more likely to retain the words in the long term.

We can make a distinction between **roughly-tuned** and **finely-tuned input**. Roughly-tuned input is only approximately at the students' level; it permits them to understand the message although there may be many aspects of this message that elude comprehension. An example of roughly-tuned input might be a teacher telling the students a story. Here, the features in italics may be beyond an intermediate student's *production*, but the whole passage is comprehensible:

> 'Well, I read something in the paper *the other day* on a very similar *theme, basically* looking at which cities are the best to live in. *It took into account various criteria,* such as cost of living, safety, education, transport system, *and so on.* And I think *it came up with* a list of about twenty, and of these, five were in Switzerland.'

Finely-tuned input is more carefully controlled. It doesn't contain complex grammatical constructions or vocabulary far beyond the students' current level, and is designed so as not to distract the students from the target grammar/vocabulary. In some cases, finely-tuned input may contain only structures and vocabulary that the students have already covered on the syllabus. Here is an example of finely-tuned input for a low-intermediate class:

> 'So, I used to work in Belgium, in Brussels, actually. And I used to travel to work by car, 'cos I used to have a Ford … you know a Ford, a type of … make of car? And it used to take me about, about twenty minutes to get to work. OK?'

The passage above, as you've probably guessed, is designed to present *used to*.

In practice, students benefit from a combination of roughly-tuned and finely-tuned input, the one for more natural examples of language use, the other to provide crystal clear examples of target grammar.

Communicative Language Teaching (CLT)

The 1970s saw the first stirrings of **Communicative Language Teaching** (CLT). This has been widely, though not universally, adopted, and in developed countries is arguably the dominant methodology. It emphasises the use of English for real communication rather than demonstration (or 'display') of target grammar and vocabulary. Using information-gap activities, role-plays, games, discussion of real issues, etc, CLT seeks to engage the student on a personal level through meaningful interaction and personalisation. TPR is often seen as a form of CLT, but one difference is that CLT, in its broader use, encourages dialogue from the start. Even with very little English at their disposal, students attempt to develop **communicative competence** using any means they can – gesture, mime, **interlanguage** (this is the student's attempts at L2, which may not be grammatically correct but form part of the developmental stage towards proficiency), etc.

CLT brought with it significant developments in terms of listening to L2. It emphasised authenticity of materials, contexts and responses. The passages students listen to in a communicative approach tend to be closer to real-life use of language than was the case in, say, Audiolingualism, which often used contrived dialogues as carriers of the target grammar. CLT uses findings from research into **pragmatics**, **discourse analysis** and **sociolinguistics** in order to show how real communication takes place, instead of an idealised version.

The other main development in listening in CLT stems from the ways in which the passages are used – in other words, what the students do with them. In CLT there is more room for personal, emotional or critical responses to the content, and less emphasis on drilling and repetition. Listening in CLT has a communicative purpose in that students are expected to use the information they hear, just as we do when we listen outside the classroom.

Hearing English in context

No matter what methodology or approach we use, a characteristic product of language teaching is *fragments*. Most methodologies around the world use a language syllabus that is incremental, so, for example, students half learn the present perfect one day, then some items of a lexical set the next, etc. Learning a language is like assembling a jigsaw puzzle. Jigsaw puzzles tend to be more easily completed when we have an idea of what the whole will look like. Similarly, listening to a piece of extended discourse gives the students a whole, complete view of what English sounds like. Listening, then, can momentarily bring together the fragments.

Listening to English in context also reminds us that **appropriacy** – the right words for the right social context – and **register** – the degree of formality – are vital factors in the goal of communicative competence. Imagine a foreign student going to a job interview in a New York bank and greeting the interviewer with, 'Hey, man, how are you doing?' The English is correct, but the register is too informal. Language use occurs in authentic contexts which involve human relationships and 'fixed' situations that may require formulaic language in order to proceed smoothly. Sometimes we teach English – and our students perceive English – as if it is an abstract system in a context-free world of its own. Listening reinforces the importance of context.

A model for speaking

Language is primarily an aural/oral phenomenon. Most students, when asked why they are studying English, say that they want to *speak* the language. Relatively few say 'I want to improve my reading/writing'.

One thing that listening can do is to provide a model, or an ideal, for students to aspire to, copy or learn from. If our students *hear* highly proficient speakers

2 **10.5** Listen to three speakers and answer the questions. What does each speaker talk about? Are they having a moan, raving about something or taking a stand? What are their opinions?

3 Prepare to moan, rave or take a stand about an issue of your choice. Use the pictures opposite to help you if you need inspiration.

presenting a budget or ordering their chicken tikka, it will help them do the same more effectively than any *explanation* or *written language summary* we can offer. Students can familiarise themselves with discourse patterns, intonation, pronunciation, rhythm, etc while listening. The example on page 20 is taken from a coursebook.

Building confidence

Many students get nervous about conversing in L2 in real-life contexts as this presents numerous difficulties for them, not the least of which is the lack of control over what their interlocutor will say. Here are some quotations from students concerning listening.

> 'It make me nervous because they speak fast and I can't always follow.'

> 'I am too shy to talk to people here because sometimes I can't understand what they say and it's very embarrassing. It's boring for them when I keep saying "Sorry, can you repeat?"'

> 'Listen is difficult. I am good in asking questions but when they reply I don't understand nothing!'

Listening practice in class can help to overcome these fears. There is an element of safety in language classes – most of the mistakes our students make and the problems they have in comprehending English won't cost them anything in the privacy of the classroom. It must be said, too, that one of the teacher's roles is to prepare students to succeed in any given listening task, thereby building their confidence. Just how teachers can do this will be the wider subject of this book.

Listening and language learning – six myths?

We began this chapter with some facts about listening. As we move on to the processes involved in listening and language learning, we find that facts often give way to grey areas and unresolved issues. There are a number of myths and half-truths that abound on the topic of listening and, in particular, the teaching of it. These often stem from an incomplete understanding of general principles, or they may be false rituals which need to be analysed and, in some cases, debunked. Let's consider them.

1 You can't teach people how to listen.
To a certain extent, this is true. Listening is an internal skill based on mapping what we hear against our expectations and what we know. But there are many things teachers can do to help students. They can provide continual exposure to appropriate listening material with carefully sequenced practice activities which give the students opportunities to listen successfully and build confidence. They can also guide students towards more efficient listening through the teaching of strategies.

2 Listening is a 'passive' skill.
Listening is not passive. Indeed, it is extremely active, but all the activity happens in the mind. Listeners guess, predict, infer, criticise and, above all, interpret.
   How and why do listeners guess? When we listen, an acoustic signal (the sound wave) is analysed according to a mental checklist of recognisable, semi-recognisable and unrecognisable sounds. But if the acoustic signal is unclear, perhaps because of background

noise or the speaker's accent, we make a guess, using context to inform our guesses. One piece of research involved participants listening to a doctored recording. They heard sentences with some initial sounds replaced by a cough, for example the *d* of *date*:

'Check the calendar and the #ate.'

or the initial *g* of *gate*:

'Paint the fence and the #ate.'

When asked, not one of the listeners noticed the missing *d* or commented on the impossibility of painting the *ate*; the listeners simply imagined the word *date* and the word *gate* based on the context. The research points clearly to the fact that our background knowledge sometimes overrides the acoustic signal we hear.

What about prediction? Listening is a process of hypothesising in real time. As one **utterance** (a unit of speech; for example, a sentence) is made, we hypothesise about its meaning. As the next utterance is made, we may be able to confirm or revise our hypothesis. And so it continues. Sometimes our hypotheses are confirmed or negated even before an utterance is complete: we hear:

'The packets of'

and prepare ourselves for a noun – the packets of what? The sentence continues:

'The packets have been delivered'

and we revise our interpretation of the *of* sound. Furthermore, at some point we have all finished someone else's sentence for them or had our own sentences finished for us. This is prediction in action, based on knowledge of the speaker, the context and how language works.

Regarding interpretation and inference, we 'fill gaps' all the time as listeners, again using everything we know about the topic and about the balance of power between speakers and listeners. People do not always say what they mean or mean what they say, but listeners try to extract the truth from what they hear. According to American playwright David Mamet, 'People speak for one reason and one reason only: to get what they want'. Whether this is true or not, utterances do not exist in some kind of neutral zone; they are always in a context – cultural, personal, situational – and they have to be interpreted by the listener. This is why not all estate agents are millionaires – listeners recognise contexts and listen critically.

Listening, then, is an activity that takes place on many levels simultaneously, from recognition of individual phonemes to recognition of patterns of intonation that alert us to irony, sarcasm, anger, delight. Clearly, it is a receptive rather than a passive skill.

3 It is easier for students to understand native speakers of English than foreign speakers of English.

This myth might be common in multilingual classes, but less so in monolingual classes. In monolingual classrooms it may be easier for students to understand each other than a native speaker. On meeting problematic sounds – for example, **consonant clusters** (several consecutive consonants) as found in words like *through* or *synchronise* – students with the same first language (L1) are more likely to deal with these problems in similar ways.

In multilingual classes, where there may be no relation between the students' native languages, a native speaker may be easier to understand as he or she speaks the type of English to which the students have mostly been exposed. Much depends, of course, on other conditions, such as the speed at which a speaker talks, experience of and exposure to the target language, and how sympathetic to the problems of second language (L2) listening the speaker is. Furthermore, it must be recognised that most interaction in English now occurs between non-native speakers who may have learnt the language using a similar syllabus and would therefore be familiar with similar structures.

A further point to make is that the type of English our students will be exposed to, naturally, affects the listening work we do in class; if our students need only to listen to English as it is spoken in India, for example, there may be little point exposing them to varieties such as British or Australian English.

4 The skills involved in listening to a foreign language are the same as those that we use for listening to our native language.

This is largely true, but there are some differences in how we apply those skills. While listening to our own language, we may do so 'with half an ear'; that is, listen without concentrating fully but still understanding the message. This is far less common while listening to a foreign language because the listener, unless highly proficient, needs to give their full attention to the message.

Another difference concerns the use of **compensation strategies**. L2 listeners, in general, need to guess more than L1 listeners, and rely more on context in order to compensate for gaps in their knowledge of the language.

5 While listening in class, students shouldn't try to understand every word.

Speech usually consists of more words than are necessary, apart from some exceptions such as formal speeches and other scripted passages. **Redundancy** is commonplace as we repeat ourselves, and use *um* and *er* while searching for the right words. Redundancy makes listening easier because it gives the listeners time to assimilate new information while ignoring things they know already – in fact, redundancy allows us to be lazy because we don't have to focus fully on every word.

Furthermore, many words such as auxiliary verbs, articles, and prepositions like *of* act as the glue that holds syntax together rather than as powerful carriers of meaning; as such, they command a listener's attention far less than 'content words' such as nouns and main verbs. It is easy to understand this sentence:

_____ Bishop _____ Birmingham bought _____ car.

without:

The _____ of _____ _____ a _____ .

However, while it is undeniable that certain types of word are more important than others for the comprehension of messages, until students have reached a basic level of competence in the language, they cannot know, from meaning alone, which words are important. It is also too simplistic to say that auxiliaries, articles, prepositions, etc are unimportant. There is a small difference between *I took the gun for her* and *I took the gun from her* in terms of phonology, but a huge difference in meaning.

The essential point here concerns **automaticity**. Once students have a command of the basics of grammar and vocabulary, they can afford not to listen to every word, because they automatically recognise which words are significant and which they can ignore. This is partly accomplished through the way stress works in English, the stressed content words being longer, louder and of a different pitch to unstressed words. The competent listener automatically ignores *the, of* and *a* in favour of *Bishop, Birmingham, bought* and *car*.

6 Students shouldn't be allowed to read the scripts of recordings.

The main argument against reading scripts while listening to the recording is that reading and listening at the same time can lead to a 'divided attention' situation, with the student focusing on the reading more than the listening. This is a procedural issue. The script could be used at the final stage of the listening sequence (the students should already have heard the recording at least twice), as a tool for solving language/listening problems and confirming – or otherwise – the students' ideas about what they heard.

The other argument against scripts is that students will come to rely on them. As Marc Helgesen elegantly puts it: 'Life … doesn't come with a tapescript.' This is true, but outside the classroom life doesn't come with grammar drills, comprehension questions, putting people into pairs, gap-fills, and most of the other techniques and apparatus of language teaching. English lessons are preparation for real language use in the outside world; the class is not an end in itself.

Overall, it must be acknowledged (and students acknowledge it regularly) that the script can be an invaluable resource. It allows students to see the difference between the written and spoken form of words. It also allows them to see which words are 'swallowed'. They can pick out and notice prominent grammar points, and focus on form. The script, in other words, can be a starting point for teaching.

Conclusions | *In this chapter we have:*

- looked at how the ears and the brain work when we listen.
- examined the characteristics of spoken English.
- talked about some of the difficulties involved in listening, which may be categorised into four sets of characteristics, relating to the message, the delivery, the listener and the environment.
- discussed bottom-up, top-down and interactive models of listening.
- suggested reasons for students listening to English: access to information, pleasure, academic, work and travel purposes.
- examined the place of listening in language teaching and developments in methodology, including Audiolingualism and Communicative Language Teaching, which have emphasised the importance of listening to L2.
- talked about listening as input and as a model for students' own speech.
- discussed how students' confidence can be boosted by successful listening in class.
- examined some myths concerning listening and the teaching of it.

Listening texts and listening strategies

Language is powerful not only because there are competent speakers but because there are competent listeners. (Sweden Graphics)

- **What makes a good listening text?**
- **Authentic versus pedagogic**
- **Strategies good listeners use**
- **Different types of listening text and different processes required**

What makes a good listening text?

On 30 October 1938, Orson Welles made a radio recording of the H G Wells story *The War of the Worlds*. The story describes a Martian invasion of the US. Millions of Americans tuned in to hear the fake news bulletins reporting that a 'huge flaming object' had landed on a farm in New Jersey. As the broadcast continued, the audience began to panic. People started running into the streets. Others were reported hiding in cellars, loading guns and packing possessions into crates. Some even wrapped their heads in wet towels to protect themselves against the Martians' poison gas. Even though the radio programme warned that it was a fictionalised account, this warning was broadcast only every forty minutes. Those who missed the warnings believed that the US was in the grip of a full-blown invasion.

Later, after the truth was revealed, the *New York Tribune* alluded to the fact that 'a few effective voices, accompanied by sound effects, can ... create a nationwide panic'.

This broadcast was clearly something out of the ordinary. Let's look at a few of its features. Firstly, it was convincing. Perfectly rational men and women believed it was true, in part because in 1938 invasions were all too plausible. Secondly, it was gripping. The listeners were hooked – people only switched off in order to prepare their escape route – perhaps because the broadcast had direct relevance to them; they believed that their country was being invaded. Furthermore, the broadcast presented new information. Anyone wanting to know what an alien looked like as it emerged from its spaceship could find out by listening. The answer, by the way, is that the alien was 'as large as a bear and glistened like wet leather'. The broadcast was also clear and unambiguous – everyone recognised the genre of the emergency news bulletin, and the language was appropriate for its listeners.

Among listening 'events', the Welles recording had a sensational impact. It was clearly great – if rather alarming – listening material for a general audience.

From this example we may deduce what makes a good listening text *for language classes*: believability, relevance to the listener, new information and appropriateness in terms of language level. In the context of language classes, we can divide these and various other factors into two groups: **content** and **delivery**. Let's deal firstly with content.

Content

Interest factor

Perhaps the most vital factor of all is interest. If the text is intrinsically interesting, and particularly if the students have a personal stake in it, they will listen attentively. Welles's audience wanted to listen because they believed their lives were under threat. In order to try to ensure that the listening texts they use in class are intrinsically interesting to their students, some teachers give lists of topics and subtopics to their classes to choose from. They then find listening materials to match their students' needs, a surefire though potentially time-consuming way of raising the interest factor. Of course, what is interesting for one person may be dull for another, but part of the role of pre-listening tasks (see Chapter 4) is to raise interest in the topic.

Entertainment factor

Related to the notion of interest and 'having a stake in the text' is entertainment. Funny, enjoyable or gripping texts contain their own built-in interest factor.

Cultural accessibility

The text needs to be accessible to the listener. Certain concepts simply don't exist in some cultures, so the situations and contexts of some recordings may be incomprehensible. For example, Hallowe'en is unheard of in most of Africa. A recording which describes gangs of ten-year-olds in witch costumes trick-or-treating their way through the pumpkin-laden streets would, therefore, make little sense in an African context. If the aims of the lesson involved learning new cultural information, fine, but if the aim was listening practice, then the passage would be unsuitable.

Here's a passage taken from UK television:

> He bowls a well-disguised googly and his top-spinner is delivered from a bit wider of the crease. At any rate, all of the batsmen are having trouble picking him.

Many people, hearing the sentences above, would be left baffled, even though the number of words they had never heard before may be small: *googly, top-spinner, batsmen.* Then there will be other words that the listener may have heard, but which are specialised terms in this context, such as *crease*, which has a completely different meaning from the crease that we have in our trousers. And then there are straightforward-sounding expressions which make no sense unless you know what happens in this particular context: what, for example, does *picking him* mean? If, however, the listener is told that the sentences describe the game of cricket, things become a bit clearer. In conclusion, teachers need to make sure that the students have the content knowledge to make the text accessible, and this knowledge extends to cultural issues.

Speech acts

A further factor to consider when asking what makes a good listening passage is the type of **speech act** it represents. Speech has a number of different functions, such as suggesting, narrating, criticising, etc. When my sister tells me how to operate the washing machine or feed her parrot, this is a fixed or static speech act in that it is predictable in structure and less variable than other speech acts. It refers to unchanging states or objects which the listener keeps in mind throughout (the parrot may gain a few words and lose a few feathers here and there, but is basically unchanging). Other fixed speech acts include airport announcements, formal introductions and most transactions in shops. Narratives and extended discussions tend to be dynamic – they flow, twist and turn. A lecture on quantum theory or a discussion of existentialism is abstract in that it deals with ideas rather than concrete things.

As long as they are not too technical, fixed or static speech acts tend to be easier to grasp. Some dynamic texts, especially narratives, may also be quite straightforward in that they sometimes have a fairly predictable structure; indeed, some writers claim that only seven story plots exist (see Chapter 7 for a discussion of stories as listening input). Abstract texts tend to be more difficult, asking listeners to hold in mind a number of (often hazy) concepts. A good rule of thumb is that, for lower levels, the more predictable and familiar the speech act is, the more easily it will be understood. Perhaps this is one reason why low-level coursebooks tend to focus on transactional dialogues, such as buying stamps in the post office, checking into a hotel, etc.

Discourse structures

There are also certain **discourse structures** which are easier than others. Discourse structures refer to the organisation of a piece of text. For example, here are some common patterns: *phenomenon – example* is when a text begins by describing a general trend and then goes on to look at a specific example of this trend. For example:

> *Extreme sports are the in-thing for the adventure mad. For those of you tired of slumping in front of the TV or hauling yourself to the sweaty gym every morning, there are real alternatives out there. The latest craze is extreme ironing. All you have to do is climb a mountain with a board, an iron and a few crumpled shirts strapped to your back.*

Another common pattern is *cause – effect*. For example:

> *Johnny thinks Martians are going to spray him with poisonous gas so he puts a wet towel around his face.*

The first part of the sentence describes the cause (Johnny's thoughts on what the Martians are going to do), while the second part describes the effect (Johnny's action). *Cause – effect* patterns are particularly important for listening because after hearing about causes, listeners tend to predict what the effects will be. Prediction, as we will see later in this chapter, is an extremely important part of listening.

Here's a *problem – solution* pattern:

> *The Martians, having landed on Earth, were cold so their leader asked to borrow some fur coats.*

This makes an interesting comparison with, say, a *situation – problem – response – evaluation* pattern:

> *The Martians arrived but there was a problem: they weren't friendly. In response, the humans organised a series of get-togethers around a camp fire. Both parties evaluated the success of these measures by reflecting on whether relations between Martians and humans had improved.*

The *problem – solution* pattern is far easier to grasp because it has fewer stages and fewer transition points where the conversation changes tack.

Density

Somewhere between our two categories, content and delivery, is the issue of **density**. Density refers to the amount of information in the text. Does the speaker repeat main ideas, backtrack, clarify points? If he or she continually moves on to the next point, without stopping to clarify, this places a greater burden on the listener. Redundancy – as mentioned in the previous chapter – gives listeners a chance to process the content of the previous utterance. The less redundancy present, the more demanding listening is. News headlines are an example of a typically dense listening passage. The text below, taken from the BBC radio news, illustrates the type of lexical density we usually associate with written English.

> *President Bush and his South Korean counterpart, Roh Moo-hyun, have reaffirmed they will not tolerate the prospect of North Korea possessing nuclear weapons, but they said the issue should be resolved through diplomatic means.*
>
> *As Sri Lankans vote in presidential elections, security is tight at more than ten thousand polling stations amid fears of a rebel attack. The front-runners for the president are the prime minister and the opposition leader.*

Language level

Also related to both content and delivery is language level. A listening text containing many new lexical items and high-level grammatical structures will be difficult. Besides grammar and vocabulary, a further aspect of level is complexity: long sentences full of noun phrases, packed with meaning, are hard for students to process. Degrees of formality also need to be considered. Very informal texts, perhaps containing slang and/or unclear articulation, may cause difficulties, as may very formal texts. Formal English is generally longer and more convoluted in its construction than 'neutral' English, and it tends to use lots of words with Latin origins. For this reason, formal English may be easier for Italian students than, say, Japanese students.

In asking the question *What makes a good listening text?* we have so far considered several aspects of content. Let's now move on to delivery.

Delivery

Listening input in the classroom comes primarily in two modes. The first is live talk, which may be student-to-student, teacher-to-student or guest speaker-to-student. One of the benefits of live talk is that the listener may have the opportunity to influence the delivery, for example through body language, facial expression, gesture, interruption or verbal interaction.

The second type of input comes in the form of recordings. These may also vary in their mode of delivery: cassette, CD or DVD, etc, but generally speaking, none of these allows the listener to influence the delivery.

In Chapter 3, we will deal in depth with the ways in which the two forms – live talk and recordings – differ for the listener, and the benefits and drawbacks of both. For now, we will address the question: *What aspects of delivery do we need to take into consideration when it comes to choosing good listening texts?*

Length

A key factor is the length of the recording. Most students can only cope with a limited amount of input. As detailed in Chapter 1, every time they listen, they need to process language at the same time as receiving more language. Even as we try to understand what has been said, more input is constantly arriving. This is tiring for students, who get overloaded with input. Elementary coursebooks usually average about one minute per listening text. This is a reflection of the difficulties of listening for extended periods of time in a foreign language. Students at slightly higher levels, however, need a balance of **intensive** and **extensive** listening. As mentioned in Chapter 1, there are many different purposes for listening, and extensive listening is usually marked by factors such as relative ease in terms of comprehension, and the use of gist questions rather than questions asking for detailed information.

Because of class time constraints, most teachers do little or no extensive listening during the lesson (an exception is teachers who use **Suggestopedia**, a methodology which involves the teacher reading long texts to relaxed students). Instead, most teachers see extensive listening as something students can do in their free time. In the final chapter of the book we will discuss ways for teachers to introduce this idea along with other ideas for autonomous listening.

Quality of recordings

As suggested earlier, in many classrooms around the world, much of the listening input comes in the form of recorded materials. In such situations, the quality of the recording is an important aspect of delivery. These days, professionally produced material is recorded in a studio and the sound quality is generally high. Teachers attempting to make their own listening material sometimes find, however, that their own recordings, made perhaps on old machines, contain distortion and lack clarity.

Speed and number of speakers

There are other issues related to the recording itself, such as speed. Rapid speech, such as that heard in BBC news headlines, is more difficult for students than the speech rates of, say, an adult talking to a young child. The number of speakers is a further issue. The more speakers there are, the more potential there is for confusion, especially when there is no visual backup for the students.

Accent

There has been much comment in recent years about world 'Englishes'. The English spoken in downtown New York is very different from English in Delhi or Trinidad or London. This raises the question of which type of English students should listen to and take as a model. Some European commentators believe that 'standard British English', such as that heard on the BBC news, is the best model, while countries with more contact with the US, such as Brazil and Japan, tend to learn a variety of American English. Others say that we need to teach international English (which has fewer idioms and colloquial phrases than, say, British English), a variety that can be understood by everyone. What is likely is that local dialects spoken by minorities will pose great problems for foreign learners when it comes to listening. For this reason, most professionally recorded materials, at least for the European market, tend to favour a southern English standard accent. There is, however, a growing belief that students should be exposed gradually to a variety of accents as they become more proficient. This belief is reflected in recent professionally produced materials.

Another factor to take into account is that, these days, there is perceived to be less need for students to speak like the English, Australians, North Americans or any other native speakers. As mentioned in Chapter 1, most English in the world is spoken between non-native speakers, and teachers generally don't need to sound like native speakers in order to provide good models for students to listen to.

We have so far looked at certain factors that make a good listening text. This leads us inevitably to the question of whether the text should be **authentic** or not.

Authentic versus pedagogic

What exactly do we mean by *authentic*? Henry Widdowson, among others, has stated that authenticity is something to do with the purpose of the text and the quality of response it elicits. One way to define authenticity may be to say that if the text exists for a communicative purpose other than teaching language, then it is authentic. Even so, this leaves us with certain questions. Is authentic language always the best model? If I say, 'Sit!' or 'Roll over!' to my dog, this is authentic, but is it a good model for non-dog-owning students? Is a highly stylised play script 'authentic'?

Situational dialogues in coursebooks are often criticised for their lack of authenticity. One commentator, Ronald Carter, says they represent a 'can-do' society, polite and problem-free, in which 'the conversation is neat, tidy and predictable, utterances are almost as complete as sentences, no one interrupts anyone else or speaks at the same time as anyone else'. Finally, he compares the question-and-answer sequence to that of a quiz show or courtroom interrogation. In other words, these dialogues represent nothing like the messiness of real communication in real situations. Below is a list of common differences between authentic and scripted speech.

Authentic	Scripted
Overlaps and interruptions between speakers	Little overlap between speakers
Normal rate of speech delivery	Slower (maybe monotonous) delivery
Relatively unstructured language	Structured language, more like written English
Incomplete sentences, with false starts, hesitation, etc	Complete sentences
Background noise and voices	No background noise
Natural stops and starts that reflect the speaker's train of thought and the listener's ongoing response	Artificial stops and starts that reflect an idealised version of communication (in which misunderstandings, false starts, etc never occur)
Loosely packed information, padded out with fillers	Densely packed information

Compare a scripted dialogue and an authentic dialogue about similar topics.

M = man, **W** = woman

W: What type of exercises are you keen on?

M: I'm keen on running.

W: Do you do it regularly?

M: Er ... three or four times a week.

W: Where do you run?

M: In the park.

M = man, **W** = woman

M: Are you in, are you in fairly good shape? Do you still keep ... keep fit?

W: [pause] I think so, yeah. In my opinion, yeah.

M: Well, what do you do exactly? To, to stay fit?

W: Mmm. Keep a routine, a routine like going ... doing something every day.

M: Uh huh ‖

W: ‖ It doesn't matter what it is but

M: (Wh) But ‖

W: ‖ What I do more is going to the gym, lifting weights ‖ and

M: ‖ Uh huh

W: (Wh ...?)

M: But you do something, one of these, every day, one or two of these every day. Is it ... ?

W: No, I do it, I do it every day.

M: One or two of those every day, one or two of those exercises?

W: No, no, I do both of them ‖ but

M: ‖ Ah, right.

W: For example, when the gym is closed on ‖

M: ‖ Yeah.

W: I do something every day. I have to do something every day.

M: Ah, right, right, OK.

Features of the authentic dialogue include overlapping sentences (this is what the ‖ symbol means); much repetition (*every day* occurs seven times in 20 seconds); misunderstanding and negotiation of meaning (the man wasn't sure how many exercises the woman did every day); false starts (*like going ... doing something*); **backchannel devices** (*uh huh*) which show that you are listening; non-standard forms (*What I do more is ...*); and a far longer conversation than in the scripted dialogue, which is 'cleaned up' of most of these elements.

We need, however, to evaluate the scripted conversation on its own terms. It isn't there as genuine listening practice; it's there to exemplify a grammar point, and it serves its purpose: it provides a clear model of the rules of question forms in the present simple. It is both easily understood, with little to distract the listener, and economical in terms of time and space.

Ultimately, then, much depends on what we wish to teach. If we want our students to practise listening, and we want to teach discourse markers and useful **chunks** (*in good shape, keep fit, keep a routine, lifting weights*, etc), the authentic dialogue will be more useful. If we want to teach question forms, we will choose the first dialogue.

Authenticity – the historical view

Perhaps, if we wish to discuss authenticity in language-learning materials, a look at the historical perspective will be instructive. It was only fairly recently, with the advent of modern recording equipment, that linguists began to analyse authentic speech patterns. Inevitably, they noticed how the dialogues in textbooks were not representative of real-life speech. In real speech, several phenomena occur which previously went unnoticed, or at least undocumented. For example, when asked a direct question, most people preface their response with a filler such as 'er'. Speakers do the same when asked to give directions, in order to alert the listener that they are about to start or to play for time or soften the tone.

Essentially, what this closer study of real speech taught us is that many of our intuitions about the way we use language are wrong, and that real language use is messier, less complete and less ordered than the examples in many scripted dialogues. The result of this research was that the usefulness of inauthentic-sounding dialogues was immediately called into question. If people don't really speak like this, why are we teaching this type of discourse? However, rather than a simple formulation of *authentic = good, scripted = bad*, the debate took wing.

There are the purists who insist that only 'real' English is worth listening to. Classrooms are places of inquiry, they say, and the investigation of real English is a part of what good language classes do. In addition to this, if our students hear only graded material, when they need to understand English as it is spoken on the street, at meetings or on television, they will be inadequately prepared to cope with features of authentic language such as patterns of discourse, fillers, redundancies, false starts, etc.

In contrast, others claim that it isn't always worth explaining the false starts, redundancies and irregular features involved in an authentic dialogue. These features may not represent typical language use, but only one – perhaps inarticulate – speaker and one listener, who between them have a deep well of shared background knowledge that cannot possibly be available to the student listening in on the conversation.

There are other disadvantages. It isn't easy to find good authentic listening materials for very low-level students. The syllable rate per minute of natural speech is very high – in other words, native speakers talk fast – and ungraded material usually means difficult vocabulary, complex sentence structures, hesitations, fillers and false starts. There are also factors such as density, length and **exophoric** reference. The latter is when the speakers refer to things outside the immediate context – they may use pronouns such as *it* – and is one problem associated with eavesdropping (or being an overhearer rather than a participant in the conversation) when you don't know the speakers' relationship or their shared knowledge. All of these factors mean that authentic material is potentially very difficult for students.

Although there is an abundance of authentic material on the Internet, most of it doesn't come in a pedagogical framework (preview questions, comprehension questions, discussion points, etc). This means that the teacher may need to spend a considerable amount of time preparing authentic materials for classroom use. Furthermore, there is no guarantee that authentic materials are any more interesting than scripted materials. As many functional-notional coursebooks proved in the 1970s and 1980s, train station announcements and the like may be authentic, but they are not content-rich, and, out of context, may be rather demotivating.

Some ELT writers have also argued that, if we are concerned with 'naturalness', what could be more natural than native speakers slowing down their rate of speech and using simplified vocabulary to a foreigner, just as they do to a young child who has not yet mastered the language? What could be *less* natural than native speakers talking at full speed to a foreigner and *not* grading their language?

A solution favoured by many materials writers is **authentic-based** language. This may include some features such as hesitation and false starts, but the dialogue is basically 'cleaned up' of any overly distracting aspects. In other words, it is scripted, but more realistically than in the past. Alternatively, there is the **semi-scripted** recording, in which actors are given a task to accomplish and may be asked to include various language points. They then improvise the dialogue.

Jan Bell and Roger Gower, author team of one successful coursebook series, wrote, 'We ... wanted our listenings to be natural and as authentic as possible ... but we did compromise and use some actors. On reflection, given the response of some non-UK markets to the difficulty of the authentic texts, we wonder now whether we should have compromised more. We put in a lot of effort to make sure the listenings were authentic but it was not appreciated universally. Perhaps we should have made more of them semi-scripted – or at least made the authentic ones shorter and easier and built in more "how to listen" tasks.'

It is probably true to say that most teachers would like a balance of scripted, semi-scripted and authentic speech for their classes. This is certainly what coursebook writers such as Bell and Gower have been attempting to include in listening syllabuses in recent years.

Before we move on, let's summarise. What makes a good recorded text, whether authentic, scripted or semi-scripted?

Feature	Questions to ask
1 Interest	Will this be interesting for my students?
2 Cultural accessibility	Will my students understand the context and ideas?
3 Speech act/Discourse structure	Does it discuss abstract concepts or is it based on everyday transactions?
4 Density	Does the information come thick and fast or are there moments in which the listener can relax?
5 Language level	Is the majority of the vocabulary and grammar appropriate for my students?
6 Length	Will I need to cut part of the recording because it is too long? Is it long enough?
7 Quality of recording	Is the recording clear? Will background noise affect comprehension?
8 Speed	Do the speakers talk too fast for my students?
9 Number of speakers	Are there many voices, potentially causing confusion?
10 Accent	Is the accent familiar? Is it comprehensible?

Strategies good listeners use

Here is Nisbet and Shucksmith's take on adult learning: 'Most adults will avoid the need to learn if they can by sticking to familiar routines (and when faced with an unfamiliar task, will not know how to set about solving it).' Anyone who has ever felt like kicking an uncooperative computer or taking a hammer to a spluttering car faces a dilemma: learn a new approach or be condemned to frustration and ignorance (and a large repair bill). Problems in listening to L2 may also require new approaches, and this is where strategies come in, and teachers help out.

What exactly is a strategy? There is no general consensus on this, although a number of writers, such as Oxford, Chamot and O'Malley, agree that strategies consist of conscious, deliberate behaviour which enhances learning and allows the learner to use information more effectively.

Strategies can be divided into three groups: **cognitive strategies**, **metacognitive strategies** and **socio-affective** strategies. Cognitive strategies are those that we use in order to complete an immediate task. For example, a student may find out about the topic (perhaps using information in L1) before listening, in order to predict content.

Metacognitive strategies are related to learning in general and often have long-term benefits. For example, students might choose to tune in to a BBC recording once a week as a strategy for improving their listening.

Socio-affective strategies are concerned with the learners' interaction with other speakers and their attitude towards learning. For example, they may choose to rehearse a telephone conversation in L2 with another student in order to develop confidence, or reward themselves with a doughnut when they successfully complete some task in the target language.

Good listeners use many strategies simultaneously and in accordance with the task at hand. They may listen regularly to a radio broadcast (metacognitive), take notes on the key points (cognitive) and then meet fellow students in the café (for their doughnut) and tell them all about what they just listened to (socio-affective).

The key point about strategies is that some of them are *teachable*. In exam situations, teachers can point out the importance of predicting. What type of word (a noun? an adjective?) will go in the gap? What type of information (a name? a number?) is missing here? While listening to radio news headlines, students may be instructed to note down key words immediately. Training students to become 'strategic' about listening is one of the most important things that teachers can do to develop their students' competence in the skill.

One point to make about listening strategies is that they are often compensatory. They cannot replace the skill of decoding words and propositions and putting the information to use. So why do we teach strategies? Because students do not always transfer L1 listening strategies to L2. Furthermore, they need to find ways to cope when faced with elements above their current level.

What makes a strategy teachable? In many cases, the first condition is that the students must recognise there is a problem and realise that they need to take strategic action. The next condition is that the teacher must be able to exemplify the strategy and show that it is effective (if it is a purely mental process, the teacher cannot show it). Finally, the strategy needs to be repeatable; that is to say, it can be incorporated into the students' armoury for dealing with such problems whenever they arise in the future.

As educators have come to realise the importance of strategies, many published materials now include ideas on strategy use. Indeed, a number of strategies are often built into the material in the form of rubrics. For example, many coursebooks include a post-listening rubric, 'Check your answers with a partner', a socio-affective strategy that helps students to build confidence.

Here are some ideas for teaching listening strategies:

Strategy	How to teach it	When to teach it/Type of text
Be ready and have a plan to achieve a given task.	Clarify what students will need to do with the information they hear by asking **concept questions** (questions that ask students to show they understand ideas rather than show that they merely recall facts). These encourage the students to verbalise what they need to do, thus clearing up any ambiguities.	Teach it before the students listen. It can be done with any listening text.
Use world knowledge to predict what will be said.	Before listening, discuss the subject and how the speaker might view it. Use KWL charts (Know/Want to Know/Learnt) to pool knowledge of the topic. Give students headlines/titles. They predict additional content before listening to the recording.	Teach it before the students listen. It can be done with factual texts, e.g. news, discussion of a topic, lectures.
Use linguistic knowledge to predict what will be said.	Use **gap-fill** exercises (students fill the gaps in a transcript). Students complete the exercise before listening. As they listen, they can see how accurate their predictions were.	This can be done either before listening or after a first listening. If the latter, it should be used to show which words naturally follow other words, rather than as a memory test. It can be done with any listening text containing common **collocations** (*take your time*, *make an effort*, *Happy Birthday*, etc), idioms or *adjacency pairs* ('How are you?' 'Fine, thanks.' 'Thanks.' 'You're welcome.').

Monitor performance while listening.	Pause at regular intervals during the listening to check comprehension (students in pairs, groups or as a whole class). Ask questions such as *Who said X? Why? What is the topic?* Ask students if their answers are logical. (Does it make sense that Russia's biggest airport is located in Monaco, as one student thought he'd heard?)	This is taught during listening. The strategy should be taught only occasionally as the teaching of it interrupts the listening experience and can frustrate students. It can be done with any listening text, especially if the students are listening for gist, but it works better with slightly extended texts.
Pick out only salient points, listening selectively and ignoring irrelevant details.	Give tasks that require listening for detail, e.g. with train timetables, cinema listings information, etc, which consist mainly of information that is extraneous for the individual listener. Use gap-fill exercises.	The strategy can be taught during the setting of the while-listening task, as the teacher explains what the students must listen for. It can be reinforced during feedback after listening. Use announcements and other lists of information.
Take notes, writing down relevant information in shorthand.	As above. People can't remember details such as telephone numbers, so they need to practise writing information quickly. Ask students to identify key words (the stressed words, which they should note) in full sentences. Give students 'Who/Where/What/Why' charts. They take notes in the columns. Explain that note-taking systems only need to make sense *to the note-taker* (notes are essentially private aids for later recall).	The strategy requires pre-listening advice on what to note down and how to write it. It also requires extended feedback after listening, as students compare their notes. Use factual texts, e.g. news, discussion of a topic, lectures and texts with information such as phone numbers and addresses. (See Chapter 5 for a detailed discussion of note-taking.)
Note an approximation of a difficult word/name. Check later.	As above, but help students to make a guess based on a phonetic approximation. News broadcasts are excellent for this as they often contain names of places and people.	The strategy requires a hint before listening – 'Even if you aren't sure of the answer, write down what you think you heard' – and then post-listening feedback. Use factual texts, e.g. news, discussion of a topic, lectures. The strategy is especially useful as practice for exam situations.

Listen for key words for topic identification.	Ask students to listen again and pick out words belonging to a lexical set. Check with the script, if available. Songs lend themselves well to this.	Teach this after the first listening, pointing out that the key words clarify the topic. Use factual texts and songs.
Check with other listeners.	Regularly include a stage at which students compare answers. This is also valuable as a way to highlight discrepancies in interpretation.	This strategy can be taught after listening, and is built into many published materials. It can be done with any listening text.
Ask for clarification.	Teach phrases: *Could you repeat what you said about … ? What did you mean by … ? I didn't catch XXX.* Give opportunities for students to use these, e.g. by telling an anecdote slightly above the students' level.	The phrases need to be taught and practised before listening. The strategy requires face-to-face communication, and works well with stories (fact or fiction) and anecdotes.
Reconstruct orally or in writing.	Do **dictogloss** activities: tell a story or anecdote at full speed several times. Students work together to reconstruct the story, gradually adding details.	The strategy is explained as the teacher gives the while-listening task. After listening, the students evaluate their success in using the strategy. Use stories (fact or fiction) and anecdotes.
Listen for transition points.	Teach linking expressions/ devices: *so*, *on the other hand*, *furthermore*, *in conclusion*, etc. Pause (a recording) after the expression and ask students what comes next.	The phrases need to be taught and practised before listening. The text can be paused during a second listening, once students have got the gist. Use factual texts, e.g. news, discussion of a topic, lectures. You can also use stories (fact or fiction) and anecdotes.

Over the course of study, students need frequent and systematic training in these strategies, and opportunities to put them into practice. This is a crucial part of planning. Inevitably, some students will use them already, but many will not. One problem is that some students dislike being told how to learn. Teachers can be fairly subtle about strategies. The best approach is to do it, focus briefly on what you did, and then move on without labouring the point. Strategy training works best as a drip-feed process (little and often) rather than a flood, and if you repeat the process often enough, students will probably begin to use the correct strategies automatically, which is the goal of all learner training.

An alternative approach to strategy training is to start a discussion on the topic of strategies so that the students can pool their ideas. Here's an example from a well-known business English coursebook.

Skills
Active listening

A How do you know if someone is not listening to you? How does it make you feel?

B Which of the following do you do to show people that you are listening to them? Can you add any other suggestions?
- look people directly in the eye at all times
- nod your head often to show interest
- repeat what the speaker has said in your own words
- be aware of the speaker's body language
- interrupt the speaker often to show you are listening
- think about what you are going to say while the speaker is talking
- use body language to show you are attentive
- try to predict what they are going to say next
- ask questions if you do not understand
- say nothing until you are absolutely sure that the speaker has finished

C 10.4 Listen to three conversations in which people are talking about customer service.
1 Make notes under the following headings:
   a) Product or service
   b) Reasons why service was good or bad
2 Listen again. Tick the words and phrases in the Useful language box that you hear. Then add other words and phrases of your own.

D Work in pairs. Describe two examples from your own experience where the service you received was:
a) excellent   b) poor.
When your partner is speaking, make an effort to listen actively. Use some of the language from the Useful language box.

Useful language

Showing interest	**Clarifying**
Really?	Are you saying ... ?
That's interesting.	What (exactly) do you mean by ... ?
Right / OK / Mmm /	Could you be more specific, please?
Yes / No	

Summarising
(So) you think ...
(So) what you're saying is ...

Showing empathy
I know what you mean.
How awful!

Repetition / Question tags
A We've reduced customer complaints by 30%.
B 30%? / Have you?

Asking for details
So what happened?
What did you do?

89

Different types of listening text and different processes required

The strategies and processes required depend on the situation, type of input and reasons for listening. Conversations, very broadly speaking, come under two types: **transactional** and **interactional**. Transactional conversations occur when one person needs something, for example a train ticket. These conversations tend to be more formulaic, whereas interactional conversations – for example, when friends sit down for a chat – are usually less predictable and more wide-ranging.

If we compare listening to a lecture with listening to a friend gossiping, we can highlight some of the differences. A lecture is more formal and may involve extended one-way discourse, whereas gossip usually involves shorter **turns** (a turn is one speaker's complete utterance before they are stopped or interrupted). While both gossiping and lecturing are transactional in the sense that the speaker passes information to the listener, gossip usually contains an element of interaction as the listener comments and asks questions. In contrast, a lecture may require a delayed response and involve note-taking for later recall. A further difference is that lectures may also involve the interpretation of pictures, charts or diagrams. Finally, gossip is pleasure oriented, whereas lectures are often part of educational programmes and contain information that listeners need to pass exams or further their careers.

All of these elements make a difference to the way in which people listen, and listeners cope with different types of listening by preparing themselves according to the conventions and expectations of the genre. They then match their behaviour to the task: perhaps they will need to convert lecture notes into an essay, or convert gossip into something altogether more lurid before passing it on to the next set of listeners.

Conclusions | *In this chapter we have:*

- looked at the type of material that students could listen to in class and some of the criteria to bear in mind when choosing material, such as interest, level, length, type of speech act, discourse structure and accessibility in terms of cultural content and format.

- examined the differences between authentic and pedagogic texts.

- looked at strategies that students can apply in order to become more proficient listeners.

- talked about different types of listening, such as transactional and interactional conversations, and the different approaches required, stating that these depend on the situation, type of input and reasons for listening.

3 | Listening sources, listening tasks

A wise man listening to a fool will learn more than a fool listening to a wise man.
(Anonymous)

- ■ **The characteristics of effective listening**
- ■ **Different sources of listening**
  Teacher talk
  Student talk
  Guest speakers
  Textbook recordings
- **Television, video, DVD and radio**
- **Songs**
- **The Internet**
- ■ **Types of comprehension exercise**
- ■ **How to create tasks**

The characteristics of effective listening

Let us consider the mythical creature called a 'good listener'. What do we mean by a good listener, and does such a thing exist? We might define good listeners as those with sensitivity to context, language and nuance, who don't view listening as the pause before they talk. This is the good listener we associate with agony aunts and psychiatrists (according to author Robert Conklin, 'Very few people would listen if they didn't know it was their turn next'). In face-to-face conversation, they may do some or all of the following:

- Use attentive body language – for example nodding frequently;
- Look the speaker in the eye;
- Use expressions such as *mhm, I see, yes*, etc, to show they are paying attention;
- Ask questions if they don't understand something;
- Try to predict what the speaker is going to say next;
- Note the meaning of silences.

But what about good listeners in L2?

One thing we need to remember is that language students, like the rest of us, are rarely good listeners all the time (hence the 'mythical creature' tag above). Some may be good when listening to a football commentary in a foreign language, but poor when the teacher plays a recording of John and Mary discussing the weather. Why? Because motivation plays a vital role. Maybe they love football, whereas John and Mary's plans for the weekend just don't come high on their 'need to know' list. Furthermore, those who have a stake in what is being said are more likely to listen attentively. Many teachers will recognise the phenomenon of students suddenly becoming outstanding listeners when the teacher is explaining how to pass the course. Hands shoot up, questions are asked to clarify issues, students write detailed notes. Conclusion? The topic and its relevance to the listener are crucial.

So, L2 listeners become better listeners when they are motivated. What else might make 'good L2 listeners' good? They tend to think ahead, predicting and grappling with the meaning of the whole text rather than fretting about unknown words. They fill gaps in a narrative. They are engaged and see themselves as participants in an interaction rather than passive receptacles of messages. They take ownership of what they hear; rather than just answering comprehension questions or completing a given task, they create their own agenda in accordance with their goals. They also have the ability to focus on valuable information that will allow them to achieve those goals (whether set by themselves or an outside party like the teacher or the coursebook) while ignoring everything else that they hear. This reduces the load on their short-term memory. They also listen to different things in different ways, adapting their strategies to the text.

Good listeners realise that ambiguity is sometimes unavoidable, and rather than becoming frustrated by this, they bear with it until ambiguous issues are eventually resolved. This is the payback for perseverance. Good listeners persevere, realising that the hypotheses they make (about the meaning of what they hear) can be checked later. In short, they are prepared to make a calculated guess, hold it in their memory and suspend judgment.

Good listeners become experts at self-monitoring. While listening, they are constantly aware of whether or not they are achieving the task. They are alert to inconsistencies in their interpretations of events, and they try to resolve the issues by collaborating with their interlocutor or revising their interpretations.

All listeners suffer moments of confusion while listening. Rather than 'switching off' and saying 'I don't understand', good listeners tend to say 'I didn't understand the bit where she said …'. In other words, they identify specific problem areas. Sometimes they are able to make a phonetic approximation of the words they didn't understand: 'I didn't understand this word, but it sounded like XXX.'

Good listeners also become aware of irony and other tones of voice. They 'listen between the words' rather than taking every utterance at face value, and recognise shifts in intonation (the way the voice pitch rises and falls).

Overall, then, good listeners are **strategic** – they are organised and they have a plan to achieve the task.

We have looked at a number of the characteristics of effective listening. Now we will move on to the type of texts students might usefully listen to and where teachers can find these.

Different sources of listening

Teacher talk

There is a Swiss saying:

> *Wenn alles schlaft und einer spricht, dass nennt der Lehrer Unterricht.*

This means 'When everyone's sleeping and one person is speaking, that's what the teacher calls teaching'!

Many teachers and students might not regard teacher talk as a way to practise listening in class. After all, it isn't formally tested; there are no marks assigned or ticks and crosses. The students do not usually brace themselves, pens hovering above the paper, to complete a task, and there are no signals that this is the listening stage of the lesson. Students themselves may not even be aware that they are practising the skill. But listening to the teacher is the most frequent and valuable form of input during lessons. One enormous benefit is that the teacher is in complete control and can slow down, speed up, repeat key points, paraphrase difficult vocabulary, and generally modify the input as desired. This is extremely useful for learners trying to get accustomed to the sounds of the new language. No other authentic input is as easy to manipulate. Teacher talk is also interactive in that it responds to students' needs and can be very motivating. At the very least, it consists of excellent roughly-tuned input.

One aspect of teacher talk is **planned input**. Here is a scenario: a teacher needs to convey some information – perhaps what time an exam will take place – and makes an announcement in front of the class. The likelihood is that everybody will listen carefully and ask further questions to clarify the points made. This is because the students, the listeners, have a stake in the information. If they misunderstand, they will turn up to the wrong exam in the wrong room at the wrong time. In other words, planned input such as this may be some of the best, most motivating of all. Some teachers in monolingual classes tend to make this type of announcement in the mother tongue. A better way would be to use it as a real opportunity for listening input, followed by a checking or clarification exercise, in which the teacher elicits the key information from the students and writes it on the board.

Semi-planned input refers to a pedagogical sequence prepared but not scripted by the teacher. Here are some examples:

 Photos: the teacher shows a number of his or her photos and talks about them. The students guess which person in the photos is being described. Afterwards, the teacher elicits vocabulary to describe people.

 Firsts: the teacher talks about three important 'firsts' in his or her life, asking the students to take notes in columns such as the ones below.

What	When	Who

Then the students compare notes, reformulate the stories and prepare to do the same speaking task in groups.

 Childhood anecdotes: the class brainstorms words connected with childhood. These are written on the board. The teacher tells a childhood anecdote. After listening, the students say which words on the board were used in the anecdote and how they were used. A good follow-up is to focus on the form of the past tense and ask students to tell a childhood anecdote themselves.

 Chat show: one teacher, Joseph R Fraher, organises a classroom chat show called *The Joe Show*, in which he interviews his students in front of a live audience (the other students) who take notes. He even has a theme tune, interviewer's outfit and spotlights rigged up, just to increase the entertainment factor!

 Biographies: another teacher, Alun Davies, suggests using teacher-generated biography as input material. He posits the idea of teacher-as-cultural-resource, and says, 'My students' proposal for more cultural input was prompted by the interest and curiosity which they felt towards me as a representative of the L2 culture'. Davies uses **realia** such as passport, wedding certificate, etc, which may not be everyone's idea of interesting documents, and he then builds lessons around these. Whether or not teachers are themselves representatives of a target language culture, this type of activity can still be valuable. If we take the basic idea that the teacher's life becomes the input material, a particularly fruitful angle for non-native teachers is that of 'language model': how they became proficient enough to teach the language – maybe through travel, a special course of study or interesting methods to learn the target language.

All of the above represent excellent ways of providing input, as they are personalised, probably relatively natural in delivery and can be a model for students to follow. The difference between planned and semi-planned input as described here is that planned input does not come with pedagogical tasks. It is the conveyance of real-world information that the students need, and there is no ulterior language- or skills-based goal. In contrast, the main goal of the sequences using semi-planned input is pedagogical: either practice of the listening skill or new language.

Finally, there is **spontaneous input**: words of encouragement, witty comments, gossip, on-the-spot classroom management. If the lesson is conducted in English and if there is an element of dialogue between teacher and students, spontaneous input is unavoidable. Imagine that a student turns up late and dishevelled to class. The teacher may say something like, 'What happened to you this morning?' This is a starting point for a dialogue that could continue in many different ways. Perhaps the student replies, 'I went to a party last night … '. What follows is a spontaneous conversation that may provide excellent listening/speaking material.

Another consideration concerns the many teachers around the world who do not have access to electricity or recording equipment. In these situations, the teacher's voice may be the only source of listening input for the students. One option is for the teacher to read out transcripts from textbooks, if they have them. This is fairly straightforward when the listening text is a monologue. If it is a dialogue, the teacher may need to act out both parts, using body language or a change of tone to signify a new speaker. A gentle twist of the upper body at the beginning of every new turn may be enough to show an audience that there is a new speaker. Alternatively, the teacher could ask a student to read out the second part, or possibly invite another speaker from outside to read the part.

Another option, if teachers wish to give their students some extended listening, is for the teacher to give a talk. Delivering longer, structured talks effectively to students is a skill in itself, which requires a good deal of planning. Here are some of the factors that need to be considered.

Quality teacher talk
- Prepare students adequately. Use pre-listening activities (these are the subject of Chapter 4). There is an adage used by conference speakers: tell the audience what you are going to say, say it, then say what you have said. The first part of the adage (tell the audience what you are going to say) gives the students notice of what they will hear.
- Get the volume and speed right. Speak at an appropriate volume, and speak naturally but not too fast. Emphasising a point usually entails a change of pitch and possibly elongation of vowel sounds (as in 'reeeaally?!'). Do these, but don't exaggerate them!

- Use clear signposting. Signal your changes of topic overtly with **macro-markers** (e.g. *now we will turn to the subject of …*, *the final thing we are going to look at today is …*) as opposed to **micro-markers** (*moving on, so, …*).

- Move in linear sequence. Don't jump around in time; tell your story chronologically. An author once said that modern novels have a beginning, a muddle and an end. Make sure your talk has a middle, not a muddle.

- Pause and paraphrase. Provide mini summaries at the end of each section. Students who missed the details the first time should get a second chance. Remember that redundancy (see page 23) can be a good thing in moderation because it means that listeners don't have to concentrate on every word.

- Watch your vocabulary. It sounds counter-intuitive, but longer, more technical words may be more easily understood by students. This is because these words often have Latin roots or they are international words. In contrast, phrasal verbs (e.g. *get by*, *run over*, *break down*) are notoriously difficult for students. Be aware of the students' range of vocabulary while you speak, and as you paraphrase, explain tricky items more clearly.

- Cut the colloquialisms. One teacher-in-training was heard to say to an elementary class 'You don't need to bother with all that malarkey'. (*Malarkey* is a colloquial word for *nonsense*, used mainly in certain areas of London.) This is an extreme example, but even the use of *pretty* as in *She was pretty smart* can cause problems.

- Watch your analogies. Many analogies are culture-specific. The researchers Jackson and Bilton noted that lectures in US universities often move from the scientific world to the everyday world. But the everyday world of Americans is not the everyday world of Brazilians or Chinese. TV programmes, cultural icons and sports terminology that 'everyone knows' may be less universal than you think.

- Make it interactive. Allow questions at the end of each section. Most listening, as we have pointed out, is not one-way, and teacher talk doesn't have to be. At the very least, maintain eye contact with your students and make sure your talk is not overscripted.

- Provide visual support. This includes **paralinguistic features** – facial expression, gestures and body language, as well as slides, illustrations and lists.

- Provide a course-related context for the talk. Use phrases such as, *Last week we saw how …*; *Yesterday we spoke about …*; and end with something like, *Next week we will look at …* . This gives a sense of progression to students and also helps them to relate new content to information already covered.

- Be aware of formality. Public speaking styles vary considerably, but they can be put roughly into three categories: informal, formal and reading. Reading in front of an audience is obviously the least interactive and usually to be avoided. A more formal style tends to come with the advantage of being tightly organised and structured, helpful qualities for listeners. An informal style can reduce the perceived distance between speaker and audience, allowing both to relax. There is some evidence that use of the inclusive *we*, and other informal references, can also help to build this rapport.

- Monitor the students' comprehension. You need to keep checking that the students are following your talk. You can do this through observation of the listeners' facial expressions and body language, or perhaps by direct questioning. If the listeners appear confused or overloaded with information, you must make allowances: for example, by recapping, slowing down or stopping altogether.

- Finally, over a whole course, make sure there is a balance between the amount of time you talk and the amount of time your students get to respond. Long monologues, in most teaching situations, are probably to be used sparingly.

Teacher talking time (TTT) used to be frowned upon. In recent years, however, many have argued for more, not less, of it for humanistic and input reasons. We have also begun to see it in terms of teacher talking quality (TTQ). Rather than measuring it by time, we can measure teacher talk by its interest, clarity, use of appropriate expressions, coherence, etc. At its best, teacher talk is excellent roughly-tuned input; it is also interactive and it responds to the students' needs.

Student talk

Just as there is planned, semi-planned and spontaneous talk from the teacher, there should be the same from the students. There are any number of things that students can speak about in groups that will develop their listening as well as their speaking skills. One of these is anecdotes, which are personal and therefore tend to be interesting, real and concrete rather than abstract. However, we should remember, as mentioned earlier, that one man's interesting story is another's yawn-inducing ramble.

One way to ensure that students really are listening to each other is to set tasks. These might include:

 Jigsaw tasks with an information gap: individual students have pictures or parts of a text. In groups, they paraphrase their text or describe their pictures and together form the whole story.

 Reporting back: before the activity starts, the teacher tells the students that they will have to report back on what was said.

 Making a presentation: the teacher asks the students in groups to present something that the other students need to judge. For example, each group presents an idea for a new magazine; the listeners decide if they wish to invest in the magazine.

 Secretaries: the teacher assigns the role of secretary to one student.

Perhaps surprisingly, some students and teachers dislike the idea of devoting class time to pair or group discussion. They say that:

1 students learn each other's mistakes.

2 students provide bad models for each other.

3 students slip too easily into the mother tongue.

4 teachers cannot monitor adequately when, say, fifteen pairs of students are all talking at the same time.

Some of these points may be valid, but students learn useful language from each other as well as errors. If they slip into the mother tongue, that is a question of motivation and can be countered by negotiating class rules early in a course. The fourth issue is only a problem for teachers who believe they must be in control at every stage of the lesson, and this is a question of educational philosophy. Certainly, within the communicative approach, which emphasises the development of fluency in class, such control is untenable and undesirable. Besides this, the best teachers find ways to listen to many conversations simultaneously!

A final comment is that the classroom provides a 'safe' environment in which students can 'experiment' with new language.

Guest speakers

The sources of input described so far are teachers and other students; these can be described as 'live' listening. Another way of giving students access to a live, authentic, real-time conversation is to invite a proficient or native speaker of English into the class. This has many potential advantages. Firstly, a new face and voice are always stimulating in a regular class. In many classes, the students do not have the chance to listen to native speakers in a relatively controlled environment. As such, live listening is a type of bridge between 'the real, outside world' and the world of the classroom. Furthermore, with a native speaker guest, there is an opportunity for students to hear about a foreign culture.

Another benefit is that the language is semi-planned or unplanned but the speakers have a sense of an audience, and may find themselves paraphrasing and recapping. In addition, if the students choose the topic discussed, it means that they have invested something in the conversation, to a greater extent than with pre-prepared coursebook recordings.

Paralinguistic features are also helpful. The students can see the body language being used and this aids comprehension. If, at the end of the conversation, the teacher or guest speaker invites questions and comments, this gives the students a chance to interact in a way that is impossible with other types of listening (e.g. radio or TV), and which is much nearer to what we usually do in daily life. For example, the students can ask for clarification of confusing points, or ask follow-up questions to deepen their understanding of what was said.

One way of planning a lesson with a guest speaker involves a number of stages, some of which are optional.

Listening to a guest speaker – an approach

1 Introduce the guest.
2 Ask the students to write down any topics they would like to hear discussed. These should probably, but not necessarily, be related to the guest's area of expertise or interest.
3 Decide as a whole class which of the suggestions you and the guest will discuss.
4 Record the conversation. It is easier to do this if both of you are seated at the front of the class, with the recording equipment either at your feet or on a table close by.
5 At the end of the conversation, ask the students to summarise what was said, in pairs or groups. Ask the whole class for feedback.
6 Ask the students if there were any new phrases that they noticed, or if there were any particular difficulties.
7 Play the recording, pausing as necessary and scaffolding their understanding by asking questions to frame the conversation and to check comprehension. Also, stop occasionally to ask what's coming next – what word, phrase or proposition. Highlight any new or difficult phrases/words by writing them on the board.
8 Ask the students to discuss the same topic in pairs/groups, followed by feedback.

An alternative to stages 2 and 3 would be to get the students simply to think of questions for the 'mystery' visitor (job, hobbies, relationship with the teacher, etc). The conversation then flows according to the answers and follow-up questions.

A potential problem is that you have to find a native or proficient speaker who is available, willing to come to the class and blessed with the ability to hold an audience. One solution is to put two classes together and have the teachers do the speaking. You will probably want classes of the same level, and you will need a room large enough to hold both classes combined. An additional benefit of this is that students often enjoy meeting other classes and seeing how other teachers operate.

Textbook recordings

One extreme view of textbook recordings can be found on Teaching Unplugged, a language teaching website: 'No recorded listening material should be introduced into the classroom: the source of all "listening" activities should be the students and teacher themselves.' This, however, means the students will be exposed to no variety of accents apart from their own and the teacher's, no topics that don't originate from the class, no native-speaker dialogues or discussions, no videos, no news broadcasts, and if the class consists solely of women, no male voices, and vice versa. The extremity of this position actually highlights many of the strengths of textbook recordings.

One of these strengths is variety. Modern textbooks contain recordings of many types: news bulletins, interviews with experts in their field, stories, jokes, songs, situational dialogues, discussions, and so on.

Besides variety, textbooks provide **listening sequences** – exploitation material that gives students a 'way in' to the recording, guides them through its difficulties and provides discussion points at the end. All of this saves the teacher a lot of work. Here is an example of a listening sequence from a well-known coursebook.

Special friends

Listening   **1**   ▶ ⬛ 75 Listen to Tim, Gus and Maxine being interviewed about their pets. Guess what their pets are from the words in the box. Compare your guesses with a partner. The answers are on page 127.

> a cat   a rat   a pig   a dog   a hamster   a parrot   a spider   a snake

2   Work with a partner. Look at the following list of pet characteristics. Tick (✓) the ones that you think were mentioned in the interviews.

a) He/She's a good companion.
b) He/She listens to my problems.
c) He/She makes me laugh when he/she does silly things.
d) We have a special bond.
e) He/She helps me make friends with other people with pets.
f) He/She frightens people away.
g) He/She keeps me fit because I have to take him/her out for walks.
h) He/She looks cool.
i) He/She parties all night long.
j) He/She gives me unconditional love.

3   Listen to the interviews again and check your answers to 2. Put *T* for Tim, *G* for Gus or *M* for Maxine if they mention that their pet has one of the characteristics.

4   Which of the characteristics in 2 would you look for in a pet? Which of these characteristics would you look for in a person? Discuss with a partner.

Textbook recordings also have a degree of integration within the syllabus – perhaps they reinforce grammar or vocabulary that has been recently studied, or they introduce or extend the topic of the unit. Furthermore, most textbooks also have the **transcripts** of the recordings in the back of the book. This allows students to check problem areas.

There is another benefit that will be apparent to teachers with access to **interactive whiteboards** (IWBs). IWBs, which are digital whiteboards with all the functions of a computer screen hooked up to the Internet, work with customised versions of some textbooks. The IWB's facilities, used in conjunction with the customised versions of the textbooks, allow teachers to do all kinds of things with textbook recordings that were not possible with older technologies. Teachers can 'summon' the transcript to the board simply by touching the screen; they can highlight a tricky part of the passage in a different colour by moving their finger across it, and then play the tricky sentence in isolation by tapping the appropriate place on the board. These facilities (and there are many more) encourage a very visual and dynamic teaching style with great benefits for the teaching of listening. At the time of writing, only a minority of schools possess IWBs and most textbooks do not have digital versions. This is likely to change in the near future.

Bearing in mind these benefits, why might teachers choose to introduce 'no recorded listening material' into their classes? One reason may be to do with **student-centredness**. In a truly student-centred class, the topics should be suggested by the students and not a third party, such as a textbook writer. Another criticism of textbook recordings is that they rarely deal with controversial or topical issues. Controversy may badly affect sales of textbooks – ELT is, after all, a business – and as a result, these books tend to play safe. Some critics have accused textbook recordings of blandness – one writer calls them 'PG-rated' (one wonders what an X-rated listening text would contain). It is also difficult for a textbook to be truly topical because of the time lapse – usually a minimum of one year – between the writing of the book and its use in classrooms.

A final aspect of textbooks is that, for both practical and pedagogical reasons, they inevitably use some scripted recordings, which, as discussed earlier, sometimes sound unnatural.

Perhaps the key point is that teachers need to *mediate* between the textbook and the class, selecting, omitting and supplementing as appropriate. If the recording lacks the interest factor for the class or it sounds too unnatural, then the teacher can always omit it or find ways to make it interesting. A recording text perceived to be above the students' level can always be given a simplified task. To sum up, the teacher needs to make pedagogical decisions about every recording, an issue that will be discussed in Chapter 7.

Television, video, DVD and radio

The advantages associated with using these media are that the material is frequently authentic, **topical**, with real-world information, and that, with television and video, there is a **visual aspect**. Being able to see the speakers, their context and body language is a huge advantage to listeners. Furthermore, there is the interest factor of seeing people in their natural habitat, a useful source of cultural information. Jane Sherman remarks, 'My Italian students ... refused to believe the English could be so eccentric as to eat biscuits with their cheese after a meal, but I showed them – in a sitcom!'

Video is dynamic in that it presents moving images – a major bonus for students with short attention spans – and for those who can't read or write well, it provides a ready-made

context. For young learners, video, with its combination of colour, action, engaging characters and story lines, is particularly appropriate.

Video can also be controlled: the pause button allows teachers to divide the recording into usable pieces. The rewind button is also a lifesaver for the confused student. In the case of DVD, we can even avoid the long wait which we endure with cassettes as they double back on themselves: DVDs will take you straight to the scene you request.

Another advantage that DVDs have over most videos is subtitles. These help bridge the gap between reading and listening skills. Some teachers and students dislike subtitles, claiming that their presence turns the process into a reading rather than a listening exercise. The answer is simply not to show the subtitles or to cover them at least for the first run-through.

The disadvantages of using media such as the radio and television include many that we have already seen with authentic materials: the level is frequently too high, the extract may be culturally inaccessible, and the teacher has to design the teaching sequence. Also, there may be a credibility problem to solve. According to Frank Lloyd Wright, 'Television is chewing gum for the eyes.' Indeed, many students, teachers and parents see TV as a medium of entertainment rather than learning. 'We can do this at home,' they say. The key is to use the medium in ways that students *don't* use it at home. These include challenging tasks. The teacher can also make the viewing collaborative, for example by asking one student to turn their back to the screen while a partner describes what is happening. Useful phrases can be picked out, highlighted and practised. Video worksheets that really guide the viewing experience can be used. Teachers can give students key phrases from the programme written on cards, which the students put into order and use to reformulate the extract. In conclusion, it is vital to treat the use of media such as radio and TV in the classroom as seriously as you would any other mode of teaching.

This brings us to the question of what exactly you want your students to watch. Many new courses these days have videos and DVDs, often a mix of authentic and scripted. These are a good place to start as they probably relate to the textbook's syllabus and topics, and provide suggested teaching sequences, such as the one on page 50.

If you want to use totally authentic material, there are a number of genres that have built-in advantages. All of the genres in the table on page 51 are short, self-contained and complete. They also have fairly common and recognisable structures which the students will be familiar with. Other benefits are listed in the second and third columns.

As to the question of which is better to use – video or audio – video has the major advantage of the visual element, as well as other advantages. Even during pauses in the dialogue, there is always something happening to engage the students. Audio presents other challenges. There is a constant flow of speech, and some would argue that audio represents a type of 'pure' listening in which students really do have to rely on their ears and brain (the following chapter will deal with the use of visuals in listening sequences). The accessibility and cheapness of audio, particularly radio, may be another advantage in some contexts.

Songs

Music brings other dimensions – art and emotion – to the classroom. Songs can be enjoyable, memorable and stimulating for the students. Teenagers, in particular, who may feel shy when pronouncing words in a foreign language in front of their peers, often feel less intimidated when the words are those of a famous singer. Another advantage is that

While you watch

SECTION ONE

(*to* **David:** Oh, OK, then.)

It is Paola's last weekend in Britain. She's staying with David in Bath. She has just gone out to the shops to buy newspapers. David has a surprise for her when she returns …

1 ▶ **Watch and answer these questions.**

a) What is David doing when Paola comes in?

_____

b) When did David buy the cappuccino machine?

_____

c) Has David learnt how to use the cappuccino machine properly yet?

_____

d) Which newspapers has Paola bought?

_____

2 Put these sentences in the correct order. Number the boxes.

☐ I'll reverse the charges.

☐ Shall we go for a walk when we've had our coffee?

☐ I'm going to call Italy.

☐ Yes, but can I make a phone call first?

☐ You don't need to.

☐ Oh, OK, then.

☐ Of course.

▶ **Watch again and check.**

SECTION TWO

(*the phone call. To* **Paola:** Ciao, Daniel.)

1 Who do you think Paola is going to call? Why?
  ▶ **Watch the video. Were you right?**

2 Match the operator's questions with Paola's answers.

Operator	Paola
International Operator Service.	The area code is 06 and the number is 586 8246.
Can I have the area code and number, please?	Calvetti. Paola Calvetti.
	Bath 622398.
What number are you calling from?	I'd like to make a reverse charge call to Rome, please.
What's your name, please?	

songs are often familiar, particularly when teachers give students the opportunity to bring songs of their choice to work with in class.

There are also a number of benefits in terms of language and skills. Songs help students focus on aspects of pronunciation such as stress patterns. Also, songs tend to contain some usefully predictable elements: the use of rhyme, for example, often helps the listener to predict vocabulary. Choruses mean we hear the same phrases with the same emphasis several times, giving students multiple opportunities to understand the lyrics. Songs often

Genre	General benefits	Linguistic features and the benefits of these
television or radio news and weather reports	topical, interesting, sometimes stories run over a period of time and in different modes (e.g. newspaper), evenly-paced delivery, clear cut-off points for pausing, headlines given first – good for prediction	vocabulary-rich, lexical sets based on topic, formal discourse – good for high levels
film clips	entertaining, dynamic, dramatic, cultural content, story line → inbuilt task (guess what happens next), easy to extend (show another clip)	various, depending on the film genre and the clip
film trailers	entertaining, dynamic, dramatic, story line → inbuilt task (guess what happens), preview is 'taster' for students to watch whole film	short turns – good for low levels
television advertisements	entertaining, cultural content, springboard for critical thinking (loaded language, bias, etc) – good for high levels, variety good for comparisons between ads – some have humour, ambiguity and short story lines	use few words – good for low levels, use persuasive language → springboard for critical thinking – good for high levels
television documentaries	in-depth look at real issues, interesting, impact (stunning visuals?), cultural content, lend themselves to personalisation (give your opinion)	lexical sets based on topic, mix of planned and unplanned (narrative and 'live') discourse – good for **awareness-raising** of formal versus informal features
episodes in a comedy series	entertaining (humour), known characters (?), cultural content – recognisable settings usually (hotel, office, home)	different tones of voice – irony, sarcasm, remorse – good for teaching intonation patterns, puns/wordplay – good for high levels
animation	entertaining (especially for children), imaginative, story line good for prediction, unambiguous characters and relationships	usually contain long dialogue-free pauses (*The Simpsons* excepted) – good for low levels/children, often simple language
television or radio talk shows/ interviews	entertaining (celebrities), few (or no) visual distractions, model for student task (peer interviews)	structured turns (question → extended answer), dynamic and unscripted, good source of discourse markers, e.g. turn-taking, topic-shifting
television or radio game shows/quiz shows	entertaining, built-in interactive participation (answering questions), clear cut-off points for pausing, cultural content, model for student task (quiz)	short turns (question → answer structure)

contain stories, too, which can be motivating. Finally, songs bring different accents, voices, cultures and ideas into the classroom.

As with all authentic material, finding the right piece isn't easy. The words need to be audible, appropriate and useful. With developments in technology, songs are becoming easier to access. One approach that teachers of teenagers are using successfully is asking the students to bring in songs on CDs or MP3 players. The teacher then applies a template for how to use the song in class. The great advantage of this is that the students choose the content. Often there is real social status to be had in knowing the English lyrics to contemporary songs – a major motivational factor! One teenagers' coursebook, shown on page 53, provides project-type templates which work with any song.

The key to using songs may lie in what you do with them. If they are seen as merely a break from routine, they will probably not carry much value with adult students beyond lightening the mood of the class (though this can be very valuable!). If they are treated as seriously as any other text, then they will be similarly valued while also containing the entertainment factor that all students – but especially young learners – need. In Chapter 7, we will look at practical ideas for using songs in class.

The Internet

The Internet is another tool in the teacher's box. Prophecies that computers will one day replace teachers have yet to come true, and show no sign of doing so. However, students who log on to a number of English language-learning websites can find much that is of use. These sites contain listening texts, questions, answers and even explanations. There are a number of benefits, including the fact that students can practise listening alone in their own time. The activities are repeatable, which means that students can work at their own pace, and there is also scope for both intensive and extensive listening. A final and important point: many of these websites are free. (See the list on page 183.)

The disadvantage, of course, is that computers generally cannot have a conversation or replicate the human interaction that allows people to learn languages, hence Picasso's comment that 'Computers are useless. They can only give answers.' This, though, is the same disadvantage carried by all non-face-to-face and even some face-to-face communication.

One recent development of Internet listening is the **podcast**. The name is a hybrid of iPod and broadcast. A podcast is a tool for publishing files on the Internet which are then sent directly to the personal audio players (usually iPods) of individuals. Podcasts allow independent producers to create something akin to a radio show which gets automatically distributed to subscribers, who can listen to it at any time they choose. There are clear possibilities for people – maybe language learners – to create their own shows which can then be heard by students in other countries as and when they wish. Musselburgh Grammar School, in Scotland, has produced foreign language recordings for students to listen to for homework (on http://mgsonline.blogs.com/mgspodcast/). Teachers can now send any .wav or MP3 files to students in what is a fairly simple process (see *How to Teach English with Technology* for more details).

It is debatable whether the limitations of listening on the Internet lie within the medium or within the attitudes of its users. Many younger students and teachers tend to be quite at ease with technology. In a nice analogy, Marc Prensky describes today's students, who have grown up with mobile phones, computers and iPods, as 'digital natives', while older teachers are 'digital immigrants' who have adopted aspects of technology but retain

Fun with songs 3

A rebus of a favorite song

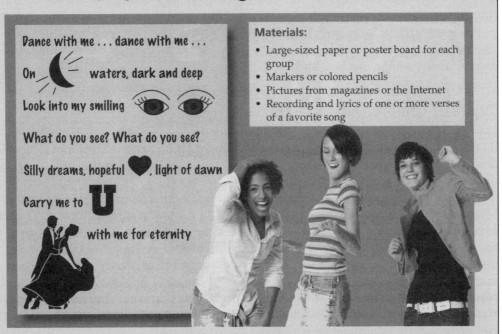

Dance with me . . . dance with me . . .

On 🌙 waters, dark and deep

Look into my smiling 👀

What do you see? What do you see?

Silly dreams, hopeful ❤, light of dawn

Carry me to U

with me for eternity

Materials:

- Large-sized paper or poster board for each group
- Markers or colored pencils
- Pictures from magazines or the Internet
- Recording and lyrics of one or more verses of a favorite song

A. GROUPS. Choose a favorite song. Choose one person in your group to bring a recording of the song to class.

B *Homework*: Find the lyrics of the song you chose in Step A. Find pictures that illustrate some of the words in the lyrics. Bring your pictures to class.

C. GROUPS. Discuss the song. Use some of the Useful language in your discussion. Create a rebus for the song. Choose someone to write the lyrics on a large piece of paper or poster board. Discuss which words you want to replace with pictures. Either draw pictures you need for your rebus or use pictures that you've found in magazines or on the Internet. Glue your pictures in place.

D. GROUPS. Exchange your rebus with another group. Figure out what words the pictures or drawings represent. Sing the song (or read it aloud) to the class using the rebus. Then listen to the recording of the song to see how you did.

Useful language:

- I think we should . . .
- I think so, too.
- That might work.
- Go ahead and try that.
- I'm not sure I agree with you.
- I'll put this here.
- That's a perfect picture for that word!
- What word is that supposed to be a picture of?

an 'accent'. Digital immigrants grew up with pen and paper and typewriters and need a manual to understand modern technology; digital natives are confident enough to let the programs teach them.

Perhaps it will take a new generation of teachers – a generation of digital natives – to utilise fully the possibilities of listening on the Internet, and to reinvent the technology so that it fits the purpose rather than following the latest trend. What is certain, given the rate at which technology advances, is that students in developed countries will have more and more options and an increasingly wide range of listening resources to choose from. Good professional teachers will keep abreast of these developments by consulting the Internet itself, which is its own greatest proponent and advertiser. In short, if you want to find out about listening on the Internet, look on the Internet.

Types of comprehension exercise

Let's assume the teacher has found or created a wonderful piece of listening material. What do they do with it now? They need to embed it into the lesson and therefore into a sequence of activities, starting with a pre-listening stage. The next thing they will plan is some type of comprehension exercise, but which?

One of the most important things to consider about comprehension questions is whether they are designed to test the student or to guide the student through the text. In a sense, all listening activities in the class test the students' abilities, but the goals of the teaching lesson and the testing lesson are different, as is the procedure. One of the differences is in the mindset of the teacher, who might like to see the listening lesson as diagnostic. *Where do the students have problems? How can I help them?* (Goodith White asks teachers to focus on 'what went wrong'.) This is a very different approach from that of testing, as we will see in Chapter 8. In the listening lesson, as opposed to the listening test, comprehension questions are useful if they scaffold learning.

In education, *scaffolding* means support from a teacher or more proficient peer. The support continues until, ideally, the student is able to 'stand' (complete tasks) alone, just as buildings lose their scaffolding once the work is completed. In practice, scaffolding often means providing a framework to understand and interpret the input.

So what types of comprehension exercises should we use? In the past, comprehension checks usually consisted of lists of questions. Current thinking suggests we need to ask our students to *do something* with the information they hear – discuss, complete notes, choose, draw, etc. If we examine a selection of tasks from widely-used published materials at the intermediate level (*New Cutting Edge, New Headway, Inside Out* and *Total English*), we can see the trends. The table on page 55 shows the twenty most common tasks in these books in total (I haven't listed the tasks in each coursebook separately because the study wasn't intended to engender a comparison between the books). These are not all comprehension exercises in the true sense of the word as some are designed to practise pronunciation or the perception of sounds (5, 10, 12 and 18). Where there is only one occurrence of a task type, I have omitted it from the list.

> Listening tasks in *New Headway Intermediate*, *New Cutting Edge Intermediate*, *Inside Out Intermediate*, *Total English Intermediate*
>
> 1 Listen to check your answers (81 occurrences)
> 2 Listen and answer the questions (34)
> 3 Listen and complete the sentences/notes (24)
> 4 Listen and make notes (18)
> 5 Listen and mark the stress (14)
> 6 Listen and tick the picture (13)
> 7 Listen. Which questions do they answer/topics do they discuss? (13)
> 8 Listen. Tick the words/expressions you hear (12)
> 9 Listen and match the people to the statements/dialogues (11)
> 10 Listen and practise/repeat (11)
> 11 Listen and notice (9)
> 12 Listen and write what you hear (9)
> 13 Listen and write answers for yourself (7)
> 14 Listen and complete the chart/table (5)
> 15 Listen and put the events in order (5)
> 16 Listen and find mistakes/differences (4)
> 17 Listen. Are the statements true or false? (4)
> 18 Listen for the difference between the two sounds (4)
> 19 Listen and mark on the map/picture (3)
> 20 Listen and read (3)
>
> There are eleven higher-order inferring questions/questions that ask for personal opinions: *Who's talking? What's their relationship? What's just happened? What's going to happen? Where are they? How do they feel? What did she think? Do you agree? Do you think she'll get the job? What impression do you get of ...? Which is the best summary?*

What conclusions can we draw from this audit? The fact that 'Listen to check' is by far the most common rubric shows the emphasis placed on students using their intuition or prior knowledge to complete an exercise before they listen. This reflects current thinking on how people learn best – by becoming active participants (sometime known as co-creators of knowledge) in the creation of meaning. Subsumed under the 'Listen to check' category are what we might call 'personalised' tasks: 'Listen to the conversation. Were your answers the same?' 'Which of your ideas were correct?' 'Listen to the questions and write answers for yourself.' In line with one of the most powerful developments in language-learning pedagogy over the last fifty years, the focus of listening tasks, at least in the books reviewed, is shifting away from de-contextualised materials and methods and towards the learners' contribution to the process.

Another striking element of these rubrics is the sheer variety. In modern textbooks it is recognised that people listen for many different purposes. Hence, we get a task asking students to listen to a weather forecast and mark tomorrow's weather on a map; we get a traditional dictation, and a dictogloss-type activity – students hear a song and write down as many of the lyrics as possible. We get tasks that ask students to make inferences ('What impression do you get of the people?'), to think critically ('Listen and decide if you agree or disagree.'), and to evaluate alternatives ('Listen. Which is the best summary?').

A further observation is that relatively few exercises ask the students to write at length while listening. Most of the 'Listen and answer the questions' exercises contain four or fewer questions, so the students don't have to hold enormous amounts of information in their minds while listening. Of the forty-two exercises involving note-taking, twenty-four consist of note completion, often asking students to write just one or two words in a space.

What about the visual element in listening? If you compare listening exercises in textbooks dating from the 1970s to the four under review, it is noticeable how different they look. In the past, the page would be filled with text, in particular, lists of questions and long explanations of vocabulary. Nowadays, these pages tend to have far less text but have photos, illustrations, diagrams and charts to complete. Visuals are used overtly in around thirty of the comprehension exercises in the audit shown in the table, but they play a background role in many more. Used properly, visuals can help students to anticipate the content of a passage or recall what they know about the topic before listening. Students can be asked to spot discrepancies between a picture and a description or to choose the picture that is being described.

There is, however, an opposite view of the role of seeing while we listen. If students are listening to a recording, they may get distracted by the things they can see, including each other. One teacher has reported using masks, of the type found on long-distance flights, to shut out all distractions. Other teachers have suggested that the students close their eyes to focus their attention. *New Headway Intermediate* asks students to 'Close your books and close your eyes', while listening to a poem, W H Auden's 'Funeral Blues'.

This view of simultaneous seeing and listening is something akin to the sixteenth-century painter El Greco's reply when asked why he never ventured outside. He said, 'I don't want the light outside to blind the light within.' For us, the light outside represents movement and colours in the classroom; the light within represents the internal process of comprehension!

Overall, the inclusion of a visual element in listening is highly beneficial for students, but for moments of intense concentration, complete darkness may work for some. My advice would be to try it; at the very least, it adds variety to classroom procedures.

Returning to the comprehension exercises in the four books, what is missing? There is little overt strategy training, although a couple of exercises do ask the students 'Which key words helped you?' Furthermore, there is very little listening for pleasure or extensive listening. There are just three examples of students listening to literature (poems and the ending of a short story) without having to do a comprehension exercise. There are eleven **higher-order questions** (asking students to interpret what they hear or infer extra-linguistic information), a number that one would expect to increase for more proficient students.

Ultimately, none of the twenty exercise types in the table is intrinsically better or worse; their suitability depends on the type of text and the reasons for listening. For teachers intent on creating their own listening comprehension exercises, the list is a place to start.

In addition to those ideas, here are some key principles:

- Questions asked by the learner will always be more interesting to them than questions asked by an outside source. Where possible, encourage students to set their own questions based on the topic.

- The task needs to fit the input. Ask the students to do something realistic with the information they hear. Whatever they do should replicate, at least in part, the reasons why the original listener would listen. This means the questions help form a bridge between the classroom and the world outside. If the students are listening to directions, get them to follow the instructions on a map. If they are listening to a description of a place, get them to say whether they would like to go there, and why or why not.

- Vary the questions so that there is a balance of intellectual and emotional response involved. Ask both higher-order and lower-order questions.

- Try to incorporate some visual material where appropriate.

- Make sure the answers contribute to the students' understanding. The idea of comprehension questions is to guide students through a listening passage, not to catch them out.

- Make sure the students need to concentrate throughout the input phase in order to achieve the task. This means we should avoid setting only two questions that are answered in the first ten seconds of a three-minute recording with nothing else for the students to do. Why? Because less motivated students will 'switch off' once the task is achieved.

And here are some things to avoid:

- testing memory rather than guiding the student to comprehension;

- focusing on irrelevant details;

- asking students to do things they wouldn't normally do with the genre of text being listened to;

- asking students to listen and read or write too much at the same time;

- pulling students out of the 'world' of the text, or going 'off topic'.

As mentioned earlier, there is sometimes a thin line between testing and teaching, and some question types may be associated with one rather than the other. Multiple-choice and true/false questions are particularly useful for testing because they are simple to mark, the answer being either right or wrong. Although multiple-choice and true/false questions can provide good pre-listening support in terms of activating schemata and helping the students to see how the passage might develop, on the negative side, these question types are seldom (perhaps never) seen as authentic by students because we don't do them in real life. They also require simultaneous reading and listening, which can be very challenging, particularly for low-level learners. In conclusion, if we want to use these question types (and they are very useful!), we need to be aware of any extra burdens we are placing on the students that may distract them from listening.

How to create tasks

With authentic materials that do not come with a pedagogical sequence (because they were not written for classroom use), the teacher will often need to create not only comprehension exercises, but also a task. What is the difference between comprehension exercises and tasks? In order to answer this question, it may be useful to look briefly at the principles behind **Task-Based Learning** (TBL), an offshoot of Communicative Language Teaching (see Chapter 1).

The main idea behind TBL is that students learn more effectively when their minds are on the task rather than on the language they are using in order to achieve it. The lesson is based on a task that students complete in groups. During the interaction, the students find that they need certain grammar and vocabulary, and thus the target language emerges from their needs instead of being pre-set by the teacher. Proponents of TBL claim that it produces a lot of communication, allowing for varied language output that is less teacher-controlled than in other methodologies, and that the students use all of their language resources to achieve the task, much as they would outside the classroom. As with most methodological approaches, there are different versions, but a common sequence is as follows:

1 Pre-task

The teacher introduces the task and maybe lets the students listen to proficient speakers attempting it.

2 Task cycle

Planning – Firstly, the students do the task. Secondly, they plan how to explain their procedures and results to the class.

Report – They tell the class how they achieved the task and compare results. The teacher may wish to play a recording of proficient speakers achieving the task at this point.

3 Language focus

Analysis – The class focuses on useful language that arose during completion of the task.

Practice – The students activate this language in a controlled or semi-controlled environment.

The task types include problem-solving, sharing personal experiences, making a list, ordering, comparing or sorting a group of items, or various creative tasks such as building or making something. To summarise the main features of tasks, we can say that they:

- involve several skills: speaking and listening but also perhaps reading and writing;
- are primarily focused on meaning rather than form, and so create opportunities for authentic language use;
- involve decision-making on the part of students;
- have an outcome, so students should feel a sense of achievement at the end;
- can often be extended, perhaps for homework or self-study;
- have a good payoff, which means they are worth setting up for the amount of language produced;
- contain some form of input and are derived from that input.

Tasks, then, differ from comprehension questions in that they usually have broader goals. As we look for materials, in the back of our minds are the key questions: *What will my students do with this? Does it lend itself to a full exploitation involving each phase: pre-, while- and post-listening?*

Below are some examples of tasks that meet the criteria above, with comments in italics. In each case, the core input comes in the form of listening to authentic material, and the tasks take place after comprehension work has been completed. The first three tasks are appropriate for any level above beginner.

 Favourites: (authentic recording: someone describing a favourite film/book/place/restaurant, etc)

Students in groups devise a radio programme in which each speaker has to talk about one favourite thing, such as a film/book/place/restaurant, etc. The students

then listen to the other recordings and prepare follow-up questions.
In this task, the personalisation is motivating and it often leads to extended discussion in the follow-up phase.

 Anecdotes: (authentic recording: students record their own anecdotes – give a theme such as travel/a first-time experience – in pairs)
During the recording phase, the students question each other to tease out as many details as possible. Afterwards, the students listen to themselves and pick out about one minute's worth – the key moment – of their story and transcribe it.
In this task, the transcribing phase leads to much 'noticing', especially concerning pronunciation, vocabulary (students tend to see their limitations) and discourse management. The teacher follows up appropriately after viewing the transcriptions.

 Five things in common: (authentic recording: someone giving biographical information)
Students prepare to speak about themselves under a number of headings: family, hobbies, work, places, etc. In pairs, they find five things they have in common. Then they change partners and repeat. (An alternative is to speak about their partner and keep changing partners. They then ask to check.)
In this task, everyone listens because they have a goal which relates to themselves.

 Business venture: (authentic recording: someone talking about a start-up company/a successful company)
The students' task is to invent a company. They prepare, in groups, to describe what the company does, where it does it, its name, and why the company will make money. The other students act as bank managers who have to decide whether to loan the new company start-up money.
In this task, everyone listens because they will need to ask questions and decide whether to loan the money.

 News: (authentic recording: the news)
After they have listened to the news and discussed the stories they have heard, tell the students that they are newspaper editors. Give them a list of twelve imaginary headlines. Specify that there is room for only six stories on the front page of their newspaper. The students work in groups to put the six most important stories on the front page in whatever position they think is justified. Afterwards the groups compare front pages.
In this task, there are many opportunities to extend or adapt: give students roles according to what type of stories they like, ask students to write or record one story, open up a discussion about newspaper content, etc.

Conclusions | *In this chapter we have:*

- **looked at some of the characteristics of good listeners, including their ability to persevere, interact with the speaker and monitor their own performance.**
- **discussed different sources of listening input, including teacher talk, student talk, guest speakers, textbook recordings, television, video, radio and the Internet.**
- **looked at the types of comprehension exercise that are most common, plus some to avoid.**
- **discussed how to create effective tasks which stem from listening input.**

Pre-listening skills and activities

People never listen without a purpose, except perhaps in a language class.
(Gary Buck)

- **Listening in the lesson – the sequence**
- **The role of the teacher**
- **What a listener needs to know before listening**
- **Activating schemata/ predicting**
- **Establishing reasons for listening**
- **Generating questions**
- **Pre-teaching vocabulary**
- **Things to avoid during the pre-listening stage**

Listening in the lesson – the sequence

Current thinking suggests that listening sequences should usually be divided into three parts: pre-listening, while-listening and post-listening. These three stages will be exemplified at length in this and the following chapters. First, however, we will deal briefly with what the three parts consist of and why this sequence is often favoured.

Pre-listening

The pre-listening stages described below help our students to prepare for what they are going to hear, and this gives them a greater chance of success in any given task. The first stage of pre-listening usually involves activating schemata (see Chapter 1) in order to help students to predict the content of the listening passage. The second stage is setting up a reason to listen. Maybe there is an **information gap** that needs to be filled or an **opinion gap** or pre-set questions, or perhaps the students have asked questions based on things they would hope to hear.

While-listening

The students hear the input once, probably listening for gist, although of course there may be occasions when they need to listen for specific information or listen in detail (see Chapter 1). They check their answers in pairs or groups. This is to give them confidence and to open up any areas of doubt. They then listen a second time, either in order to check or to answer more detailed questions. It is important that the students should be required to do different tasks every time they listen (listening to check answers is slightly different from listening to answer questions).

How many times should students listen to a passage? Some commentators say 'once'. They point out that in real life we may not get second and third chances. For teaching purposes, however, multiple opportunities to hear the input give students a safety net which helps to reduce their anxiety. There are a number of other factors concerning the passage that come into play: difficulty, length, the pedagogical focus and the potential for boredom. It may be the case that students only need to listen again to the part that they found difficult. If the focus is on close language analysis, it might be necessary to repeat several times, whereas if the focus is on listening for gist, it won't be. Hearing the same passage three times is probably the maximum before feelings of boredom begin to set in. Furthermore, if a listener has been unable to decode a word or phrase after hearing it three times, the problem is probably not one that can be solved by repeated exposure to the same recording.

With longer passages, teachers might consider 'chunking' the text by pausing it at various intervals. This can help to make extended listening more accessible and to avoid overloading the students.

Post-listening

The whole class checks answers, discusses difficulties such as unknown vocabulary, and responds to the content of the passage, usually orally, sometimes in writing. This may be done in plenary (with the whole class) or in pairs or groups.

A final stage may involve the 'mining' of the recording for useful language, a particular grammatical structure, vocabulary or discourse markers, for example.

Here is a summary of the sequence:

Pre-listening	1 Activate schemata: What do I know?
	2 Reason: Why listen?
	3 Prediction: What can I expect to hear?
While-listening	1 Monitor (1): Are my expectations met?
	2 Monitor (2): Am I succeeding in the task?
Post-listening	1 Feedback: Did I fulfil the task?
	2 Response: How can I respond?

The above is the most common sequence for a listening lesson, although the duration of each stage will vary. Why has this sequence developed? Both research and instinct tell us that students have more chance of succeeding when they know something about the topic and are mentally attuned to what they may hear. These are, after all, the conditions under which most listening takes place outside the classroom. Also, as stated in the quotation that begins this chapter, we listen with a purpose and with certain expectations, hence the development of classroom exercises that ask students to listen purposefully. During the post-listening phase there is now an emphasis on helping students with difficulties, and reflecting on performance. The post-listening stage also developed with the realisation that listening provides excellent input and that this input needs to be analysed. We should note, of course, that the sequence described here – pre-, while- and post-listening – is not the only one, and alternatives will be discussed in the next chapter. It should also be mentioned that although the three stages of the sequence have been placed in different chapters, they need to form an organic whole – a seamless flow of activities that fit the text and the teaching situation. Further guidance on lesson planning will come in Chapter 7.

The role of the teacher

The illustrations above show eight jobs that have something in common with the English teacher conducting a listening lesson. How are these jobs related to the teacher's role? Here are some suggestions:

1 A tailor: The listening text must 'fit' the class just as a suit or dress must fit its wearer. Topic, level, genre, etc must all be appropriate.

2 A stand-up comedian: Or perhaps a storyteller. As mentioned in Chapter 3, the teacher is often the best source of input. Teachers who can 'hold' an audience have a valuable skill (just make sure you've stopped speaking before the audience has stopped listening).

3 A sleuth: Before class, teachers need to be able to analyse the language in a recording as closely as Sherlock Holmes analysed clues. These are the type of questions to ask: *Will my students understand this idiom? Can they deal with the variety of verb tenses here? Will they be able to decode all the contractions in this passage? Do they need to? Will they get the joke?*

4 An engineer: When using recordings, the teacher needs a working knowledge of the way in which the equipment works and, more pertinently, the way in which the equipment sometimes *doesn't* work.

5 A spy: While the students are listening, the teacher should be watching their hands and faces. Are the students writing the answers? Do they look confused? Who is nodding intelligently? Why is one student looking at the wrong page?

6 A doctor: Teachers need to be experts at diagnosis. What went wrong? Why? Was it the speed, the vocabulary, the accent, the topic or the fact that it's Friday evening and the heating is on too high?

7 A firefighter: If *everything* goes wrong and the listening passage is too difficult, the teacher needs to get everyone out of trouble, just as a firefighter might lead the way to safety.

8 A tour guide: Teachers can point out what's interesting (that piece of spoken grammar, this bit of slang, the metaphor that also occurs in the students' mother tongue) and ignore everything that isn't. And, like good tour guides, they should make sure everybody is with them before moving on.

Naturally, the role a teacher chooses to adopt depends on many factors, including what type of class it is and whether the lesson is at a pre-listening, while-listening or post-listening stage, but it is likely that, at one stage or another, teachers will find themselves in most or all of these roles.

What a listener needs to know before listening

In 1980 Cole, Jakimik and Cooper did some research on English native speakers' perception of speech. They played a recording of a strange, de-contextualised and somewhat archaic sentence: 'In mud eels are, in clay none are.' The researchers then asked the listeners simply to report back on what they had heard. The listeners proved totally incapable of understanding the sentence. They reported hearing such nonsense as 'In muddies sar in clay nanar' and 'In my deals are in clainanar' and other sentences that sounded like something out of a fantasy novel.

For teachers of listening, Cole and Jakimik's research is relevant because it shows us that, without a clear context, connected speech often becomes inaccessible – simply noise – even to people listening to their own language.

What type of contextual information do we need? At least some of the following: Who is speaking and who is listening? Why? What is their relationship? Where are they and what are they trying to achieve? If we think about the differences between a president speaking to his people, a mother phoning her son or children nattering in the playground, it becomes clear that the context affects several factors such as vocabulary used, tone of voice, body language and patterns of discourse.

There are a number of other things that will be useful to know before we begin listening. One is the speaker's voice and way of talking. This includes pitch (high or low voice), accent, volume and what musicians call *timbre* (something like tone). Speaking styles also vary greatly: some people use metaphors liberally, others use monosyllabic words in short sentences; yet others may use speech that resembles writing in its complexity and syntax – e.g. university professors in lecture mode or political experts on TV news programmes.

Also useful to know is information about the passage we will hear. How long will it be? What is its function (ordering, persuading, negotiating)? What structure does it assume (a monologue, a three-way argument)?

Information concerning the topic is another important factor. Is it something the listener knows about and can relate to, or does it require specialised knowledge and vocabulary?

All of this information allows a listener to predict what a speaker will say and how they will say it. As mentioned in Chapter 3, 'good listeners' often know what is coming next, and are constantly making hypotheses about how the passage will develop, as well as constantly narrowing the range of possible interpretations as they confirm these hypotheses.

How can we get all of this information across to our students? Some of it can be stated explicitly by the teacher. Other information, such as the function and the intended audience, may be clear from the way published materials introduce the listening passage. But often it is the case that teachers need to prepare the students by using certain pre-listening techniques, some of which are listed in the table below. These techniques and activities are the main subject of this chapter.

What students need to know before they listen	How students/listeners can find out
the speaker's voice/way of talking	use 'tune-ins' (a short 'taster' allowing listeners to become accustomed to voices)
length of text	explicit (stated by the teacher)
intended audience and audience's role (participatory, critical, appreciative, etc)	inferred or stated by the teacher/materials
relationship between listener and speaker (friendly, hierarchical, etc)	inferred or stated by the teacher/materials
function of text (entertain, inform, etc)	inferred
information about the topic	brainstorming, discussion, pre-reading, research projects
specialised vocabulary	pre-teaching, pre-reading
what they need to do	written into the materials, or stated by the teacher (and checked via questioning of the students)

Activating schemata/predicting

We have already discussed schemata and how the use of pre-existing knowledge provides motivation and allows our students to anticipate content (Chapter 1, page 15). We will now look at six practical ways to activate the schemata and to get students to predict what they will hear. The activities involve: 1) brainstorming; 2) visuals; 3) realia; 4) texts and words; 5) situations; and 6) opinions, ideas and facts.

1 Brainstorming

Linus Pauling once said, 'The best way to have a good idea is to have lots of ideas.' He should know – he won the Nobel Prize for Chemistry and the Nobel Peace Prize. The first goal of brainstorming is to generate large numbers of ideas based on a topic or a problem. Initially, all contributions are accepted without criticism. The next stage involves whittling the ideas down to those which may be practically applicable. Brainstorming is a particularly useful thing to do before listening to factual passages with one main topic. Here are a few ways to do this in class in order to activate the students' schemata:

From one to many: the most basic form of brainstorming is probably the most common – students work alone, making notes on paper, before sharing their ideas with the group.

 Poster display: one of a number of variations on the above, this activity involves students in groups making a poster based on a given topic. A time limit on this activity tends to keep the students focused. The logical conclusion to the exercise is to do what we usually do with posters: stick them on the wall. The teacher and students then wander around the classroom looking at the posters. The listening passage will touch on many of the words/ideas in the posters and, of course, the students will be prepared for these words/ideas, having thought about them, written them down and read them.

Teachers might like to show their students word webs (see below), which are excellent for posters.

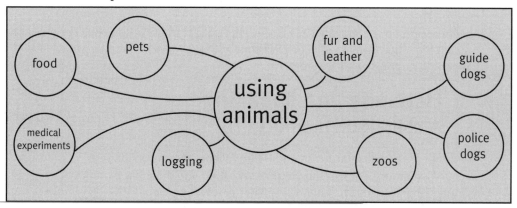

Brainwalking: this is based on the poster display activity above, but the students walk around the room, adding to or enlarging the ideas written by their classmates.

 Board writing: the students work in groups and each group is allocated a section of the board and given a different coloured board pen or piece of chalk. If the students are all brainstorming the same topic, they first note down their ideas on paper in their groups, and then one scribe from each group comes up and writes the group's ideas on the board. An alternative is to give the students different questions based on the same topic. They may then work in groups to formulate ideas first or shout out ideas for their own scribe. The final stage is for the students to sit down and appraise all of the contributions on the board before listening.

 Shout to the scribe: a variation of the above is for the students to call out ideas which the teacher writes on the board. This saves time and ensures correct spelling and grammar, which the students may choose to copy down.

2 Visuals

Used in pre-listening activities, visuals have many advantages: they are immediate and evocative – hence the axiom 'a picture is worth a thousand words'. Furthermore, many students have a visual learning style; they learn better when seeing images that correspond to the things being taught. (See Chapter 1 for comments on Multiple Intelligences theory.)

Visuals can help activate the schemata relating to any theme and any type of listening passage.

 Pictures: pictures can be used to help students recognise the lesson theme. In a coursebook there may be no overt reference in the rubric to any pictures on the page, but a picture still sends out a message about the topic of the lesson. The students can simply look at the picture and guess what the listening text will be about. One personalised way to use pictures is to ask: What does it remind you of?

 Guess what's happening: in this activity, the students make guesses in groups about what is going on. Pictures which contain some kind of mystery are the most suitable for this. Usually the pictures will contain something intriguing, perhaps discordant or out of place. There should be multiple interpretations possible in order to get the students to think creatively. They generate as many ideas as they can, share them with the class and listen to find out what is really happening (see below for an example).

A variation on the 'guess what's happening' idea is to use a film clip. The students watch a sequence from a video or DVD but without sound. They explain what is happening or guess what is being said.

Listening and speaking
A childhood memory

1 a You will hear Justin and Helen talking about a childhood memory. Look at the pictures. What do you think happened?

Helen

Justin

 Picture story: in this activity, the students are given a story told in pictures. Their task is to tell the story in groups (see page 67 for an example).

A well-known alternative is for the students to see the pictures but in the wrong sequence. The task is to put the pictures in the correct order so that the story becomes clear. Another possibility is to put the students in groups, then give each student one picture from a sequence. In turn, they describe their pictures (hidden from other students) in order to piece together the story. The extended listening stage occurs when the students hear the true story. This activity is particularly popular with young learners.

2 Listening and speaking

1 What is the Past Simple of these verbs?

> break into   steal   eat   drink   feel   fall   wake up

2 **T 44** Look at the pictures about a burglar and listen. It's a true story!

Complete the sentences with verbs from the box and your own ideas.
Don't write! Practise saying the story until you can remember it.

Picture 1
On 1 June 1992, a French burglar … a house … He … living room and …

Picture 2
Then … kitchen. He opened … cheese.

Picture 3
… hungry, so … Next … champagne.

Picture 4
… thirsty, so … Then … felt …

Picture 5
… upstairs for …, but … tired … fell …

Picture 6
When … the next …, there were … bed!

3 Complete the questions about the story.

Example
When *did he break into* the house?
On 1 June, 1992.

a How many pictures _____ ?
Two.

b What _____ see _____ ?
Some cheese.

c How _____ bottles _____ ?
Two.

d Why _____ upstairs?
Because he wanted a rest.

e When _____ up?
Next morning.

f How many _____ ?
Four.

4 Write the story for homework!

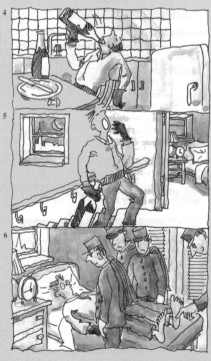

Students as artists: as a pre-listening activity and a way to activate the students' schemata, we can also use the students' own drawings. We simply state the topic and allow the students to make a representation of it. As a follow-up, we may wish to display the illustrations for all to see. This activity is especially useful for younger learners.

 Guided visualisation: this is an idea that has its roots in therapy. The first step of a guided visualisation is usually to ask the students to close their eyes and imagine something. Depending on how far we wish to take the activity, we can continue to ask our students to refine their images, adding aspects, movement and detail. At the end we might incorporate a feedback stage in which students share what they visualised.

One guided visualisation involved a group of teachers attending a presentation. They were each given a leaf and asked to examine it and to view the main stem as a symbol for themselves. The veins of the leaf (which feed into the main stem) were to represent all of the people who had influenced them as teachers.

The participants then closed their eyes and visualised these great influences – usually favourite teachers – in action. This visualisation formed the pre-listening stage of the presentation, which was about professional development and the notion of 'good teachers'.

The link between visualisation and creativity may appeal to some students (and teachers!) but not to others. Einstein's famous visualisation of himself riding a beam of light led to the theory of relativity, but there is little empirical evidence to attest to the effectiveness of visualisation as a pre-listening technique (and it would be quite a challenge for a researcher to provide such evidence). However, numerous conference participants have claimed to be stimulated by the process, and classes with open minds – which means children, in particular – tend to enjoy it.

 Diagrams: students look at a chart, table or graph. This provides a conceptual framework for their listening. Their task is to complete it or change incorrect information.

An alternative activity involves using a Venn diagram, as shown here. Find a listening passage that compares two things (for example, two sports). The students draw a Venn diagram and label the two circles (one for each sport). As a prediction

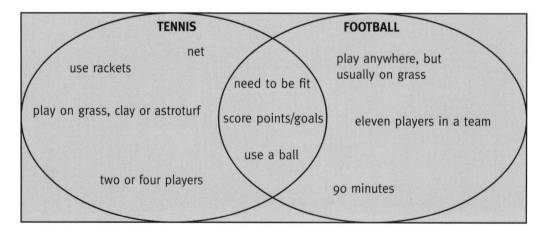

activity, the students then write down things or qualities that they associate with each sport. Those things or qualities that are common to both sports go in the intersecting area of the Venn diagram. Diagrams such as these are often understood by learners on business English courses, and also teenagers who may have studied such diagrams in other subjects in the curriculum.

3 Realia

One of the more striking uses of realia occurred in a project for teaching English to engineering students. As part of their coursework, the students were asked to write a manual for making a box kite. Naturally, they had to construct the box kite themselves (it was literally a hands-on project), and at the end of term they saw how successful they had been: some kites flew and others crashed! This project can be used to illustrate the primary function of realia in language-learning situations: it acts as a link between the world of the classroom and the outside world. In this example, realia is used in the context of engineering, but in general English classes, it is especially well suited to listening to anecdotes and stories.

How can realia help students with their listening? Objects in general bring with them memories and associations that can spark off students' ideas (does anything spring to mind when you see or touch a pair of rubber boots? A radio? A toy car? A doll?). These memories and associations are aspects of our schemata. All students can benefit from the use of realia, though it must be said that younger learners, in particular, love handling real objects.

 Using photos: one enjoyable, personalised exercise involves the teacher bringing in photos of friends or family. The students' pre-listening task is to guess who the people are. The teacher then describes them. An alternative is for teachers to bring in photos of themselves at different ages. This tends to be an amusing activity because of the ways in which fashion and hairstyles (and people) change. The realia here can be a rich source of language. The pre-listening task involves the students making guesses about what type of person the teacher was at each stage; for each photo they guess the teacher's age, favourite things, hobbies and perhaps favourite music at the time.

 Guides, maps, brochures: we can use these types of realia, as well as numerous others such as menus, calendars, entertainment sections of magazines, etc, for authentic purposes. For example, maps and guides can be used as stimuli for conversations about places and travel or features of towns and cities. Brochures are particularly useful if the teacher can collect a number of them concerning the same product or service but from different sources. One teacher trainer collected brochures from half a dozen language schools and asked her trainee teachers to examine the principles and methodology behind the courses on offer (Communicative approach? Audiolingualism? Principled eclecticism? Unprincipled charlatanism?). What does this have to do with pre-listening? Looking at brochures 'sets a scene'; we do it because we are interested in a service or a product. The brochure is seldom the final piece of the jigsaw. Instead, it is a 'taster' which leads us to seek more information; this can come in the form of a listening passage, perhaps a description of an experience related to the product or service on offer, or a video or DVD clip.

Other objects: teachers can bring in objects that form part of a story, and students guess what the story is about. In the spirit of the box kite project described earlier, teachers can also bring in pieces of an object to be assembled. One teacher of very young learners, Yuko Torimitsu, describes how she brings in objects to be made with pieces of Lego (a futuristic car, a mansion, a robot). The students in groups are given their own pieces, and their task is to construct the same object while listening to the teacher describing how to do it. Alternatives to this are to hide the target object from the students who are doing the constructing. One student from each group is allowed to see the target object and gives the instructions to the other group members, while not actually touching the pieces.

4 *Texts and words*

There are many times in daily life when we read before we listen: viewers and listeners consult TV and radio guides or read reviews of films before going to the cinema; university students read set texts before attending lectures. Texts may give us vital information or motivate us to investigate a topic further. Short reading texts can also be useful as an introduction to the topic (e.g. the text in Chapter 7, page 116, which describes ways to motivate employees), to highlight any controversial themes or to pose a question that gets students thinking.

 Court case: one idea is to present the details of a court case but without revealing the final judgment. A good example is the story about the lawyer who insured his cigars (Chapter 7, page 114). Students can read the first part of the text, predict the judgment and then listen to find out.

 Gap-fill exercises: the idea of gap-fill exercises is that students read transcripts with blanked out words or phrases. Their task is to fill the gaps. Some may see this as a grammar or vocabulary exercise rather than pre-listening, but if we wish our students to listen for detail or to listen intensively, it is an effective exercise. Here's an example (from 'Wonderful Tonight' by Eric Clapton):

It's late in the _____ .
She's wondering what clothes to wear.
She puts on her _____ ,
And _____ her long blonde hair,
And then she asks me,
'Do I _____ alright?'
And I say, 'Yes,
You _____ wonderful tonight.'

A variation on this is to delete some rhyming words from a song or poem (in the example above, we could delete *hair*). The fact that the missing words rhyme with words that the students can see provides a useful clue.

Another variation is to doctor the text so that it contains incorrect phrases. An amusing exercise is to put 'soundalike' absurdities.

It's lady in the evening.
She's wondering what nose to wear.
She puts on her May cup,
And washes her long blonde hair,
And then she asks me,

'Do I cook alright'?
And I say, 'Yes,
You cook wonderful tonight.'

Before listening, the students underline anything that doesn't seem right. As they listen, they make the necessary changes. One of the benefits of this type of activity is that it can be used with any type of listening passage; the teacher simply needs to manipulate the transcript.

 L1 first: most of the ideas in this section involve using texts in the target language. This activity is different. A very useful exercise, if it can be set up, is to ask students to listen to the news in their own language first. With monolingual classes this can be done easily. With multilingual classes it might be necessary to make arrangements such as getting the students to read the news on the Internet.

When the students listen in English afterwards, because they know the content already and therefore the cognitive load is lightened (this means there is some space left in the brain!), they are able to focus mainly on language issues. After hearing the news in their own language, the students will find themselves able to guess far more accurately than usual, and they will also start to recognise cognates (words that are almost the same in L1 and L2), an important listening strategy. For advanced students, the activity also provides a good way to compare news coverage from different sources. Aspects such as political bias may become evident as students learn to process messages more critically.

Key words: the teacher provides a list of key words from the passage. The students use these words to predict what will happen in the text, as in the examples below. Again, we can use the activity with any listening passage as all extended discourse includes key words.

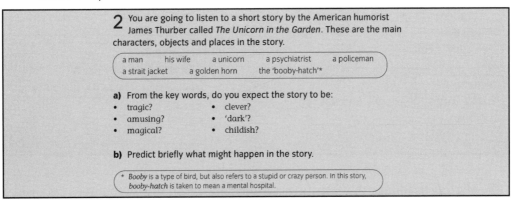

2 You are going to listen to a short story by the American humorist James Thurber called *The Unicorn in the Garden*. These are the main characters, objects and places in the story.

| a man | his wife | a unicorn | a psychiatrist | a policeman |
| a strait jacket | a golden horn | the 'booby-hatch'* | | |

a) From the key words, do you expect the story to be:
• tragic?   • clever?
• amusing?   • 'dark'?
• magical?   • childish?

b) Predict briefly what might happen in the story.

* *Booby* is a type of bird, but also refers to a stupid or crazy person. In this story, *booby-hatch* is taken to mean a mental hospital.

1 These words are from a true story. In pairs, predict what happened.

to stock up	a trolley	the checkout
the ice cream counter	a bunch of flowers	a cheque book
directory enquiries	embarrassed	

2 [▣1] Listen to the whole story.
    1 Note down three things you learn about Jane.
    2 What happened ...
       • at the ice cream counter?   • at the checkout?
       • later that day?   • on their date?

5 Situations

Certain situations – answering the telephone, ordering in a restaurant – are recognisable to most students in most countries, and this familiarity can be used to help predict the development of, say, a dialogue or a story (see the section on discourse structures in Chapter 2, page 27). These typical, routine situations, represented in people's minds, are sometimes called **scripts**. If the script seems completely alien to the students, it may lend itself to a discussion of cultural differences. British travel writer Nick Middleton tells a story of how, while riding through Ethiopia, he came across a group of herdsmen, who – as is the custom – asked him how his cows were. Not having any cows, Middleton muttered an evasive answer, at which point the herdsmen, not trusting a man without cows because this didn't fit their script, started fingering the machine guns around their shoulders. Middleton made a swift exit. The more mundane scripts that most of us live with allow us to anticipate the way certain transactional conversations will flow.

 Functions: the teacher can explain that the situation is making a business phone call, for example. The students then guess how the call will proceed: it will start with a speaker saying the name of the company and 'How can I help you?', etc. We may ask our students to try to write the dialogue first before listening. As an aid for our students, we can provide a flow chart giving the functions of each turn, as in the example below. The activity is appropriate for any formulaic transactional dialogue.

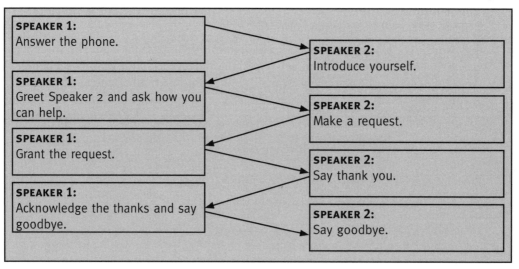

 Mystery headlines: this activity uses a different type of situation: a news story and a headline. The students are given the headline and they make guesses about the story. Below are some ambiguous headlines that have appeared over the years (this type of thing can be found on numerous websites such as www.sterlingtwilight.net and http://people.brunel.ac.uk). The students' task is to unravel the ambiguities to work out what happened, before listening to check.

Miners Refuse to Work After Death

Squad Helps Dog Bite Victim

Drunk Gets Nine Months in Violin Case

Deaf Mute Gets New Hearing in Killing

Diet of Premature Babies Affects IQ

Foot Heads Arms Body

 Problem-solving: students are presented with a problem. Their pre-listening task is to come up with ideas for solving it, or a list of questions to ask. After this, the students listen for the answers. Here are a few examples of lateral thinking problems. The answers are below in italics.

1 Mickey gets home. Lola is dead, lying in a pool of water. Tom is sitting in an armchair, looking pleased with himself. There is broken glass on the floor. Tom killed Lola, but he is not charged with murder. Why not?

2 A man lies dead in a field of snow. There are no footprints. He has a pack on his back. What happened?

3 A man goes to a coin collector with a very old, rare coin that he wants to sell. It shows a king's head and an inscription saying 220 BC. The coin collector tells him immediately it is a fake. How does he know?

Answers
1 *Lola is a goldfish and Tom is a cat.*
2 *The man's parachute didn't open.*
3 *BC means 'before Christ'. When the coin was made, they cannot have inscribed BC on it because they didn't know that Christ would be born. (Of course, this problem can only be solved by students familiar with Judaeo-Christian culture.)*

6 Opinions, ideas and facts

Using the students' views and opinions both activates and broadens their schemata. Asking them to grapple with ideas or concepts, do their own research or teach other students is a good way to involve them before they listen. These activities are particularly suitable for listening passages about factual topics.

 KWL charts: these were mentioned briefly in Chapter 2. Students are given a topic and a chart with a *K* column, a *W* column and an *L* column. *K* stands for *Know*. In this column the students write what they already know about the topic. *W* stands for *Want to know*. Students write questions here that they would like answers to. *L* stands for *Learnt*. After hearing the recording, the students write what they have learnt about the topic. KWL charts are common in many secondary school contexts, particularly in the US, but can be used profitably in ELT or ESL contexts with older students, too.

 Speed writing: the teacher gives the students the subject of the listening passage, then asks them to write continuously on this subject for a set period of time (between two and four minutes is usually enough to produce usable texts). This activity has the benefit of creating student-generated material, something that potentially has numerous offshoots: peer correction, peer comparison, collaborative writing, etc. Once the texts are completed, they can be put to use as pre-listening material in a variety of ways. For example, a simple comparison can be made between what the students wrote and what they then hear. Speed writing works with any type of literate student, although teachers of young learners might consider reducing the writing time or getting them to do it collaboratively.

 Group writing: the teacher names a topic and divides the class into three groups. Group 1 writes five questions about the topic, Group 2 writes five imperatives, Group 3 writes five sentences using negative constructions. The groups re-form so that in each new group there are now questions, imperatives and negatives. The students share their ideas and listen to see if they are answered or mentioned. Here is an example (after some peer- and teacher-correction) from an intermediate class, on the subject of New York:

Group 1 questions: Is it a dangerous city? Is the subway system easy to use? Why is it called The Big Apple? Why is it so famous? Is it expensive?

Group 2 imperative sentences: Go to the Museum of Modern Art. Take lots of money because it's expensive. Don't smoke in the bars! Walk in Central Park. Go to Times Square at New Year.

Group 3 negative sentences: New Yorkers aren't friendly. There isn't as much crime as there used to be. It doesn't take long to get there from Europe (eight hours). I have never been there. I wouldn't want to live there.

The activity works with all types of student, though the topic needs to be at least half-familiar!

 Quotations: with slightly higher-level learners, the teacher can give a list of quotations which the students discuss. They then relate the quotations to the content of the listening. Here are some quotations about education, which can be discussed before a listening passage about the same topic:

> *If you think education is expensive, try ignorance.*
>
> *Good teaching is part preparation and part theatre.*
>
> *The goal of education is to replace an empty mind with an open mind.*

Texts for language learning currently tend towards the factual; they deal with real events and issues more than in the past. Where invented characters used to dominate, now materials tend to be 'real world', for reasons dealt with earlier in the book (see the discussion on authenticity in Chapter 2). This means that dealing with facts may be an important aspect of the pre-listening stage. Here are some activities that use factual knowledge:

 Backgrounding: one class of teenagers listened to Mark Twain's novel *Huckleberry Finn* over a term. They prepared for this by doing a project on slavery in the US. This had the benefit of introducing some of the major issues of the book, some geographical names (such as the Mississippi) and other vocabulary.

Other information that can help prepare the students includes learning about the author or cultural information relevant to the context of the listening passage.

 Quizzes: students can be asked to do a quiz and to listen for the answers. This is very motivating because we naturally want to know whether our answers are correct or not. It is a classic 'Listen to check' set-up, which, as we saw in the previous chapter, is the most common rubric in published listening materials.

Advance organisers: these are initial statements or questions about a topic, which the students read and discuss. One type of 'advance organiser' consists of '1 to 5' statements. Students are given a list of statements based on a topic, and they say how much they agree on a scale of 1 to 5 (1 = completely disagree ➝ 5 = completely agree). They might then listen to someone else's viewpoint. Advance organisers of various kinds are used frequently in secondary schools, across different subjects, but can be transposed successfully to the ELT classroom.

The ideas above are all ways to activate the students' schemata and prepare them to predict content. We frequently use several modes at the same time: for example, we might use a picture and a short text, a list of questions along with a chart, etc. The key thing is to provide a 'way in' that arouses our students' interest and gives them at least some of the information they will need in order to understand the text.

Establishing reasons for listening

Once our students' schemata have been activated, we need to give them a purpose for listening. Here we look at a few general principles:

1 Make the purpose realistic (the task must reflect the type of listening text).

2 Make the goal achievable.

3 Get the students involved. If they have invested time, effort and thought in the material, they are more likely to listen successfully.

Setting questions beforehand is the most common way of establishing a reason for the students to listen. There are, of course, many different types of questions we can set. One particularly useful type is sometimes known as a **signposting question.** Just like a real signpost, this points the students in the right direction and ensures that no one gets lost. Signposting questions make listeners aware of the key points of the text and guide the students through it. Here is one practical method for getting the students to generate a simple signposting question.

 From title to question: the teacher gives the students a title which encapsulates the listening passage. They then use as many of the same words as possible to turn the title into a question. For example, the title *How to look after a rabbit* can be turned into the question *How do you look after a rabbit?* Alternatively, the students are given a title or heading and they create as many questions about it as possible in a given space of time. Two minutes is usually sufficient to produce a good number of questions but not long enough for boredom to set in.

The next section explores in more detail some techniques involved in questioning.

Generating questions

Ever since Socrates engaged his Athenian students in question-and-response routines 2,500 years ago, questioning has been a staple of education in modern democracies. We realise now that the best and most motivating task of all, as suggested in the previous chapter, is when we listen for the answers to our own questions.

A number of the activities in this chapter are designed specifically to get students generating questions (Group writing, KWL charts, From title to question) and others can be adapted to do so (Pictures, Guess what's happening).

What about questions posed by teachers or materials? One thing we do know is that, in modern pedagogy, questions come thick and fast from the teacher. White and Lightbown's 1984 study found that teachers asked around 200 questions per class, while Long and Sato noted 938 questions in six elementary ESL classes in 1983. One factor that these studies highlighted was the need to be aware of the differences between certain types of questions. **Higher-order questions**, mentioned briefly on page 56, are those which ask students to analyse something (*Do you think the play touches on any contemporary issues?*) or personalise the issue, maybe even going beyond the immediate topic. Higher-order questions tend to produce deep thinking as they are often open-ended and may have more than one answer. In contrast, **lower-order questions** ask students for very basic factual information and usually have just one correct answer (*Who does Macbeth kill first?*). At the least authentic end of the scale are **display questions**, encapsulated by Mehan's famous classroom data, a dialogue that went like this:

TEACHER: What time is it, Denise?
STUDENT: Two-thirty.
TEACHER: Very good, Denise!

This type of question – where the teacher is asking for a correct form rather than for any thought – clearly has no place in pre-listening activities, but higher- and lower-order questions can be useful for students as a way to activate their schemata. A good question is an invitation to think. Teachers who examine a listening passage before class, finding interesting themes, sensing potential incongruities and noting cultural issues, should consider presenting these in the form of questions for students to discuss before they listen.

Pre-teaching vocabulary

If the teacher thinks that there are a number of words that will be unknown to the students, and that these words are essential to the meaning of the passage or to the completion of the set task, it is probably better to pre-teach them. Besides being an essential step towards an understanding of the passage, pre-teaching words may also give students confidence as well as potentially useful information about the topic.

When making the decision about whether to pre-teach an item of vocabulary or not, there are several factors to consider. One is the time it takes to teach the word. Another is whether the word itself is worth the effort. If the word is of **low surrender value** (which means it is of very limited use to learners), it is probably not worth teaching it. If the teacher decides it is worth the effort, efficiency is the key. Teach the word in a familiar context (or get the students to look it up), check that the students grasp the concept, check the pronunciation and get them to do something with it: put it in a sentence and personalise it. Ideally, students will have the opportunity to say the word – we are more likely to recognise sounds that are known to our mouths as well as our ears – but remember that the goal is for the students to be able to recognise the word in connected speech. For this goal to be achieved, the more the new word is processed by the students, the more likely they are to be able to recognise it during the actual listening.

Another consideration is the number of words to be pre-taught. A short answer is: the fewer, the better. Are there any limits or guidelines? It depends on many factors: whether the students have good memories or not, their previous exposure to English, whether the words themselves are memorable or not, and, as stated above, the amount of processing the students do with the words. As a rough guideline, we could say that pre-teaching more than four words is probably too much for most classes.

On the negative side, recent research has found that the effectiveness of pre-teaching vocabulary is questionable. The researchers Chang and Read, in a study of 160 Taiwanese students, concluded that pre-teaching vocabulary was considered the least effective of a number of pre-listening techniques.

Describing a situation that many teachers may recognise, an online educational forum contains the following anecdote:

> 'I remember a colleague, a teacher trainer, telling me how he was watching a class where the teacher was painfully pre-teaching the vocabulary for a listening activity. It took something like twenty minutes or so. Just as the teacher was about to play the tape, a late-arrival entered the class. The late-arrival seemed to make just as much sense of the text as did the other students, despite having missed out on the pre-teaching. It makes you wonder what was really happening in those twenty minutes.'

The problem is that newly-learned vocabulary is usually not accessible to the student in mid-listening phase. Most students cannot think quickly enough because they need to process the spoken form of the word and its meaning simultaneously. If the students have come across the vocabulary for the first time a few minutes before listening, they may not a) recognise the word in connected speech, or b) be able to recall its meaning during the high-pressure, real-time processing that takes place when we listen. The essential thing about learning vocabulary so that it becomes automatised is that students have several opportunities to process the word over time. The type of situation in which students 'meet' words moments before hearing them in fluent speech does not cater to this need.

Another problem revealed in Chang and Read's study is that pre-teaching vocabulary tends to encourage students to focus on the target vocabulary rather than the meaning of the passage as a whole.

A final, more positive reason for not pre-teaching vocabulary is that guessing unknown words is a valuable skill in itself, and one that the students should practise regularly.

Overall, then, teachers are urged to think very carefully about which words to pre-teach, how to pre-teach them and whether the meaning of unknown words can be inferred and checked in the post-listening phase.

On page 78 are two examples from published materials of ways to pre-teach vocabulary before listening. Notice the different approaches: the first asks the students to do something with the words, although it doesn't deal at all with meaning, while the second provides a dictionary definition and asks the students to read the poem before listening.

Lexis: daily activities

1 Work with a partner. Complete the table by matching the verbs (*watch, do, have, go, listen to*) with the nouns to make ten different daily activities.

a) *do*	b) ___	c) ___	d) ___	e) ___
• the washing up • the ironing	• to the park • for a walk	• a cup of tea • lunch with friends	• the radio • the birds singing	• television • films and sport

2 ⏹ 🔊 22 You are going to listen to eight people (*1–8*) saying what they do when they want to relax. Check your answers to 1.

SECTION 2

Before listening

b) Work with a partner and compare your answers.

c) You are going to read the poem aloud. Which words will you stress? Where will you pause?

> **smithereens** /ˌsmɪðəˈriːnz/ *n* (plural) a lot of small broken pieces

d) Practise reading the poem.

2 [📻 3.2] Listen to Roger McGough introducing and reading the poem. How does his reading compare with yours? (e.g. Does he read it more quickly or more slowly than you? Does he stress words you didn't?)

Smithereens

I spend my days
collecting smithereens.
I find them on buses
in department stores
and on busy pavements.

At restaurant tables
I pick up the leftovers
of polite conversation.
At railway stations
the tearful debris
of parting lovers.

I pocket my eavesdroppings
and store them away.
I make things out of them.
Nice things, sometimes.
Sometimes odd, like this.

3 You are going to listen to Roger McGough talking about how he writes his poetry. Imagine you were able to earn your living writing poetry.

a) What kind of poems would you like to be able to write (e.g. love poems, poems about places)?

b) What kind of daily routine would you have? (e.g. Would you write at night?)

Listening **c)** What advantages and disadvantages would there be in this kind of life?

d) Find another student who has similar ideas.

Things to avoid during the pre-listening stage

Having considered a number of good characteristics and examples of pre-listening activities, let us look at some things to avoid.

1 Don't let the pre-listening stage drag on. Make it short and fast paced.

2 Don't give away too much information to the students. Part of the interest of listening lies in 'catching' new information that you then use to solve a problem, confirm an idea, develop a thesis, etc. The idea of pre-listening is to introduce the topic rather than to give all the answers.

3 Don't 'do a listening before the listening'. Launching into a teacher monologue introducing the subject is the same as asking the students to do two listenings. During the pre-listening phase, let the students do as much speaking as possible. Keep in mind Christine Nuttall's axiom, 'Never say anything yourself if a student could say it for you.'

4 Don't just talk about the general topic; if the idea is to introduce the listening passage, the conversation should stick, more or less, to the content of the passage. The pre-listening activity must be entirely relevant to what the students will hear.

We will finish this chapter on a fanciful note. Although we would not normally use such a short recorded text, let's imagine that the teacher wishes to prepare a group of students for the sentence we saw at the beginning of the chapter: 'In mud eels are, in clay none are.' The teacher's preamble might go something like this:

> 'So, look at the picture.' [Students look at a picture of an eel.] 'Does anyone know what type of fish this is? That's right. It's an eel. Listen. Eel.' [Students repeat; T writes *eel* on the board.] 'Now, does anyone know where eels live? In water, you said? That's right. Where else? That brown substance is called mud. Does anyone know the type of mud that we use to make pots or vases? That's right: clay!' [Students repeat; T writes *clay* on the board.] 'Now we're going to listen to a very old recording of an expert on eels. It's very short. The sound quality isn't great and he speaks rather old-fashioned English. Anyway, the question I'd like you to answer is this: Where can we find eels? Are we ready?' [T plays recording: 'In mud eels are, in clay none are.']

This preamble manages to avoid the four no-nos: it is short, it doesn't give away too much information, it allows the students to contribute, and it is focused on what the students will hear.

Conclusions | *In this chapter we have:*

- looked at the most common sequence of listening lessons – pre-listening, while-listening and post-listening.

- talked about the different roles the teacher may assume, according to the stage of the lesson.

- highlighted the type of information that is useful to know before we listen, such as context, the function of the dialogue, the speaker's voice and the speaker–listener relationship.

- looked at activities which help to activate the students' schemata and allow them to predict what they will hear.

- discussed ways to establish reasons for listening.
- discussed the issue of whether to pre-teach vocabulary or not, concluding that it is worth doing so under certain conditions (if the items are crucial to the meaning).
- looked at ways to generate questions.
- suggested some general principles concerning pre-listening skills and activities.

While-listening skills and activities

No man ever listened himself out of a job. (Calvin Coolidge)

- **Why use while-listening activities?**
- **Listening for gist**
- **Listening for detail**
- **Inferring**
- **Participating actively**
- **Note-taking**
- **Dictation**
- **Listen and do**

Why use while-listening activities?

The history of English language teaching is full of shifts in approach, fads, false trails and the sound of babies being thrown out with the bathwater. While-listening activities reflect this as much as any other aspect of language teaching, and down the ages we have persuaded students to do a whole range of things when they listen: transcribing everything that is said, word for word; curling up in an armchair and closing their eyes while the teacher reads a text; manipulating coloured wooden blocks on cue; falling asleep at night to the sound of English on tape, hoping that the language will worm its way into their dreams.

All of the above may be valid in certain contexts, but most current thinking points to one central idea: that students must, in some way, use the information that they hear. The content should demand a response. It should make them think and react. And the activities that teachers ask their students to do should contribute to, or help shape, this response.

Before we look at some while-listening skills and activities, let us consider a question: When all the research tells us that listening is an extremely active process in which the mind works very hard, why ask our students to do yet more in the form of a task? Why get them to do *anything* while they listen? There are two main reasons. The first is that well-designed activities can help students to understand the listening passage. Such activities:

- provide a focus, showing students what is important about any given passage;
- allow them to perceive the text's structure (causes and effects, problems and solutions, etc);
- help them to 'chunk' the listening into sections or units of information;
- provide clues as to how they might respond;
- keep them concentrating throughout the passage;
- contribute towards the entertainment factor of the lesson by highlighting points of interest, irony, humour, etc.

The second reason for setting while-listening tasks is that we want our students to show evidence of understanding or non-understanding. This allows us to recognise the points at which we need to intervene, clarify or provide further practice.

As we discuss the activities, it may help to bear in mind the distinction between responses that involve production and those that involve recognition only. Productive responses include note-taking, writing answers to questions, correcting errors and completing tables, charts, diagrams and sentences. Recognition responses include answering multiple-choice and true/false questions, ticking words and phrases that are heard, matching and choosing pictures.

With recognition responses, the students have less to do and therefore experience less distraction from listening, whereas productive responses demand other skills besides listening. A written response, for example, may require a focus on any or all of the following: grammar, spelling, punctuation and cohesive devices. The time it takes to write also puts pressure on the students' short-term memory. In other words, by the time they are writing, they may have forgotten much of the information in the listening passage. An oral response also demands more of the learner than solely comprehension. It may not always be clear if the students' problems lie in their comprehension of the passage or in the fact that they don't speak L2 well enough to explain their thoughts. The latter situation, of course, describes a speaking problem rather than a listening problem. To summarise, it is always wise to remember that the purpose of listening is comprehension, not production.

As we look at a number of while-listening activities in the following pages, the distinction between the two types of response will be helpful for readers in considering a number of questions. For example: For which level of student is the activity appropriate? How long would the activity take, and what is the ratio of time spent listening to time spent responding? How much integration is there with other skills? How free or controlled are the students' responses in the activity?

Listening for gist

On their first encounter with a passage in the classroom, students usually listen for gist – the main idea. Before we can develop any discussion of themes, analyse language used, examine features of pronunciation, etc, the students need to have grasped the overall communicative intention of the speaker. This forms the basis and the context of all other work that we do on the text.

Here are some examples of typical gist questions:

What problem are they discussing?
What does the speaker think of the topic?
Look at the pictures. Who are the speakers talking about?

A simple gist exercise is to ask for basic information under the headings *What? Who? Why?* (see the similar What/When/Who table in the section on teacher talk in Chapter 3, page 42). This works for most listening passages.

Listening for detail

If we tend to ask our students to listen for gist the first time they listen, we usually ask them either to listen in detail or to listen for specific information the second time (see Chapter 1).

In recent years, psychologists have discovered some rather interesting t ability to focus on details at the expense of other information. In a 19 experiment at Harvard, participants watched a video of some students p Their task was to count the number of passes made by one team. Afte asked to answer some extra questions: *While you were doing the counting, u... anything unusual on the video? Did you see anyone else (besides the six players) on the viuce.* It turned out that 46 per cent of the participants had been so engrossed in the task that they had not noticed a man in a gorilla suit walk onto the court, stop to face the camera, thump his chest and walk off again. This was an astonishing example of selective looking. The oral/aural equivalent which we will now discuss is **selective listening.**

While listening to announcements in an airport, we filter out almost everything we hear because only one flight announcement is relevant to us: our own. If there are 200 people in the departure lounge, some are listening for London, others for Milan, others for Caracas, a selection driven by the listener's needs rather than the speaker's. The skill of extracting the information we need, as mentioned in Chapter 1, requires an ability to ignore most of what we hear and focus only on what is relevant. How can we practise it?

 Bingo: in this activity, which is particularly enjoyable for young learners, the teacher writes a list of words on the board, all of which occur during the listening passage. These should be content words – nouns and some verbs, not words such as *of* or *and*. The students, working alone, choose and write down seven of these words (or however many the teacher feels is appropriate). They then listen to the passage. Whenever their words come up, they tick them. They shout *Bingo!* when they have ticked all seven. This activity is excellent for selective listening though it actually prevents listening for global meaning. As such, it should only be done after an initial listening has established the gist.

 Times, dates, numbers: many listening passages are full of times, dates and numbers. We can ask our students to note them down, also making a note of their significance. A real-life application of this exercise is writing down a phone number or address.

 Spot the difference: the students look at a picture and listen to a description of it. The oral description contains a number of differences from the picture. The students listen for these differences, and mark them on the page.

'Spot the difference' is perhaps slightly more challenging than 'Times, dates, numbers'. Students listening for differences cannot afford to switch off at any point because what they are listening for could be one of many things, and they don't know when it will occur. With the 'Times, dates, numbers' activity, we usually know what we are listening for (a departure time, for example) and so can filter out extraneous information.

 A story told twice: similar to 'Spot the difference', this activity hinges on students listening for changes to something they have already come across, in this case a story. The teacher tells the story twice. The second time a number of details are changed, as in the example below.

Version 1
Billy Morris walked into a chemist's with a note that said, 'I have a gun in my pocket. I will shoot if you don't give me the money.' The assistant threw the note

into the bin, without reading it. He tried the Italian shop next door. 'I'm sorry, sir,' said the owner, 'I can't read English.' Next he tried the Chinese restaurant. The manager said, 'I need to get my glasses,' and went to a room at the back and called the police. Five minutes later they arrived and arrested Mr Morris.

Version 2

Billy Morris walked into a supermarket with a note that said, 'I have a gun in my bag. I will shoot if you don't give me the money.' The assistant threw the note into the air, without reading it. He tried the German shop next door. 'I'm sorry, sir,' said the owner, 'I can't read English.' Next he tried the Japanese restaurant. The manager said, 'I need to put my contact lenses in,' and went to a room at the back and called the police. Five hours later they arrived and arrested Mr Morris.

The students' task is to note down all changes as they listen. Alternatively, they can make some kind of gesture or movement (hands up, clap or stand up).

 Mixed focus: the students listen to the same passage but they focus on different information, or 'tune in' to different speakers. For example, if the recording consists of two people giving an opinion on something, listener 1 listens for speaker A's opinion, while listener 2 listens for speaker B's opinion. There are numerous variations on this, depending on the material being used. For example, at a high level, one group of students can be asked to listen for idiomatic language while the other listens for adjectives. In the listening passage below, the idiomatic language is in italics and the adjectives are underlined.

When I heard about all the *fuss* surrounding this artwork I was <u>curious</u> to see it and when I did, my <u>first</u> thought was, '*God, she's <u>messy</u>!* The bed was <u>unmade</u>, the sheets <u>dirty</u>, *there was all sorts of rubbish* – cups, plates, magazines strewn everywhere. *It was pretty revolting really* – particularly in a <u>nice</u>, <u>clean</u>, <u>white</u> gallery. Then my <u>second</u> thought was, '*Well*, it's quite <u>interesting</u>, *but I mean*, what if somebody *sneaked in* and made the bed while nobody was looking?! Would it still be art?'

 Hoarse whisperers: this stems, in part, from Colin Cherry's research into what he called 'the cocktail party effect'. The effect occurs when we are in a crowded room (for example, at a cocktail party), engaged in conversation with someone, and suddenly we hear our name from another side of the room. We then 'tune in' to the other conversation to find out what so-and-so is saying about us. The phenomenon shows that we are able to shift our focus when we listen.

The activity involves a simple information gap – one student has information written down that his or her partner needs. The partners sit on opposite sides of the room and whisper the information to each other. They soon find that they have to whisper loudly in order to be heard above the competing whisperers. The activity is good practice for discriminating sounds under adverse conditions, lip-reading, pronunciation and using or comprehending gestures.

Inferring

Inferring is a thinking skill in which we make deductions by going beyond what is actually stated. It is all about making analogies to situations that we recognise. Inferring is closely linked to schema theory in that it requires a 'model' in our heads of how the situation might unfold.

To a certain extent, we cannot help inferring every time we listen. If someone says 'I took a book out of the library' we infer that they went up to the desk and checked out the book, using a library card or some kind of ID (rather than, say, putting the book into a sack and leaping through the window). This is inferring on a basic level, which everyone does. Without it, we would have to explain every detail of every experience, as if talking to a Martian, and conversation would be a chore.

So what actually happens when we infer at a higher level? Firstly, the situation must demand an inference. Either something latent remains unsaid or there is a hidden truth below the surface of the situation. In other words, there is a 'gap' which the listener fills in.

Gaps in narrative were originally brought to prominence by reading theorists, who claim that these omissions force the reader to imagine or to help create the text. Indeed, this 'co-creation' of texts is one of the reasons that we enjoy reading. Gaps, however, are applicable not just to reading but also to listening. On page 86 is a text that lends itself well to inferring. Notice how some of the questions ask the students to go beyond what is on the page/recording (the students are asked to listen and read at the same time).

Here are some activities to practise inferring.

 Pause and predict: essentially, this involves creating gaps in the text, which the listener tries to fill. The teacher pauses the recording or narration frequently and asks students what they think will come next and why. There is an example of this activity on page 114 (the story of the cigar-smoking lawyer). One of the beauties of the activity is that as the text gradually reveals itself – its story line, tone, theme, style and register – the listener's guesses tend to become more and more accurate.

 Not her, not him: each student is given ten to twelve pictures of people. Every picture must be on a separate sheet of paper. The teacher then describes one of the people slowly, without telling the students which one. As the students hear the unfolding description, they are able to eliminate various candidates (inferring who *isn't* being described). They turn over the pictures that don't fit the description. The activity requires some practice on the part of the teacher, the key being to reveal information gradually.

 Twelve questions: for an extended listening passage, you can use this diagram or something similar.

Many of the questions will be unanswerable, but the act of thinking about them makes students aware of the idea of inferring. It allows them to recognise that we can sometimes 'know' things without them being stated explicitly.

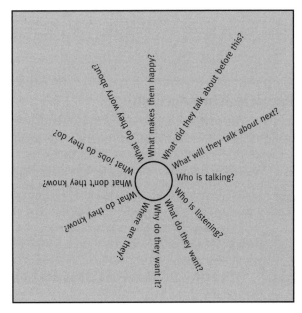

Reading and Listening

1 a **3.2** Read and listen to a short story. Answer the questions.

1 Who do you think had the idea to go birdwatching?

2 What type of town do Thomas and Rosie live in?

3 Is Thomas good at spelling? How do we know?

4 What type of person is Rosie? How do we know?

5 What does the father think of Thomas's description of the birdwatching trip?

6 Why was Rosie 'disgraced'?

7 How does the father feel about his children?

8 Which of these words would you use to describe the story? Circle one or more of the words.

surprising   surreal   traditional
shocking   funny

Birdwatcher

At 2.32 on the afternoon of 10th July, eight-year-old Thomas Smith saw a large yellow-beaked eagle rise from the roof of the local post office. His sister, ten-year-old Rosie, didn't see it because she was busy
5 applying her mother's lipstick to her small, but very pretty, mouth, and in any case she wasn't all that keen on birdwatching.
'Rosie,' said Thomas. 'How do you spell eagle?' His pencil was poised above a notebook which
10 had a picture of an owl on the front and on which Thomas had written 'BuRds'. B-u-r-d-s.
'Eagle?' said Rosie. 'I-d-i-o-t.'
'Very funny.'
'E-e-g-l-e.'
15 Thomas wrote it down. Eegle. 2.32, 10th July. Kingston Road Post Office.
They crossed the street, slipping between the fat cars all stopped still in the summer heat, fingers tapping outside windows. It was at this point that
20 Thomas heard the distant shriek of seagulls and recognised the sound at once. The previous summer they had spent a week with their parents at a seaside town eating huge sausages in pools of grease and getting red-faced in the sun, and had been woken

25 every morning by this same sound.
'Rosie, how do you spell seagull?'
'Same as eagle but it starts with an s.'
At 2.58 Thomas and Rosie paused for a minute while Rosie searched her handbag for the blue eye
30 shadow that she had removed from her mother's drawer. It was called Aquamarine Dream. At this moment, Thomas noticed a penguin waddling down the High Street. Thomas watched it go by, the penguin merrily traipsing through the cigarette butts
35 and chewing gum stains fossilised on the pavement, and Thomas wrote 'Pen Win' in his notebook.
Later, while the disgraced Rosie was shut up in her room, her mother's makeup returned, Thomas sat at his father's feet and explained about the eagle
40 on the post office roof, the ostrich outside the library, the vulture in Rosemary Gardens snacking on a discarded bag of popcorn. And his father ruffled the boy's hair and laughed to himself and thought about the wonders of the child's imagination. And
45 the man felt at peace with the world and with his two naughty children, at least until 3.11 a.m. the following morning when he was woken by an enormous white swan sitting at the end of his bed, its yellow eyes glaring.

Participating actively

Active participation might include transferring what is heard from one medium to another, using skills such as drawing, or tracing a route on a map. As there are similar activities in other sections of this chapter, we will focus here on activities which ask the students to listen and respond either verbally or by categorising aspects of what they hear.

 Listen and describe: the teacher tells a story but stops regularly and asks the students to write or give a description. For example, the teacher begins, 'I was walking close to my home when I met a girl. What did she look like?' The students then write a one-line description, e.g. 'She had green hair and big hands' (from a young learners' class).

The activity works well as a way for students to generate language. At the end, the teacher should tell the whole story with no interruptions, as this provides an extended and more enjoyable listening experience.

Interrupted storytelling: as with 'Listen and describe', the students listen to a story. While doing this, they keep interrupting by asking questions. Here is the teacher–student interaction from a low-intermediate class. The class has been studying expressions with *have* and *go* (*have a drink, have a problem, go home, go abroad*, etc) which are reinforced using the interrupted storytelling activity.

TEACHER:	Now I'm going to tell you a story. But I want you to keep interrupting me by asking questions using the expressions we looked at today and the structure 'Did you ...?' OK, just shout out your questions whenever you think of them. For example, 'Did you go crazy? Did you have a drink?' OK, are we ready? A few years ago I'd been working very hard and I decided to take a break ...
STUDENT:	Did you have a holiday?!
TEACHER:	Yes, I did! I really wanted to go somewhere warm because I was living in England which is rather cold ...
STUDENT:	Did you go abroad?!
TEACHER:	Yes, I did! I went to Goa in India, which is very beautiful but also a great place to party.
STUDENT:	Did you go crazy?!
TEACHER:	Not exactly.
STUDENT:	Did you have a problem?
TEACHER:	No, I didn't, but thank you for asking ...

With intermediate or lower levels, the activity usually works best if the students are given a particular grammatical structure for their questions because it simplifies their task.

 Truth or lie: this activity is useful in that it gets students to focus on meaning and then evaluate what they hear in terms of everything they know about the speaker and the situation. The activity is similar to note-taking, which we will discuss in more detail below. The students divide the page into two columns – *Truth* and *Lie*. The teacher tells a story based on the truth but with fictional embellishments. The students take notes either in the *Truth* column (if they think that part of the story is true) or in the *Lie* column. Alternatively, the teacher can use bits of information – perhaps biographical – for the students to classify as *Truth* or *Lie*. The natural follow-up to this is to get the students to dictate their own sentences to each other, and then speak about them.

 Information transfer: the students complete a diagram or drawing based on what they hear. Here is a simple, low-level information transfer activity: the students each have an illustration of an empty plate. In pairs, they take turns to describe what they ate for lunch that day while their partner attempts to draw the food on the plate.

A higher-level activity might be to get the students to describe an average day in terms of time spent on activities. For example, a student might say, 'I sleep for eight hours. Of the other sixteen hours, I spend about two hours a day eating, and about an hour travelling ...,' etc. Their partner listens carefully and draws a pie chart of the speaker's average day. A pie chart is a circle divided into slices, like a pie. The size of the slices, which are labelled 'sleeping', 'eating', 'travelling', etc, depends on the time spent doing each activity.

Note-taking

In terms of improving the listening skill, note-taking promotes a higher level of attention. It forces students to pick out the important points in a talk or lecture because they cannot write down everything they hear. For many students, particularly those in tertiary education, note-taking is an important life skill as it enables them to record information for later use.

It is beyond the scope of this book to examine in detail ways in which to teach note-taking (which is, after all, a type of writing), but there are a few general ideas in the table below.

Techniques for note-taking	Elaboration/rationale/examples
Choose only important information.	Do not try to write everything. Density of information usually means efficiency in note-taking.
Paraphrase (use different words that mean the same thing, but which say it more economically).	Using your own words means that you process and personalise the information.
Use titles and subtitles.	Subtitles divide the talk into clear sections, making its structure more transparent and making recall easier.
Use spaces.	Spaces can denote changes of topic or new sections. They also give us 'breathing space' from the density of the page when we review our notes later.
Use abbreviations.	Create your own shorthand (*for example* can be written as *e.g.*; *your* can be written as *yr*). Cut vowels from words in note form (consonants are more useful for recognising words). Use texting abbreviations that are familiar from mobile phones.
Use symbols and numbers.	Use mathematical operators such as + and =. These are quicker to write. Use numbers to organise lists. Use symbols that are familiar from texting on mobile phones.
Use emphatic markers.	To emphasise information, underline, highlight, write in CAPITALS or write in a different colour.
Use diagrams.	The mind doesn't necessarily work in straight lines. More visual representations can be effective (e.g. stem-and-branch diagrams, word webs).

Notes are essentially private records, as suggested on page 36, and ultimately, note-taking is an individual skill in the sense that different people do it differently, but it can be practised and improved. Here are some ideas:

Guided note-taking: instead of starting with a blank piece of paper, the students are given subheadings, numbers or unfinished notes to guide them. Subheadings show the structure of the listening passage and help students identify transition points, i.e. changes of topic or other developments in the discourse. Numbered lines, which are left blank, can serve as prompts, revealing how many key points must be noted down. Unfinished notes provide reference points which help keep the students on track. Here are some examples.

Listen to a lecture about Picasso and take notes under the headings.

Early work

Blue period

Cubism

Listen to a lecture about Picasso's different styles of painting. As you listen, take notes.

1 early works

2

3

Listen to a lecture about Picasso and complete the notes.

In his early days he copied ____
Dark, sombre paintings represent his ____
With Georges Braque he began ____

 Phone messages: this is among the more realistic note-taking exercises. The students work in pairs. One reads a pre-prepared phone message. The other simply notes it down. If your school has internal phones, you can add further realism by putting the pairs in different rooms. This replicates some of the features of authentic phone calls: lack of visual input and distorted sound. Alternatively, get the students sitting back-to-back so they cannot see each other. A standardised 'phone message template' such as this example will add to the authenticity.

WHILE YOU WERE AWAY ... ☎

Caller ....

Phoned at ....

To speak to ....

Message:

Hidden picture: the students each have one picture of a person, which they keep hidden from their classmates. They describe the picture and their classmates take notes. Each set of notes describing an individual picture is numbered by the students. Afterwards, all the pictures are stuck on the board and the students have to match their notes to the pictures. Several teachers have noticed that the students feel a real sense of achievement during this activity when their classmates ask them to slow down!

 Chart summary: the students complete a chart as a way of summarising the text. The chart should require a few words only in each section. This has the advantage of being visually clear and amenable for review.

Note-taking has both day-to-day and academic uses. In our daily lives, we may take notes from a phone call or a meeting, make shopping lists while in conversation with a spouse or partner, or scribble tasks to be achieved or ideas on the back of an envelope. There are, of course, big differences between this form of note-taking and the skill as used in tertiary education in particular. In the latter, the register tends to be more formal, the duration of the input is longer, and the schemata more specific in that the topic is an academic subject usually requiring some expertise on the part of both listener and speaker.

The growth of academic English around the world has led to a number of research projects on academic listening (which generally means lectures) and note-taking. One of the findings that is applicable to language teachers concerns lecture style. Of course, ELT practitioners are not necessarily lecturers, but many of us tell stories and deliver monologues of different kinds from time to time. The list on pages 43–45 shows ways to do this more effectively.

Dictation

Dictation is probably the best-known activity for intensive listening, but it fell out of fashion soon after the arrival of the Communicative Approach. There are a few reasons for this. One is that, done traditionally, it isn't communicative. Another is that it can be dull; transcribing requires no creativity or emotional investment on the part of the transcriber. Also, as expected with a word that shares a root with *dictator*, it tended to be associated with teacher-controlled methodology and **Grammar-translation**. This was at a time when learning was becoming more student-centred, at least in theory.

Many teachers realise, however, that dictation has great benefits as an activity type. Davis and Rinvolucri list ten good reasons for using it in class, including the fact that students are active during and after the dictation, that it is good for mixed-ability (because it is entirely receptive, requiring no output from the student) and large classes, and provides access to interesting texts. Another benefit is that it is a multiskilled activity, potentially involving listening, writing, reading and speaking. It is a great way to focus the attention of over-animated students or daydreamers at the back of the class. Furthermore, dictation is a very flexible activity, with numerous variations which we will look at in this section.

Firstly, we will deal with some questions that teachers might ask when planning a dictation, and some answers.

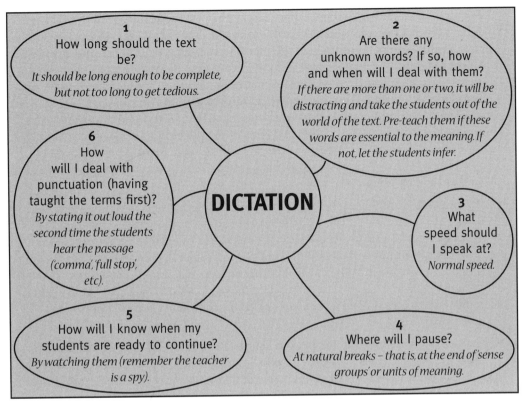

Here is one common approach to using dictation in class:

1 Read the passage at full speed. The students listen only.

2 Read the passage in chunks, leaving time for the students to write.

3 Allow a few minutes for students to check individually.

4 Read the passage again at full speed.

5 Allow a few minutes for students to check in pairs or groups.

6 Give feedback to the whole class (hand out the passage or write in on the board).

Dictations have an in-built danger: that students will slip into 'robot mode', writing down what they hear without actually thinking about the content. This problem is similar to that of weak readers or young children reading aloud – they decode words without considering the meaning of the whole sentence, and therefore pause in the wrong places and emphasise the wrong words. Dictations done badly reduce the listeners/writers to machines; they act as nothing more than speech transcription devices. Here are a number of dictation-based activities that demand interaction or decision-making on the part of the students.

 Interactive dictation: before beginning the dictation, the teacher makes sure the students know these phrases: *How do you spell that? Can you repeat that? Can you slow down a bit?*, and any others they may need. During the dictation, the students are encouraged to interrupt the teacher to ask those same questions. A good way to induce shy students to interrupt like this is to read the passage exaggeratedly fast. This forces the students into action because they will be unable to cope unless they take the initiative.

Dictogloss: this involves the teacher reading the passage at full speed several times. After a few readings, in which the students make notes, the task is to work in groups to reproduce a version of the passage that is written in good English and contains all the main ideas of the original. This involves much discussion and collaboration about areas of grammar, link words, sentence structure, etc, which tends to be very involving. At the end, they compare their version with the original.

The main point of dictogloss as a listening activity is to force our students to confront the difficulties of connected speech. The technique allows opportunities for the class to focus on features of pronunciation such as elision and assimilation (see page 11). It also keeps the students focused on meaning and its relation to form (rather than on memory).

 Picture dictation: the teacher describes a simple picture and the students draw it. The next step is to get the students working in pairs doing the same thing with other pictures. A nice touch is to use famous works of art that the students may recognise. Paintings with clear lines and not too much detail work best: da Vinci's Mona Lisa, Van Gogh's chair, Warhol's can of soup, etc. A final stage is to display the students' drawings next to the pictures of the originals on the walls. The students wander around as if in an art gallery and make comments either orally or in writing.

 Gapped/Whistle-gap dictation: as in 'Pause and predict' on page 85, the teacher reads the passage but leaves gaps or whistles to denote a gap. At this point, the students must write something plausible; it doesn't have to be correct, but it must make sense. There is an example below, with answers.

> A year ago I went to a conference in Brighton and met a [whistle 1] couple. They were from the area and they told me they had a [whistle 2] in the city, with a [whistle 3] room. We spent three wonderful days together and they invited me to [whistle 4].
>
> **1** Real answer: young. Some students' answers: happy, mature, gay
> **2** Real answer: flat. Some students' answers: house, home, friend
> **3** Real answer: spare. Some students' answers: bed, living, big
> **4** Real answer: stay. Some students' answers: dinner, a party, live with them

Afterwards the students discuss their answers with the teacher and decide which are possible/impossible, and why.

 False facts dictation: this activity involves making deliberate factual mistakes in the dictated passage. The mistakes could refer to general knowledge or to something the class has studied recently. Some teachers use the activity to review texts, dictating a summary with, say, five factual mistakes. The students either make the corrections silently, before checking in groups, or noisily, shouting out every time they hear something erroneous. Here's the beginning of a 'False facts' dictation done with an upper-intermediate class that had watched the film *Green Card*. The false facts are underlined.

> *In Green Card, the main character is a piano player from France. At the beginning of the film he gets <u>divorced</u> because he needs a green card to stay in the United States. The woman marries him because she wants to rent a flat which is only available to <u>single women</u>.*

Grading dictation: like 'False facts', this activity keeps the students out of 'robot mode' by asking them to evaluate the sentences they hear. They draw a line with *often, sometimes, hardly ever* and *never* written in sequence. The teacher dictates a number of personalised sentences which the students write wherever they think appropriate on the line. So, for example, if the teacher says 'I get up before 6.00 a.m.', the students guess how frequently the teacher does this and transcribe it on the correct place on the line (*often* or *never*, etc).

Alternatively, you could use a variation of 'Truth or lie' (page 87), with a column for truths and one for lies. You dictate various sentences about yourself: 'I don't eat meat', 'I've had dozens of pet cats', 'I learned to swim when I was a baby', etc, which the students write in the correct place.

 Running dictation: a good way to start a class, running dictation involves a text stuck on a wall outside the classroom or out of view of the students. In pairs, the students decide who will be the runner and who the scribe. The runner goes to the wall, memorises a chunk of text, runs back to the scribe and dictates it. After a minute or two, the scribe and the runner change roles. The activity is extremely lively, with students running to and fro.

A variation of this activity involves the students working in groups of three: the first student, the reader, reads and passes on a message to the second student who tells the third student, the writer. The activity becomes a version of 'Chinese whispers', in which fascinating mishearings occasionally occur (similar to 'It's hard to wreck a nice beach' on page 12)!

 Running translation-dictation: this activity works only with monolingual classes. The procedure is the same as for 'Running dictation', but the text is in the students' language. The runner has to translate the phrases into English for the scribe. One of the more interesting phases of the activity occurs when the students compare their translations afterwards, justifying the words they used, discussing nuances in meaning, and collaborating to find the best words.

There is much controversy about using translation in class, an issue beyond the scope of this book. Perhaps one solution is to use it sparingly for specific purposes, such as raising awareness of cognates and false friends (those words which look the same as a word in L1 but have a completely different meaning).

 Transcribe: this isn't exactly dictation, and like many of the activities here, it isn't exclusively focused on listening. Students record themselves giving a short presentation. They then transcribe what they said. An optional extra activity is to transform the transcription into a formal essay.

The main benefit of transcribing is that it leads to much **noticing**. Students are often shocked when they transcribe their own talk, perhaps realising the limitations of their vocabulary range or that they sound hesitant when speaking. Transcribing alerts students to how far they still have to go as language learners, and it forms a kind of heightened critical listening experience, one that is similar to what happens during oral exams (the examiner listens critically). As such, transcribing has the additional benefit of showing exactly what students need to work on, whether it is aspects of grammar, pronunciation, discourse markers or vocabulary.

The initial shock mentioned above needs to be cushioned by teachers. They should provide psychological support by explaining that native speakers also make countless errors, slips of the tongue and false starts, and that this is perfectly normal even in L1.

Listen and do

On page 18 we looked at Total Physical Response (TPR) and how effective it can be for low-level learners and as a change from normal classroom routines. The activities below are variations on TPR and work well with young learners and energetic older learners. As with dictations, they are useful for mixed-ability classes in that many of the activities don't require an oral response. Also, the spoken parts, such as commands, tend to be very short. This means that the listener may only need to understand a few words. Finally, the collaborative nature of some of the activities allows weaker students to work successfully with stronger ones.

 Simon says: this children's game involves the students obeying only the teacher's commands which are prefaced with 'Simon says', e.g. 'Simon says "smile!"' 'Simon says "put your hand on your head!"' etc. If the teacher gives an order that is not preceded by 'Simon says' – e.g. 'Jump up!' – the students mustn't do it. If they do, they are out.

 Last one is out: the students stand in a circle and follow the teacher's commands. The last person to do so is out of the game.

 Stand up if …: this is a very simple drill-like listening activity that can energise a class. The teacher simply says imperatives beginning with *Stand up if you … .* For example, Stand up if you are wearing blue/like potatoes/own a dog/have been to the cinema in the last month, etc, and the students follow the instruction before sitting down again. One useful element of the activity is that teachers can tailor the activity to practise any grammar point. If you wanted to practise the present perfect plus *ever,* you could say *Stand up if you have ever: eaten sushi, been to the US, played an instrument,* etc.

An alternative is to get one of the students who stood up to ask the next 'Stand up' question. This means the students will get speaking as well as listening practice. A follow-up activity is to get the students to make notes about their experiences concerning some of the imperatives. This leads easily into a group speaking activity.

 Change chairs if …: this is an alternative to 'Stand up if …' which works better with slightly smaller classes. The chairs are put in a circle – exactly the same number of chairs as there are students. The teacher stands in the middle and says *Change chairs if you drink coffee.* The students get up if the answer is 'yes' and sit in a newly vacated chair. After a few examples (*Change chairs if you have a pet/go swimming,* etc) the teacher says a 'Change chairs if …' sentence and sits in a free chair. One student will be left standing. This student then has to invent a sentence, say it and quickly find a free chair. Another student will then be left in the middle. This student, in turn, makes a new sentence. As with 'Stand up if …', the activity involves lots of energy and amusement as the students scramble to sit down. It's also a great way to review target grammar or vocabulary. Don't let it go on too long, however; three or four minutes is usually enough.

 Blind man's bluff: this is a pure, if somewhat unnatural, form of listening. One student is blindfolded. Their partner has to direct them to a target object that the teacher has placed somewhere in the classroom. The partner uses the voice only; there is no touching allowed. As regards the target object, a small bar of chocolate is always popular. For bigger classes, students can work in groups – one person blindfolded and several guides.

 Grab the word: choose about fifteen key words from the listening passage and write them on individual cards. Stick the cards on the wall or board, or if there are a lot of students, place the cards on the desks after making duplicate copies. The students listen as you read the passage or play the recording, and they grab the words when they hear them. The winner is the person who grabbed the largest number of cards. As an alternative, instead of grabbing the words, the students put the words/phrases in order. A tip: warn them beforehand that the activity is violent! Though not strictly true, this tends to get them in the mood!

 Mime: this is recommended for young children especially. Teachers often have their own store of favourite songs that lend themselves well to miming, or you can search the Internet. The lyrics to songs such as 'Fifty Ways to Leave your Lover' and 'I am Sailing' include numerous movements: *slip out the back, Jack/ hop on the bus, Gus/ I am flying/ like a bird across the sky*, etc. Get the students to read and listen to the song, then listen and sing along. Teach the verbs, and then get the students to act them out or perform choreographed gestures in time with the song.

 Just do it: as with the box kite project and the Lego lesson that we read about in the previous chapter, students can be asked to create something physical while listening to instructions. This type of listening activity requires various resources and therefore demands a lot of the teacher. Experienced teachers find ways to make and store the materials so that they can be used again and again. This makes the initial outlay of time and effort worthwhile.

Conclusions | *In this chapter we have:*

- looked at the reasons for using while-listening activities: we need to know what our students have understood, and the activities themselves can help students to understand the passage better.
- suggested that listening for gist is the first thing we will usually ask students to do. It is the most basic requirement of listening.
- discussed listening for detail, and the ability to focus on specific information.
- discussed inferring, and its relationship to schema theory.
- looked at ways of participating actively, and in particular getting our students to respond verbally or to categorise information.
- looked at note-taking, which, like many of these activities, involves a number of skills. We also mentioned that note-taking is an important academic skill which can be improved with practice.
- discussed dictation and a variety of activities associated with it, stating that dictation goes in and out of fashion, but has certain timeless qualities when used appropriately.
- discussed 'listen and do' activities based on TPR, which can be very motivating.

6 | Post-listening skills and activities

Listen a hundred times; ponder a thousand times; speak once. (Turkish proverb)

- ■ **Reflecting**
- ■ **Checking and summarising**
- ■ **Discussion**
- ■ **Creative responses**
- ■ **Critical responses**
- ■ **Information exchange**

- ■ **Problem-solving**
- ■ **Deconstructing the listening text**
- ■ **Reconstructing the listening text**

Reflecting

Here is the sequence of a typical listening lesson described so far. The pre-listening stage prepares the students, primarily by getting them interested in the topic, activating schemata and working with top-down ideas. At this stage we also give the students a listening task.

Following this, we go into the while-listening stage. The students are now 'on-task', engaged in real-time processing of the input.

What comes next? Post-listening activities. What do they involve? Besides checking the answers, we go into detail, looking at both top-down features such as the exact setting of the passage or information about the speakers, and bottom-up features such as individual words or phrases. We also look at what the students found problematic, a process sometimes called troubleshooting. Here are some of the questions involved in troubleshooting:

- Where was there a breakdown in communication, and why?

  - Was it caused by features of pronunciation? Perhaps the students failed to hear the difference between *can* and *can't*.

  - Was it unknown or unrecognised vocabulary that caused the problem? Perhaps the students didn't know the key word or failed to recognise the spoken form of a word like *psychology* or *knowledgeable*.

  - Was it the speed at which the speaker talked? Perhaps the students failed to segment the words from the flow of rapid speech, hearing, for example, an acoustic blur of *Whaddyathinkaboudit?* instead of *What do you think about it?*

  - Was it a problem related to syntax? Perhaps the students didn't know that *would have been* refers to the past.

    o Was it world knowledge? Perhaps the students didn't know an acronym, a name or a place. (For a fuller discussion of potential problems, see 'Why listening is difficult' in Chapter 1.)

This approach to post-listening work sees classroom listening as *diagnostic*. In the long term, like good doctors, we offer remedies – strategies, techniques, exposure to more grammar, vocabulary and discourse markers, and above all further listening practice.

We also find out what the students *didn't* struggle with, and how they came to their answers. Does their success represent improvement at the skill, perhaps increasing ability to recognise rapid speech or successful strategy use, or was it a lucky guess? Students' correct answers tell us nothing about how they came to those answers; we have to infer this information. If we could find out what goes on in the mind of the successful listener, listening pedagogy would be revolutionised!

The long-term goal of teaching listening is to ensure a successful *process* (intelligent use of top-down and bottom-up information, and good strategy use) as much as a successful *product* (the correct answer). The post-listening stage is where students can reflect on their listening experience without the pressure of having to process real-time speech or do a task.

Checking and summarising

The first thing our students speak about, in pairs or small groups, will probably be the answers to pre-set questions. Many students are too shy to speak out in front of the class, and small groups are less daunting, as well as enabling more people to speak for longer. This stage not only gives students confidence, but it also brings out any conflicting interpretations of the input. The teacher's role in this type of post-listening activity is to monitor the students' discussion, perhaps asking for textual evidence of their ideas, confirming or denying these ideas and answering queries.

Following groupwork, the teacher will probably elicit answers from the whole class. This is standard procedure in many classrooms that use a version of Communicative Language Teaching, and comprehension questions are important, for the reasons stated in previous chapters. But we must remember that they feature in language classes and just about nowhere else. Is there anything more authentic and 'real life' that we can do after we have listened?

One answer to that question may lie in focusing on the students' responses. In student-centred teaching, we begin from what the students can offer. Following a listening passage, we might ask, 'What did you understand?' or say, 'Work in pairs and try to summarise what you heard'. Why might this be useful? Firstly, it focuses on what the students succeeded in doing. Almost certainly there are things they failed to catch or understand, but by starting with what they achieved, we work from strength rather than weakness.

Secondly, asking students to summarise means they are doing something with the information, a situation that reflects most of the listening we do outside the classroom.

Thirdly, summarising focuses on what is important – the gist – but allows students the freedom to elaborate and add details as they remember them. We frequently find that students, while summarising, take delight in recalling funny or interesting details or particular turns of phrase that they picked up. Here are two students discussing a passage about an American traveller's first impressions of Europe.

S1: So he liked the small shops.

S2: Yes, and something about a beret.

S1: He also talked about the beret.

S2: What did he …?

S1: He said it was the first time he saw someone wear a beret and expect to be taken seriously!

S2: Ah, yes!

This interaction was not prompted by the traditional format of comprehension questions that have one answer, right or wrong. The students were asked, instead, to discuss anything they found memorable about the passage. The outcome of this task hinges on what the student/listener deems important, rather than what an external party – such as a teacher or a materials writer – feels is important. You could describe this as an egalitarian way of producing a summary!

Here are some other techniques for summarising:

 Take it in turns: one student says one thing they understood about the passage; their partner does the same; then the first student says a second thing, and so on. This is a very simple idea, and effective in that it evens up the speaking time and provides for a structured response: whenever it is their turn, the student will offer one unit of information. It also gives quieter students an opportunity to speak.

 Break it down: we ask the students to write a summary of the listening passage in fifty words, and then hand it to their partner who cuts it down to thirty words. Finally, the thirty-word summary is handed back to its original writer, who cuts it down to ten words. This is a writing activity as much as a listening one. More pertinently, it is a *thinking* activity. It engages the brain on different levels. The first level is content – the students must include the main information every time, and this involves creating a hierarchy of facts from what they heard. The second level is form – the students have to decide which words can be omitted without losing the sense of the summary.

 Note comparison: in the previous chapter we looked at the importance of note-taking as a while-listening activity. Here we focus on the post-listening comparison of the students' notes. The students take notes as they listen, and then compare what they have written. This has the dual purpose of a) checking for facts, interpretations and missing information, and b) sharing ways to make notes more effectively. The final stage is for the teacher to elicit the information, which is then written on the board as a model of how to take notes. At this stage of the lesson, different interpretations can be discussed and ironed out.

 Group summary: after listening to a narrative or a discussion of a topic, the students get into groups of four. Each group member has a pen and paper. Individually, they write the first sentence of their summary. They then pass their paper to another member of their group, who reads the first sentence and writes a second. They in turn pass the paper to a third member, who reads and writes, and so on. At the end, there are four summaries with four different contributors. The students compare and discuss the summaries in light of the listening passage.

Discussion

Engaging input means engaged students, a prerequisite for learning to occur. Any extended listening passage which is not purely functional in nature (i.e. *not* buying a ticket, going to the bank, ordering in a restaurant, etc) should be interesting enough to inspire comment or debate, or perhaps to round up a discussion, providing clarification of something the students talked about before listening. Indeed, much post-listening discussion revolves around how far the listeners' expectations were or were not met.

Texts containing conflict, contentious areas or challenging topics naturally lend themselves to discussion. Of course, as mentioned in Chapter 2, the notion of interest is entirely subjective, but good teachers know what their students are interested in and can cater to their tastes.

This brings us to the notion of personalisation, mentioned in the section on Communicative Language Teaching in Chapter 1. With many good listening passages, students feel motivated to listen because they see their own ideas and situations reflected in the input, and hear views that confirm or challenge their own. This leads inexorably to a personal response. Whenever students react to oral input with phrases such as *Well, in my country …* or *I disagree with …* or *A similar thing happened to me …*, the communicative teacher smiles inwardly – the input has caused a reaction.

In fact, it is not only the topic that might encourage a reaction. There are some techniques which create the conditions for post-listening discussion by virtue of the way materials or students are managed. Some of these, such as information exchange and comparison of texts, will be dealt with later in this chapter.

Discussion is usually considered a genre of speaking (although it doesn't work without listening), so we will not go into detail about ways to teach it. (See *How to Teach Speaking* for ways to teach discussion.) Suffice it to say, there are numerous techniques for structuring discussions. These include sequencing, ranking, grading, saying if something is true or false, and saying to what extent you agree. The techniques that we use should reflect the content of the input. If a listening passage deals with, say, inventions, the discussion that follows could involve ranking the inventions in some way. A listening passage including strong opinions about, say, the merits of living in cities leads naturally to an 'agree or disagree' discussion, and so on. An example of a post-listening discussion is shown on page 100.

How can teachers create their own post-listening discussions? Of course, it depends on the subject of the listening passage, but here are some ideas.

 Personalise: ask if the situation is the same for the students. How is it different? In multilingual classes particularly, teachers can ask if the situation is the same in the students' various countries. Cross-cultural discussions of this nature are often very fruitful and motivating as many students enjoy learning about their classmates' culture. For higher-level students with more language at their disposal, the teacher might ask what they would have done in the same situation, and why.

 Questions: the teacher can devise a number of questions based on the topic of the listening passage. An alternative, perhaps for higher levels, is for the teacher to devise two sets of questions based on the topic. The class is divided into two. The groups discuss their own questions before pairing up with someone from a different group and explaining the gist of their group's original discussion.

Listening and speaking

1 a **1.6** Listen to three people talking about someone who they fell out with. Match the speakers 1–3 to the photos A–C below.

b Listen again and complete the notes.

Speaker	1	2	3
Who do they talk about?		*Romina – best friend*	
How long have they known/did they know each other?			*1 year*
Why/When did they fall out?			
How is their relationship now?			

c Check your answers with a partner.

2 Discuss.

1 Do you ever have arguments with your friends?

2 Have you ever fallen out with a close friend? What happened?

3 What do friends/family usually argue about?

Statements: the teacher can devise a number of statements based on the listening passage. The students discuss whether they agree or disagree. Another way of doing this is for the students to mark the statements with a number: 0 means they disagree completely, 1 means they don't really agree, 2 means they agree with some reservations, 3 means they agree completely.

 Sorting lists: the teacher can list a number of aspects based on the topic and get the students to rank them in order of importance, desirability, cost, etc. Alternatively, depending on the text, the students discuss 'dos' and 'don'ts' based on the topic, and come up with their own list.

 Pros and cons: the teacher finds an area of debate contained within the topic or touched on in the listening passage and gets students to discuss pros and cons. It may be useful for the students to brainstorm these in groups before the discussion begins. Pros and cons debates can be extended so that they take the form of role-plays. Two or more students argue for or against something. The difference is that the teacher gives instructions as to which students argue for or against the issue, and the students then take on a role, pretending to be characters who may have different views from their own.

Discussion is rich with opportunities for students and teachers to personalise and bring something of themselves – their background and life experiences – to the class. Indeed, the idea of the student as a resource with a personal history, views, stories, etc is one of the most powerful to have emerged in language classrooms in the last few decades. The student as a resource is similarly vital when we consider creative responses.

Creative responses

Creativity is often associated either with geniuses or unusual children. Ronald Carter argues persuasively that this should not be the case. 'Creativity,' he writes, 'far from being simply a property of exceptional people, is an exceptional property of all people.' There are small acts of linguistic creativity almost every time we open our mouths. These, however, remain largely unrecognised. The result is that students and teachers – and people in general – often claim not to be creative or to have no imagination. This is a psychological barrier that exists because of a narrow view of what creativity means. Every time we find a way to use up the last potato in the cupboard or invent a game to keep the children from dying of boredom on a car journey, this is creativity.

Carter also notes that creativity is usually associated with writing rather than speaking. This is unquestionably true (which speakers are regarded as being as creative as Shakespeare, Dante or Gabriel García Márquez?), but, as Carter points out, in the presence of witty friends, comedians and children with their chants ('I scream, you scream, we all scream for ice cream!'), we realise that creativity is an extremely common oral phenomenon. We will, therefore, consider creative post-listening activities that involve both writing and speaking. Here are some that involve writing.

 Genre transfer: one way to engage students in a deeper processing of a listening passage is to ask them to re-fashion the text, for example by transferring it to a different genre. This might involve turning a spoken text into a written version. A piece of gossip can be transformed into a tabloid-style news article, complete with quotations from the transcript. We can listen to a person chatting about their daily life and then write their diary entry.

 Moral or headline: the students listen to a story and think of either a moral or a headline. Here is an example, plus some of the headlines that one high-level class wrote.

> *A car thief started a six-year prison sentence after stealing thirty-six cars in order to clean them. All the cars were stolen from car showrooms. The court was told that John Blain, a cleaner who doesn't own a car, walked into car showrooms and asked to test-drive a car. He then drove from the showroom and didn't return. Every car was later found at the side of the road, absolutely spotless inside and out. Blain washed and cleaned each one before leaving it. He was once called 'the man you would most want to steal your car' by one judge. Blain's wife, Mary, a forty-eight-year-old nurse, said after the case that their marriage was over. She told reporters, 'He looked after the cars better than me.'*

'Clean cars mean broken marriage'
'Man drives wife away'
'All washed up – the man who couldn't put the brakes on his cleaning habit'

 Write on: the students listen to a story and then write a continuation. In order to do this, they must be aware of the main ideas and key features of the original input: its tone, style, characters and story line.

One advanced high school class, after much preparation, watched Samuel Beckett's play *Waiting for Godot*. The play has two acts (two halves); the students' post-viewing task was to write a third. Because the students had sufficient preparation, they were able to achieve the task very effectively. The following year another class watched the same play and wrote *Waiting For Godot – The Hollywood Version*, complete with guns, romance and a happy ending.

The second task differed from the first in that the texts produced (by the later class) were not continuations but parodies. As a way to highlight salient features of any text, parody writing is a very useful exercise, though highly demanding.

Here are some creative response activities that primarily involve speaking.

 Sound effects story: the students hear some sequenced sound effects. These can be found on the Internet or on commercial CDs, or even recorded by resourceful teachers. While listening, the students note down the verbs that are represented by the sounds. So, for example, if the sound was someone crying, the students would write *cry*; if the sound was applause, the students would write *clap*. Then they build a story around these verbs. For stronger classes, the final stage after some rehearsal is to tell the story to the rhythm and speed of the sound effects as they occur on the recording.

 Hot seat: the students listen to some kind of narrative or situation in which there is conflict. After a lot of solid comprehension work with the recording, one of the students takes on the role of one of the protagonists. This student sits in the 'hot seat', in front of other students whose job is to interview them. The activity works well as long as the student in the hot seat remains 'in character'. For this reason, the teacher might want to demonstrate by sitting in the hot seat for a minute or two first. The rest of the class will also benefit from a few minutes to prepare questions.

 Illustrate: this activity is particularly enjoyed by children. The students listen – it might be to a situation, story or description – and then draw an image that represents the passage. They then explain their illustration in terms of its significance, and how it reflects what they heard.

Critical responses

Creative thinking and critical thinking are often linked. Effective questioning – one of the prime elements of critical thinking – is a creative activity because it involves the critic bringing their own thoughts to bear on the material with which they are confronted. In this sense, any criticism entails the creativity of a personal response.

One of the most important elements of a critical response to a listening passage is an awareness of the speaker's viewpoint, biases and prejudices. We should remember David Mamet's words, quoted earlier: 'People speak for one reason and one reason only – to get what they want.' Language use is often far from neutral. It frequently conceals ideologies, subtexts and cultural bias. A hallmark of truly attentive listening (and thinking) is constant mental questioning of speakers. Here are the types of questions we might ask:

Question	Examples	Further comment
Do I believe the speaker?	'Don't walk under that ladder! It'll bring you bad luck.'	How do I know this is true? What evidence is there? Can I trust the speaker's sources? Does the speaker know their subject?
Do I trust the speaker?	'I didn't do it! Nobody saw me do it! You can't prove anything!' (Bart Simpson)	How is the utterance influenced by the speaker's motives? Are they telling the truth?
Are there any omissions? If so, what and why?	One well-known figure, during a trial, famously claimed, 'I didn't lie – I was economical with the truth.'	The things speakers leave out may be more important than the things they say. Even silence can be loaded with meaning (in communications theory there is an axiom, 'One cannot not communicate'). Listeners need first to perceive the gaps, then to fill them in, and finally to decide why the speaker left something unsaid.

Could the speaker have said it differently? If so, how? Would this have changed the meaning?	'Weapons of mass destruction *have not yet been found*.' (Government spokesperson, UK)	The way we say things can conceal or distort the message. For example, the passive voice can be used to distance the speaker from the message. Words come with connotations. Skilled speakers (e.g. politicians and lawyers) know this and may exploit it.
What does the speaker's imagery and use of metaphor show us about their attitude to the subject?	'A *flood* of immigrants'; 'a *deluge* of foreigners'; 'our cities are being *swamped*'.	We form images in the mind as we listen. Metaphors, through their vividness, enable us to do this immediately. But we must question them: Are they positive or negative? Static or changing? Connected to nature or artificiality?
Is the speaker's use of language designed to include or exclude listeners?	'Rents 911' – US telephone slang for 'my parents are here so I can't talk now'. 'Nickleby' – pronunciation of acronym for the US education policy, No Child Left Behind.	Users of jargon, dialect, acronyms and neologisms (invented words) may be trying to exclude others from their circle or, alternatively, trying to establish their membership of a closed group. This might apply to any group, from teenage gang members to university professors.

Should we teach our students to listen and respond critically? Critical responses enrich our encounters with language, whether L1 or L2. They are a part of language appreciation and interpretation. Words may communicate less or more than the speaker wishes. Gary Buck writes, '[A] mistaken assumption is that listening comprehension consists of understanding what words and sentences mean. It doesn't. It consists of understanding what speakers mean.' One almost inevitable development as language students become more advanced is a growing awareness of not only the meaning of what is said, but *the way* it is said. At higher levels, students should start to perceive a number of rhetorical effects that speakers use – irony, sarcasm, metaphor and loaded language – words with strong emotional connotations. Critical listeners will look below the surface of the words to find deeper meanings.

In spite of the comments above, there is some debate over whether this approach is suited to language classes. A great deal depends on the type of students we have and the context. Professional adults and university students may already possess the skill of responding critically. Furthermore, they may not consider it appropriate for the English lesson. They might view language classes as means of learning only systems of grammar and vocabulary rather than ways in which these might be manipulated by biased speakers. Young children may lack the sophistication, world knowledge and level of language to be able to discriminate between trustworthy and untrustworthy speakers in English.

Perhaps, then, it is not a question of explicit teaching. Rather, we provide opportunities for students to notice features such as bias and inconsistency. We ask students to agree or disagree with what they hear, probe the speaker's intentions, examine language use in the light of what we know about the speaker, distinguish between facts and opinions, comment on how and why the text deviates from their expectations, and notice persuasive tactics used by writers (e.g. loaded language, overgeneralisation, 'bandwagon appeal' – where you persuade someone to do something because 'everyone else is doing it'). As a guiding principle, we emphasise the importance of interpretation.

Information exchange

Interpretation may also come into play when we exchange information. This post-listening activity is one of the most important reasons for listening in any language. Without it, we would still be in the dark ages because information fuels progress, and shared information is what allows societies to function and develop. We must acknowledge, however, that the shared information needs to be relevant to our students. There is a danger that ELT sometimes overemphasises the exchange of unimportant messages, and this may lead to what Pennycook describes as 'the ever-increasing trivialisation of learning and learners'.

One way to render the exchange of information in language classes more concrete is by using 'jigsaw' listening activities.

 Jigsaw: one student listens to a recording of part of a story while a partner listens to another part. After listening, they work together to share what they heard, their combined knowledge allowing them to piece together the story. An alternative is to have different recordings based on the same topic. The students then compare the two viewpoints.

 News jigsaw: one version that works for high-level learners involves each student listening to a different radio news broadcast in English – BBC, NPR, VOA, etc. They discuss what they heard on the news, focusing in particular on differences. How were the headlines different? What importance was each item accorded in terms of position in the broadcast? What angle did the programme take? The activity often leads to the type of critical listening described above, as students learn to recognise speakers' agendas and signs of bias.

Problem-solving

One of the more engaging activities is to pose a problem and use a listening passage to help solve it. To adapt the Turkish proverb that opens this chapter, if the students have pondered the problem 'a hundred times', they will undoubtedly be motivated to listen carefully and afterwards find a solution with their classmates.

There are a number of problem-solving task types that go well with listening materials. These are listed, along with some of their strengths as post-listening activities, below.

1 Listing

Example rubric: *List all the ways to … (get from A to B/save the whale/get fit).*

Listing is good for brainstorming in groups. Real-world applications are possible.

2 Sorting

Example rubric: *Put … (the words/food types/people) into groups.*

Sorting demands that students see connections between different items and is good for vocabulary acquisition, in particular.

3 Ranking

Example rubric: *Say which is the best, the second best, the worst, etc.*

Ranking typically has no correct answer. Students need to justify their ideas, and the potential conflict may lead to good discussions.

4 Ordering according to criteria

Example rubric: *Say which is the heaviest, prettiest, most expensive, etc.*

This is a very flexible task, which can be used with many criteria and at most levels.

5 Designing something

Example rubric: *How can it be designed to fit the criteria?*

This is motivating for visual/kinaesthetic learners and also for lateral thinkers.

6 Solving moral dilemmas

Example rubric: *What should they have done? What would you do?*

This can lead to meaty discussions on values. Moral dilemmas also sometimes provide opportunities for discussion of cross-cultural issues.

7 Solving mysteries

Example rubric: *Who was the killer? How was the result achieved? Who ate all the pies?*

This is a very motivating way to use listening input as mystery story lines are often engaging. Lateral thinkers often enjoy solving mysteries such as those on page 73 in Chapter 4.

Deconstructing the listening text

If we want to examine listening texts for their salient features – grammar, vocabulary, cohesive devices, discourse markers, pronunciation, etc – to a certain extent we need to pull them apart.

There are basically two ways of doing this. One involves playing short segments of the recording and stopping them so that the students can focus on the desired features while these are still in their short-term memory. If the target feature is, for example, an item of vocabulary, the teacher might play the sentence in which it occurs, ask for a paraphrase or synonym to check the meaning, do some work on pronunciation and round this up by writing the information on the board. The students then write the target vocabulary down in their notebooks. The approach is similar for grammar, cohesive devices and discourse markers: the segment that the teacher repeats should give a clear context for the target feature while being brief enough for the students to hold in their short-term memory. To focus on pronunciation, as a basic procedure the teacher can play a segment and ask the students to repeat it.

The other way is by using a transcript. Transcripts tend to be hidden at the back of books, unused and unloved. In recent years, some materials writers have made an effort to exploit them, but for a number of reasons transcripts still remain underexploited. One problem is that book configurations do not allow sufficient space for large print transcripts. Another is the lack of teacher education on how to use them. A third problem is the element of controversy surrounding their use; many teachers believe that transcripts facilitate cued reading rather than listening.

There are, however, compelling reasons for using transcripts, as we saw in Chapter 3. Their main appeal, apart from the fact that they represent an invaluable source of connected speech, is that they show the students the language in the recording. They appear in physical space rather than time. Sound is ephemeral, and conversations in recordings are gone with the wind, whereas transcripts allow students to look again, re-read and check. As such, transcripts provide opportunities for students to see the difference between the way words are written and the way they sound. Features such as elision and assimilation are far easier to teach if there is a visible context on paper. Transcripts can be marked up, annotated, kept as reminders of vocabulary or other features, while recordings cannot. Below is a summary of the reasons for exploiting transcripts.

Seven reasons to exploit transcripts

Features	Elaboration
pronunciation	elision, contraction, assimilation and other aspects of connected speech, sentence stress, intonation for mood and attitude
speed	where and why speakers speed up and slow down
vocabulary	students relate the written form to the sound of the word in connected speech
features of good listeners	backchannelling (*mhm, I see*, etc), paraphrasing, asking follow-up questions
features exclusive to speaking	fillers, false starts, hesitations, repair strategies
discourse markers	signals for speech functions such as changing the subject, softening an opinion, returning to the main point, etc
graphophonic relationships between words	words that are related in spelling and meaning but differ greatly in sound (syllable shifts, silent letters, etc), e.g. *sign* and *signal*, *suspect* and *suspicious*, *nation* and *nationality*, *know* and *knowledge*

Here is how one coursebook attempts to exploit the transcript.

A final word of warning: deconstructing a text needs to be done judiciously. If we try to point out every interesting feature, our students will become either bored or overwhelmed. Many aspects of

7.5 conversation feature showing you are listening
a When Tom is telling the story, John uses some words and phrases to show that he is listening and interested. Underline these phrases in the tapescript.

phonology that listeners need to be aware of – elision, for example – exist below the level of meaning. Practising such features will only stimulate most students for a few minutes at a time, and teachers need to judge whether such features should become a part of the students' production or if it is sufficient for them to be aware of these features as listeners. Deconstructing texts for items of language can inadvertently have negative effects – something like catching a beautiful airborne bird in a net, pulling it apart to see how it works and then tossing it into the air hoping it will fly again. It won't. Neither will the text.

Reconstructing the listening text

Just as we deconstruct texts, we can get our students to reconstruct them. The teacher's role is to provide fragments of the text or a damaged or abbreviated form of it. By putting it back together, students have to deal with many aspects of language: grammar, vocabulary and discourse features of spoken English, for example. Some of the activities that involve reconstructing texts have already been included in previous chapters. For example, earlier we looked at dictogloss and writing down key words in order to reconstruct the text later. Here are a few more:

 Gap-fill: this is one of the most common text reconstruction activities. Some words in the text are blanked out, and the student has to fill the gaps. This is a technique often used in testing, but it can be used for teaching, particularly if you blank out parts of idioms, prepositions or collocations (pairs or groups of words that are commonly found together, such as *have breakfast, make a call, wide awake, sleep well*) or **adjacency pairs** (e.g. 'A: How are you? B: Fine, thanks.' 'A: Thank you. B: You're welcome.').

 Storyboard: Storyboard is a computer program (made by a company called WIDA) which works on roughly the same principles as the game 'Hangman'. The whole listening text or dialogue is blanked out, leaving only the title, punctuation and spaces in place of words.

The students listen to a passage. They are then presented with the blanked out version. They type words that they remember hearing during the listening stage. Because of the way the computer program works, the students need to type the word once only at the bottom of the screen and it appears wherever it occurs in the text. For example, words like *to* and *of* may appear many times, and the students won't need to keep typing them in. Indeed, they should type in these words first because these are the glue that holds the language together; once they are in place, everything else becomes easier because the structure of each sentence is clear. This restructuring activity is excellent for developing awareness of patterns of vocabulary and grammar, and it is also very enjoyable.

Is it possible to create our own version of Storyboard, without the technology? Yes. Storyboard is just a computer version of a gap-fill exercise. A few minutes' word processing is all it takes to write out a blank version of a script (all you have to do is count the number of words correctly). The students then complete the transcript in groups. Two tips: 1) make sure the students know the passage well by the time they do this activity, otherwise it will be rather daunting; and 2) do the first couple of sentences as a whole class, so that they can see what is expected.

Disappearing dialogues: the students listen to and then recreate a dialogue, which the teacher writes on the board. The students act it out in pairs. After this, the teacher erases certain key words. The students once again act out the dialogue (this time playing different roles, for variety) before the teacher then erases more words so that only a skeleton framework is left of the original dialogue. As the students act it out for a third time, they find themselves relying far more on memory and the chunks of language they have acquired in the previous stages. The class rounds up the activity by reconstructing the dialogue from memory, with the teacher acting as scribe. Here's an example:

Stage 1

ARTIST:	Did you manage to sell any of my paintings?
GALLERY OWNER:	Well, there's good news and bad news.
ARTIST:	What's the good news?
GALLERY OWNER:	A man came in and asked if your work would become more valuable after you died.
ARTIST:	That sounds normal enough. What did you reply?
GALLERY OWNER:	I said, yes. Then he bought ten paintings.
ARTIST:	Fantastic! What's the bad news?
GALLERY OWNER:	He was your doctor.

Stage 2

ARTIST:	_____ you manage to _____ any of my paintings?
GALLERY OWNER:	Well, there's _____ _____ and bad news.
ARTIST:	What's the _____ news?
GALLERY OWNER:	A man _____ in and asked if your work would _____ more valuable after you died.
ARTIST:	That _____ normal enough. What _____ you reply?
GALLERY OWNER:	I said, yes. Then he _____ ten paintings.
ARTIST:	Fantastic! What's the _____ news?
GALLERY OWNER:	He was your doctor.

Stage 3

ARTIST:	_____ you _____ to _____ any of my _____?
GALLERY OWNER:	Well, there's _____ _____ and _____ _____.
ARTIST:	_____ the _____ news?
GALLERY OWNER:	A man _____ in and _____ if your work would _____ more _____ after you _____.
ARTIST:	That _____ normal enough. What _____ you _____?
GALLERY OWNER:	I _____, yes. Then he _____ ten _____.
ARTIST:	Fantastic! _____ the _____ news?
GALLERY OWNER:	He _____ your _____.

 Re-ordering: this is a different type of text reconstruction that works particularly well with dialogues. The teacher cuts the script into strips. After they have heard the dialogue and done some while-listening activities, the students put the strips in the correct order. The activity is useful for highlighting the formulaic, predictable nature of functional exchanges, which contain features such as adjacency pairs.

Conclusions | *In this chapter we have:*

- looked at the importance of using the post-listening period to reflect on the successes and difficulties encountered while listening. We also discussed troubleshooting and the view of listening in class as a diagnostic activity.

- suggested that checking and summarising are very common post-listening activities, and mentioned some alternative ways to do these.

- looked at the use of discussion after listening, stating that the content of listening passages should be interesting enough to inspire discussion.

- examined a number of creative responses to a listening text.

- talked about the importance, particularly at higher levels, of critical responses, stating that these constitute a part of truly attentive listening. We also put forward the idea that people's speech acts need to be interpreted for features such as bias and omissions.

- looked at the fact that information exchange activities are a core part of any communicative language course.

- talked about the use of listening texts to solve problems, and how this can encourage attentive listening.

- looked at ways of deconstructing the listening text for linguistic features.

- examined ways to reconstruct the listening text to allow a focus on features of spoken English.

7 | Preparation and planning

Expect the best, plan for the worst and prepare to be surprised. (Denis Waitley)

- ■ **The teacher as planner**
- ■ **Listening in the syllabus**
- ■ **Choosing and adapting published materials**
- ■ **Authentic materials: radio, film/TV, songs**

- ■ **Anticipating problems**
- ■ **Young learners**
- ■ **ESP (English for specific purposes)**
- ■ **Six essentials for planning listening lessons**

The teacher as planner

There are two types of planning: short-term (looking at issues such as the individual lesson) and long-term (looking at issues such as the syllabus). We will first discuss the teacher's short-term role.

The teacher's short-term role

All lesson planning takes place after a process of reflection, in which teachers ask a number of questions. The first question is usually *What should the students learn in the lesson?* The answer depends on many things, such as the goals of the course, the students' ongoing needs, whether there is an external syllabus imposed by the school or a board of education, and what stage the class is at. Of course, students do not always learn what teachers teach – in fact they often learn lots of other things – but professional teachers still need to have learning goals in mind during the planning stage.

The next question, which leads directly out of the first, is *How will I anchor the lesson in what students know already?* Language education is incremental in that we teach step by step, beginning with what the students know and then building on it. This means that the students are able to go from partial understanding to a more complete understanding, and it prevents the demotivating scenario in which they are suddenly faced with a mass of totally incomprehensible input.

Once we have decided what the students will learn, we assemble the material necessary, all the while asking *Will this be at the right level of difficulty? How will I deal with the students' range of ability? How will I check the students' understanding? What classroom management techniques will I use?*

As we prepare the material and think about the questions above, we naturally begin to think about which activities to include. If you peek through the keyhole of most genuinely communicative classrooms, you will see students doing things: conversing, role-playing, making notes, singing, designing posters, writing on the board. They do not have to do all of these things in one class, but a balance of activities – some quieter, others more action-packed, all engaging – is, in most cases, a good thing.

Once we know what activities will be used, we might ask *What stages will I divide the lesson into?* We need to know roughly how long each activity will take, and also how one activity will slide seamlessly into the next so that there are no sudden incongruous shifts. While thinking about the staging of the lesson, the teacher is also asking *What is my role at each stage of the lesson?* As we saw in Chapter 4, teachers have many roles; as we plan the lesson, we anticipate which role we will play at every stage. When it comes to listening, teachers will also be aware of the differences between the listening lesson and listening in the lesson, a distinction that we deal with in the next chapter.

Most teachers like to start and end lessons strongly, so we might ask *How will I begin and conclude the lesson?* Many teachers begin with short games to warm up the class, and finish with round-up activities, such as error correction slots, in which they write some of the students' errors on the board and get them to self-correct.

A final question, particularly when we are teaching a lesson for the first time, is *What is my plan B if problems arise?*

When these questions have been addressed, teachers then devise their plan, in full knowledge of the fact that the plan is provisional. Once the listening stage of a lesson is underway, teachers have many decisions to make; for example:

- *How many times will the students need to hear the recording?*

- *Where will the pause button be needed next time?*

- *When might other types of teacher intervention be necessary?*

It may be possible to plan all of this, but often these three questions require on-the-spot decisions which experienced teachers tend to make with ease and confidence. They may even be unaware that what they are doing is making decisions because it comes so naturally. At every step of the lesson, experienced teachers are monitoring their own performance, seeing through the eyes and hearing through the ears of their students, considering alternative courses of action and guessing what the consequences of these will be. Above all, experienced teachers recognise that a lesson plan is a starting point. Rather like a game of chess, each move brings with it a multiplicity of new options. What we are really describing here is flexibility. While planning is absolutely vital, the teacher must be flexible enough to change the plan whenever necessary. The lesson is a dynamic process in which the teacher has an ideal in mind but knows it may be necessary to diverge from it.

If the teacher's role in any one listening lesson involves much on-the-spot decision-making, long-term planning is different in that it requires a great deal of conscious thought and reflection.

The teacher's long-term role

Teachers need to consider long-term issues such as *What information about the English language will help my students' listening?* For example, stressed words are the main content words, discourse markers show a change of topic or tone, lexical sets indicate subject matter and patterns of intonation reveal the speaker's attitude. Teachers also need to equip students with the type of knowledge they believe is not transferable from L1, such as intonation, cultural aspects like conventions of turn-taking and politeness, and other discourse features. Much of what the students need, of course, comes from teaching the language itself independently of the listening skill, and is linked to pronunciation and the difficulties of recognising words in connected speech.

Listening in the syllabus

Providing that instruction is in English, *some form of listening in L2* takes place in all lessons and forms a core part of any course. A complete listening syllabus will include planned, unplanned and spontaneous speech, monologue, dialogue and three-way conversations, fixed situational discourse (e.g. buying a ticket) and free-flowing discourse (e.g. 'chat'), and a mix of formal and informal discourse. There will be a balance of extensive and intensive listening, too. In truth, few teachers plan as meticulously as this, and the type of input depends on several factors: the materials available, exam requirements, institutional constraints and the needs of the students. We will discuss the latter in subsequent sections of this chapter. The key thing for most general English classes is variety – of genres, text lengths, topics, voices and tasks. In order for this balance to be achieved, teachers first need to be aware of the shortfalls in any given syllabus. They can then set about the task of compensating and supplementing with other listening materials.

Let's now turn to the planning of a single lesson with listening as a major component.

Choosing and adapting published materials

Teachers often feel the need to adapt materials, a skill in itself. In previous chapters we looked at criteria involved in choosing suitable listening passages, although many teachers are constrained by the need to use a given textbook which dictates the syllabus. Other constraints may be lack of time to find alternatives, lack of access to technology and lack of resources. For teachers in these situations, the textbook will probably provide the bulk of the recorded material for their class. Here we will focus on ways in which teachers can adapt textbook material.

Why adapt published materials? Because during the planning stage (and sometimes during the lesson itself) the teacher realises that the materials are not a perfect fit for the class at that particular moment. What type of adaptations may be necessary? We often adapt listening material in order to:

 Make the sequence easier: one way to do this is to preview the content, including some of the key vocabulary, providing extra information about what the students will hear. You can do this simply by explaining – 'You're going to hear a man and woman discuss the environment' – or other means, such as providing a short text that gives background information.

You can also change the task to simplify the whole sequence. For example, instead of asking students to answer questions that require a detailed understanding of the recording, you can get them to answer simpler questions such as *What is the topic? How many speakers are there?* or *What job does the speaker do?* Tasks that require little in the way of oral or written response are easier to achieve.

We can also chunk a long text, breaking it down into manageable sections. This means we stop the recording at a number of points and help students with their interpretation of events. Here's an example of how to do this.

M: Did I tell you about this really funny lawyer story that a friend of mine sent me on email the other day?

W: No, go on.

M: Well ... the way it goes is that ... there's this lawyer in the US ... North Carolina or somewhere ... and he buys this box of really rare and very, very expensive cigars ...

W: OK ...

M: And because they're so expensive he decides to insure them ... against fire amongst other things.

W: Fair enough.

M: Yes ... except that, within a month, having smoked his complete collection of these fantastic cigars and without having made even his first payment for the insurance policy, the lawyer made a claim against the insurance company.

W: What on earth for?

[TEACHER STOPS RECORDING AND ASKS: WHAT DO YOU THINK THE LAWYER CLAIMED AGAINST THE INSURANCE COMPANY?]

M: Well, in his claim, the lawyer stated that the cigars were lost in a series of small fires.

W: How ridiculous!

M: And unsurprisingly, the insurance company refused to pay for the obvious reason that the man had smoked the cigars in the normal way. But then, the lawyer sued the insurance company ...

[TEACHER STOPS RECORDING AND ASKS: WHAT DO YOU THINK 'SUE' MEANS? WHY DID THE LAWYER SUE THE INSURANCE COMPANY? DO YOU THINK THE LAWYER WON HIS CASE?]

... and won! When he gave his decision, the judge agreed with the insurance company that the claim appeared ridiculous BUT concluded that the lawyer had a policy from the company in which it guaranteed they could be insured against fire, without defining exactly what did or did not count as 'fire'. And so the company would have to pay the claim.

W: No! You're kidding.

M: But that's not all! You see, rather than going through a long and expensive appeal, the insurance company accepted the decision and paid $15,000 to the lawyer for his loss of the valuable cigars in the 'fires'. But now comes the best part!

W: Go on ... I can't wait ...

M: Then ... after cashing the cheque, the lawyer was arrested! The insurance company had him charged with twenty-four counts of arson! With his own insurance claim and evidence from the previous case being used against him, the lawyer was convicted of deliberately burning his insured property

[TEACHER STOPS RECORDING AND ASKS: WHAT DO YOU THINK 'ARSON' MEANS? WHAT HAPPENED IN THE END?]

and so – can you believe it? – he was sentenced to twenty-four months in jail and a $24,000 fine.

 Make the sequence more challenging: to do this, we can simply reduce the number of 'crutches' that support the students: visuals, pre-listening activities, guiding questions, etc. For example, at the beginning of the sequence, we can tell the students to keep their books closed, listen (no writing allowed) and try to answer some questions. In the extract shown on page 115, the students are asked to read and listen at the same time. A more challenging activity would be to close the book and listen.

Make the sequence more personalised or relevant for our students' needs: pre-listening questions can often be adapted so that our students give their opinions of a topic and then listen to see if the speaker shares those opinions. This gives students more reason to listen. In the listening sequence here, we could easily personalise the pre-listening task by asking the students to talk about their own hobbies.

The growth in the number of specialised courses such as **ESP** (English for specific purposes) reflects the fact that 'one size doesn't fit all'. Nurses need a certain type of English, academics another, tourists yet another. The diverse needs of our students

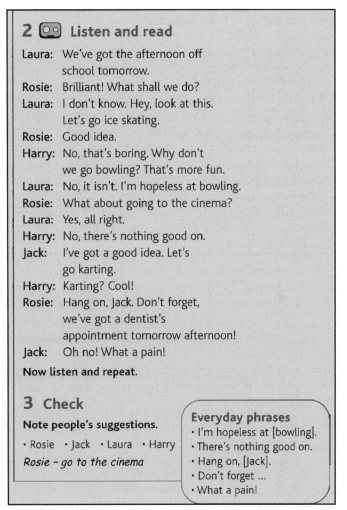

are at the heart of the syllabus and the lesson plan. If a class consists of a group of secretaries, what will they need to do with the information they hear? Probably write it down and transmit it later. So if the textbook asks them to draw a picture while listening, the task may not be valid for *them*. So we adapt. We ask the secretaries to do something more relevant, such as note down the four important points the speaker makes. This is an example of 'personalising' material to fit the needs of the students. We will discuss ESP in more detail later in the chapter.

 Extend the sequence: one way to extend the pre-listening part of the sequence is by adding something related in terms of topic but from a different source. The task for a recording from a business English coursebook is shown at the bottom of page 116.

The short text at the top of page 116 could be read and discussed before Exercise 1 in the extract. It acts as a way into the subject of what companies can do to motivate their employees.

Perks of the job – Good motivators?

Some companies have interesting ways of motivating their staff. New Belgium Brewing, a US company, offers its workers a case of free beer every week. After one year's service, employees get a bicycle, and if they stay at the company for five years they get an all-expenses-paid trip to Belgium to taste beer!

There's even more adventure on offer for employees at Brogan and Partners. The company takes its sixty workers on a mystery holiday every year. So far, trips have included Amsterdam, Iceland and the Caribbean.

An insurance company called Acuity has a great way to keep staff at work: it has a pond full of fish. The 850 employees are welcome to go fishing and they can take home everything they catch!

Even more incentive to stay at work is provided by four hospitals in Ohio. They employ concierges to do personal errands for employees. If you are busy at work, a concierge will buy your groceries and put them in the fridge, walk your dog or queue to buy you tickets for a concert.

There are many ways to extend the post-listening sequence. As mentioned in Chapter 6, one way is by using the transcript. We can ask our students, for example, to listen and read at the same time. Or we can add a further task to this, such as: *Underline any expressions connected with time/sport/shopping.* We can also add more discussion questions or develop speaking tasks such as role-plays based on the recorded input.

| Preview | **What motivates you to work harder?**

Choose three factors from the list. Explain your choices to a partner.

1 the prospect of earning good money in the future
2 competition with others
3 working in a friendly environment
4 having fun while you work
5 receiving praise
6 meeting a challenge
7 working on something that is interesting and exciting
8 feeling confident that you can do something well

| Listening 1 | **1 Listen to Dilys Breeze, a human resources manager, talking about motivating workers in her company. Which of the factors in the list above does she mention?**

2 Listen again and complete the text.

Most people feel motivated when they know they are making a
¹_____ and doing something ²_____ .
People need to receive praise. They want to feel that others
³_____ their problems or suggestions. And most want to
develop their ⁴_____ and ⁵_____ new things.

3 Tick what managers should do, according to Dilys Breeze.

stimulate ☐   encourage ☐   criticise ☐   support ☐
listen ☐   shout ☐   help ☐   instruct ☐

| Speaking | **Did you have similar ideas to Dilys Breeze?**

Shorten the sequence: sometimes teachers may feel that the recording is unnecessarily long or their students are unable to concentrate for more than a short period. The simplest way to shorten the *text* is to explain to the students that they will hear *part* of the recording. Then find an appropriate cut-off point and press the Stop button.

To shorten the whole listening sequence we may need to omit something else. It may be the case that there is a vocabulary focus that could be done at home or comprehension questions that the teacher feels are unnecessary (Penny Ur suggests that many coursebook writers ask for too many responses from the students, and suggests reducing the demands). Much depends on the priorities of the class at that time.

Re-order the sequence: discussion questions that appear *after* the oral input may be more valuable *before* the input as a way to activate schemata. Some teachers may feel that vocabulary which is pre-taught in the book (before being heard on the recording) should be dealt with after listening so that the students have had a chance to hear it in context.

Change the focus of the sequence: perhaps the class needs to focus on a particular area – vocabulary, grammar, discourse markers, strategies – that the textbook exercises don't cover in this sequence. Once the students have listened for meaning, they might then go on to investigate the linguistic features of the text. One good way to do this is to doctor the transcript. Five or ten minutes on a computer is usually enough to produce a transcript with gaps.

Students often have particular problems comprehending names, verbs and idioms, all features that could be 'gapped' in a text. Or perhaps the teacher may wish to omit all the prepositions, articles or halves of collocations (it depends on the teaching goals of the lesson) before asking the students to write the missing words in the gaps while listening. Below is an example of a short listening text plus the gapped version, focusing on weak forms.

> A woman goes to a doctor complaining of pain.
> 'Where does it hurt?' asks the doctor.
> 'Everywhere,' says the woman.
> 'Can you be more specific?'
> So the woman touches her knee with her finger. 'Ouch!' she says. Then she touches her nose. 'Ouch!' Then she touches her back. 'Ouch!' Finally she touches her cheek. 'Ouch!' The doctor tells her to sit down, takes one look at her and says, 'You have a broken finger!'

> _____ woman goes to a doctor complaining _____ pain.
> 'Where _____ it hurt?' asks the doctor.
> 'Everywhere,' says the woman.
> '_____ you be more specific?'
> So the woman touches her knee _____ her finger. 'Ouch!' she says. Then she touches _____ nose. 'Ouch!' Then she touches her back. 'Ouch!' Finally she touches her cheek. 'Ouch!' The doctor tells her _____ sit down, takes one look _____ her and says, 'You have a broken finger!'

Besides gapping texts, we can also underline or highlight features. One textbook does just this to focus on word and sentence stress, as in the example shown here.

 Bring more variety to the class: a common feature of young learners' textbooks is the focus on responding to input by doing something physical. They listen and draw or listen and move or listen and put things in the right place. There are numerous activities of this type that an imaginative teacher can create. Here are a few ideas: the students write six 'content' words that they expect to hear in the recording on separate strips of paper, stick them on the wall and tick them

> **5 | Listening: *I'm just phoning to tell you about tonight* (page 113)**
>
> A: heLLO.
> B: HI, it's ME. i'm just PHONing to TELL you about toNIGHT.
> A: oh, OK. GREAT. so WHERE do you WANT to MEET?
> B: well, we're THINking of MEEting in the SOcial. do you KNOW it?
> A: um ... i'm NOT really SURE. MAYbe. WHERE is it again?
> B: in BLACK PRINCE ROAD, JUST near the PARK.
> A: oh, i KNOW the PLACE you MEAN. it's got TWO floors. an UPstairs and a DOWNstairs.
> B: THAT'S it. WE'RE going to be in the UPstairs bit.
> A: OK. GREAT. what TIME are you MEEting?
> B: i'm not SURE yet. is SEven OK for YOU?
> A: it's a bit EARly, ACtually. i NEED to go HOME and get CHANGED first.
> B: OK. WELL, let's say EIGHT o'clock, then. is THAT OK?
> A: yes, that's GREAT.
> B: OK. i'll PHONE around and TELL everyone else.
> A: OK, and i'll SEE you LAter.
> B: OK. BYE.
> A: BYE.

when they hear them. They can also be asked to stand up when they hear a number (any number) on the recording, or put their hands up when the speaker answers any of the comprehension questions that have been set.

A criticism that has been levelled at textbooks is that they tend to focus on left-brain activities (based on logic and analysis), even though many students prefer right-brain activities (based on creativity and intuition). For more creative students or those with a kinaesthetic learning style, the type of 'listen and act' activities described above are very appealing.

 Raise awareness of features of natural dialogue: this can be achieved by using the transcript or by isolating the target expressions from the recording. Here is an example from a coursebook.

 Get the material to match our personal beliefs about language learning: we may have a number of beliefs that conflict with those of the materials writer. For example, some teachers may object to the idea that

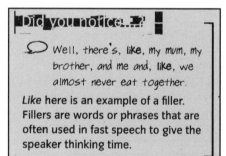

Did you notice ...?

> Well, there's, like, my mum, my brother, and me and, like, we almost never eat together.

Like here is an example of a filler. Fillers are words or phrases that are often used in fast speech to give the speaker thinking time.

students should read and listen at the same time during their first exposure to the input. These teachers will adapt by asking the students to close their books. Other teachers may feel that students should always have a purpose for listening, and therefore need a gist question. Others may feel that trying to teach pronunciation by isolating sounds from their context of connected speech is futile. They will adapt by putting the target features into a context which they then model to the students.

All of the ideas in the section above are based on pre-recorded passages in textbooks. We will now look at ways in which teachers can find and use authentic materials.

Authentic materials: radio, film/TV, songs

In Chapter 3 we stated that 'teacher talk' is a valuable form of authentic input, and the easiest to produce. Other authentic input has to be found, physically organised and, usually, adapted. Fortunately for teachers and students, listening material is easier to find now than ever before.

How to find authentic listening materials

Three sources of authentic recorded listening material are the radio, the television and the Internet. The net has some significant advantages over both the radio and television. One of these is that the content is archived rather than schedule-based. If you want to catch the TV show *Who Wants to Be a Millionaire?* you need to be either sitting in front of your television at exactly 8.30 p.m. or to have set the video for that time; otherwise you miss it. If you want to watch a **download** from the net or listen to a podcast, you can do so at any time. (With the caveat that not all listening material on the net is archived and that websites do get abandoned on the information highway just like rusting cars on real highways. This means you may need to download files quickly before they disappear.)

The biggest advantage of all, though, is the choice of material. The net is ever-expanding. Of course, more doesn't mean better, but teachers who are willing to spend some time searching, and who have honed their searching skills, will find a great deal of usable material. Some of it needs adapting, but some comes in a framework with features such as transcripts, vocabulary worksheets and comprehension questions.

How to find it? We find it much as we find anything else on the net: by searching. If we type in, say, 'ELT listening downloads' into Google, currently the world's most popular search engine, we are directed to about 86,500 websites. These will be of varying quality and usefulness, though of course one person's junk is another person's jewel. The first few pages are the most likely to offer us what we are looking for, although there may be hidden treasures for those who persevere.

A more fruitful and less time-consuming method is to visit frequently a number of trusted websites that regularly offer new material. The list on page 183 is a good place to start. Most of these contain large archives of recorded material but usually without the pedagogical framework, although some are directed specifically at language students.

How to exploit a recording

1 Radio

In Chapter 2 we looked at the numerous benefits of using authentic material such as radio, film, TV and songs. Here we look at some activities to exploit them.

The effort we put into exploiting a recording may depend on whether we see the material as reusable or a 'one-shot' lesson. A great topic that will not age, with a high quality recording may become part of our teaching resources for years to come, and so we take time to develop a full framework of discussion and language-based exercises around it. Other material – for example, a daily news bulletin – may be specifically of the here and now and is, therefore, less likely to be reused with future classes. For this type of material, if there isn't time to create a detailed worksheet, a simple formula like the one below will do the job. It also has the advantage of being usable with any news story.

Listen to the news. Complete the columns with notes.

	Who?	Where?	What?	When?
Story 1				
Story 2				
Story 3				

Teachers with more time can write fuller worksheets such as the one opposite for an advanced class. This is also based on the BBC radio news. Notice the balance of top-down and bottom-up activities included in the worksheet.

Schools that record the radio news on a daily basis have a valuable asset that isn't difficult to set up. The news provides excellent listening practice for high-level students working alone or in class.

2 Film/TV

We can exploit film and TV for listening by using a number of teaching techniques: manipulating the equipment to create a 'knowledge gap', managing the students so that they need to collaborate to piece together the content, and getting the students to make guesses about what they will see. The majority of the activities suggested below use one of these techniques. Naturally, there are ways of exploiting film and TV which are similar to those seen elsewhere in the book, so here we will focus on those activities that use aspects specific to the medium of film (e.g. moving images, real present characters in action) rather than just the audio. As with so many listening activities, other skills frequently come into play.

 Vision on, sound off: the students watch a short section without sound. They guess the gist of the scene or the words being spoken. They can be asked to write the dialogue in groups. After this, they watch the scene with sound and compare what they wrote.

 Vision off, sound on: the screen is covered, or the students turn their backs, and they listen to the sound. They might then be asked to say what is happening and who the speakers are, or to write down ten objects they expect to see on the screen, or even to draw the scene as they think it appears.

 Pause and predict: at certain points in the film or programme, the teacher pauses the action and asks the students to say what is happening and to guess what is about to happen. For this activity, the teacher needs to know the exact moment at which to pause.

 Watch and describe: the students sit in pairs, back to back. One of the pair is watching the action, without sound. He or she describes everything that is taking place on the screen and the other student writes rapid notes. After a few minutes, the activity stops and the non-viewing partner relates everything he or she

BBC News

1 Match a word from A with a word from B to make collocations.
A nuclear   presidential   resolve   tight   polling   approve   prime
B reforms   security   elections   weapons   minister   stations   an issue

2 The words in Exercise 1 come from the news headlines. What type of news stories are they?

3 Listen to the three headlines and make notes.

1   President Bush and Roh Moo-hyun (South Korea) ...

2   In Sri Lanka ...

3   In Italy ...

4 Listen again. Compare your notes in groups.

5 Complete the text with a word in each space.
President Bush and his South Korean ____ , Roh Moo-hyun, have reaffirmed they will not ____ the prospect of North Korea possessing nuclear weapons, but they said the issue should be resolved through ____ ____ .

As Sri Lankans ____ in presidential elections, security is tight at more than 10,000 polling stations amid fears of a ____ ____ . The front-runners for the president are the prime minister and the ____ leader.

The Italian Senate has approved ____ reforms of the country's constitution. The ____ will strengthen the powers of the prime minister at the same time as transferring _____ over health, education and local policing to the _____ .

Complete transcript (not included on worksheet)
President Bush and his South Korean counterpart, Roh Moo-hyun, have reaffirmed they will not tolerate the prospect of North Korea possessing nuclear weapons, but they said the issue should be resolved through diplomatic means.
As Sri Lankans vote in presidential elections, security is tight at more than 10,000 polling stations amid fears of a rebel attack. The front-runners for the president are the prime minister and the opposition leader.
The Italian Senate has approved radical reforms of the country's constitution. The measures will strengthen the powers of the prime minister at the same time as transferring authority over health, education and local policing to the regions.
(BBC1 News 5.30 p.m. 17 November 2006)

understood about the scene. In their pairs they make deductions about the people and action involved. Then the whole class watches to check.

 Act and watch: the students are given a transcript of a scene without being told anything about the characters. In groups, they act out the scene. After this, they

121

view the filmed version of the scene to compare. The students are often surprised when they watch the film or programme; words on a page have a wonderful way of being transformed in the mouths of actors surrounded by props and scenery!

 Watch and act: this is the inverse of the previous activity. The students view the scene and then use the transcript to act it out. The focus of the activity is on students listening for natural intonation and pronunciation before trying to reproduce them, but it is up to the teacher how much detail he or she wishes to go into. Teachers and students with a penchant for drama in class can work out the whole blocking sequence (where the actors stand and move in relation to each other and to the scenery) and even use props.

 Say who said it: the students are given a number of quotations from a video clip. First, they say who said it (only possible if there are several characters), before putting the quotations in the order in which they occur. This lends itself well to a follow-up speaking activity: using the quotations to reformulate the scene.

 Complete the story: similar to the activity 'Write on' in the previous chapter, the students watch until they know the set-up and the situation that needs to be resolved. The teacher stops the video. The students now guess the ending. They might do this in groups, either in writing or orally. An alternative is to show the beginning and the end and get the students to say what happens in the middle, although you would probably not do this if the ending is a surprise because it would spoil the viewing experience!

3 Songs

Many of the numerous activities that work well with songs have appeared elsewhere in the book, so they are summarised briefly in the table opposite.

How to get authentic input from other sources

At the time of writing, songs, TV/film and the radio are probably still the most popular sources for authentic listening material in classrooms around the world, although the Internet may well catch up soon. There are, however, a few other sources. More and more museums and galleries these days have a listening component in the form of a rentable audioguide, using headphones. These provide a lecture-style commentary that is calibrated to the visitor's stroll around the museum, an excellent source of input for many reasons. If I'm standing in front of Picasso's *Guernica* and listening, rather than sitting in a classroom and listening, the recording (not to mention the painting) comes to life.

One London-based school introduced an innovative new programme of events for its students that used the same type of authentic input as provided by the audioguide. The English Language Cultural Experience was a project set up by the Camden School of English. They took the students to a different museum or gallery every day. This meant that the students' surroundings became the subject matter, a kind of 3D real-life replacement for the topics in textbooks. The students' choice of destination – London, in this case – became their classroom. They used teacher-prepared worksheets, did some listening and spoke about everything they saw, heard, felt and touched in the museums. The project received outstanding feedback from the students.

How might such an idea work outside an English-speaking country? For a start, you could reverse the roles. The students prepare to introduce a place of cultural interest to a foreign visitor, using English as the medium of communication. Naturally, this type of

Using songs in ELT
Pre-listening activities
<ul><li>Complete each line with one word (fill the gap).</li><li>Guess ten words you'll hear based on the title. Or guess what the song is about from the title.</li><li>In pairs, students have alternate lines from the song (student A has the even-numbered lines, student B has the odd-numbered lines). Guess what the other lines are before listening to check.</li><li>In groups, pick a song and use news reports, drama, storytelling, poster-making, etc to present the song before the class hears it.</li></ul>
While-listening activities
<ul><li>Sing along.</li><li>Listen for pleasure. The inner voice will be singing along!</li><li>Mime the story or actions contained within it.</li><li>The teacher provides ten words from the song on pieces of card. Stick them on the wall and grab them as you hear them. Variation: the teacher gives an extra word which isn't in the song.</li><li>Clap out the rhythm of the song.</li><li>Put down the lyrics (written on strips of card) as you hear them.</li><li>Write all the words you hear that are connected to the topic (e.g. telephoning, cooking, travel).</li><li>Fill the gaps.</li><li>Underline the 'soundalike' mistakes, e.g. *The girl with colitis goes by* / *The girl with kaleidoscope eyes* (from 'Lucy in the Sky with Diamonds' by The Beatles). Correct them after listening.</li></ul>
Post-listening activities
Creative activities <ul><li>Write a letter or diary entry from a character in the song.</li><li>Write another verse.</li><li>Illustrate the song (young learners).</li></ul> *Reformulation activities* <ul><li>Re-order the lyrics on strips of paper.</li><li>Brainstorm words you heard.</li><li>Paraphrase the song.</li><li>Compare two songs on the same theme and teach vocabulary from your song.</li></ul>
Bottom-up language work: pre-, while- or post-listening
<ul><li>Match the beginning of a line to the end.</li><li>Replace words with other words that rhyme.</li><li>Correct the handout, which contains wrong lyrics.</li><li>Delete the extra words contained in the transcript.</li></ul>

project takes a lot of setting up. Students need to buy into the idea and to prepare well. Practical issues such as the number of students involved and whether the class can meet outside the school also need to be taken into account. It may be the case that a virtual tour, using artefacts or the Internet, is more practical, but the fact that the students' surroundings are used as the topic can provide excellent motivation.

How to create your own authentic materials

If teachers wish to provide some listening material but can find nothing suitable that has been professionally recorded, one option is to do it themselves. There are different ways in which they can do this.

No media:

The teacher speaks to the students in a live situation, perhaps bringing in another speaker, as in the live listening technique described on pages 46–47 in Chapter 3.

Recording during the lesson:

The teacher speaks to the students and records this. The recording can be played back as and when required. Cassette recorders are one possibility for this. Podcasts are another. These are becoming more popular, particularly in tertiary education where lecturers upload their lectures onto the Internet for absent or dozing students to listen to later. (See *How to Teach English with Technology* for an in-depth discussion of podcasting.)

Recording before the lesson:

The teacher records a talk/discussion in the staffroom or some other place and brings the recording into the class. This type of listening is often semi-scripted. We may ask a colleague to discuss a topic with a particular language level in mind (e.g. intermediate learners), using certain discourse patterns, structures or vocabulary. It is a feature of our profession that teachers often make unusually good actors!

Here we should add that creating materials – of any kind, not only listening materials – is an excellent path to professional development. It brings into focus many aspects involved in both teaching and learning, such as assessing students' needs, structuring and pacing lessons, grading language, choosing ways to introduce, practise and recycle vocabulary and grammar, drafting different versions of input and, not least, seeing the lesson in terms of what students will make of the material.

How to store this material

Language schools in technologically advanced countries often have an area for storage of useful materials in the staffroom. There might be a bank of cassettes, videos and CDs kept where they are easily available for the teachers. The material needs to be labelled clearly, indexed and regularly updated, if possible. For personal materials, it is best to keep worksheets in both paper and electronic form for rewriting and amending as well as for easy access. Again, everything should be labelled and kept in a file to make later retrieval easier. For schools in less technologically advanced countries, teachers will probably take more responsibility for looking after their own material rather than storing it in a common space.

How to plan a lesson using student-created materials

If the school has a language laboratory, this is ideal for students to create their own material. One idea is for the students to plan and rehearse an anecdote. First, they are given 'thinking time' to choose their topic and possibly make notes. Then they go to the language laboratory and individually record the anecdote at a console. They should be given several attempts to do this so that they can produce something that represents the best of their speaking ability. After this, they move around listening to each other's anecdotes, possibly answering or preparing questions or taking notes. Following this, the listeners should have a chance to interact with the tellers of the anecdotes that they heard. This can be facilitated by putting the students into groups of three and having each student listen to the anecdotes of the other two in his or her group.

Students can also create their own listening/viewing materials on video. This is often quite time-consuming project work rather than something that can be achieved in one lesson, and requires some preparation both in terms of content and use of the technology. News programmes, presentations and skits are possible genres for this type of treatment.

Kern describes a class project in the US called 'Découvrir Berkeley' (Discover Berkeley). The project involved students in groups presenting the town of Berkeley – the location, its academic programmes, etc – in French, and sending the results, including video footage, to a class in France. The final step – sharing the project with students from another country – gives the task a real purpose and the students a sense of accomplishment. Kern suggests projects with titles such as 'Discovering _____' or '_____ Uncovered' because of the overtones of investigation – intriguing for both creators and audience.

Students can also create a podcast. For this, you will need an MP3 player, Internet access and a bit of know-how. One advantage of podcasts is that they can be produced and edited to a very high level, like a radio show, using a free program such as Audacity (see the list of web addresses on page 183). They can also be posted onto the net – sometimes onto a **blog** (a weblog) – and used/enjoyed by people, including language students, all over the world.

Overall, there are advantages and drawbacks to the use of technology in student-created materials. Creativity is a great motivator, and students get a sense of pride and achievement at having made something tangible using English. The collaboration involved in this type of project is also valuable as it provides a context for a lot of language use, providing all discussions are held in English.

The drawback is that teachers may need to spend time learning how to use the technology, if it's available in the first place. No one should use technology for the sake of it, but as with all new developments, things become easier with time and practice. (Earlier generations of teachers used to have sleepless nights over language laboratories, cassette recorders and the like.) Ultimately, the question to ask before embarking on these types of lesson is: *Does the technology add enough to make this worthwhile?* In other words, is there sufficient payback in terms of student motivation, use of English and overall outcome? Much will, of course, depend on the type of students you have. If they are willing to embrace the use of technology, that's a great bonus.

Anticipating problems

Anticipating problems is a vital part of planning any lesson. Most teachers can recall moments of confusion and stress when they squirmed because things weren't going as expected. Expectations are the product of experience, and before the lesson teachers probably have a mental model of what will happen. This is based on a number of factors: how *they* were taught, previous lessons they have taught, lessons that they have observed, procedures they have read about, the methodology used in the school, and, above all, what they know about their current students. They get to class with the model in their heads, start teaching and suddenly find that the students are half-asleep, the equipment doesn't work and most of the country's workforce appears to be drilling holes in the road outside. If only they had anticipated these problems!

In Chapter 1 we established that there are four main types of problem associated with comprehending listening input. The table below shows some possible pre-emptive measures, things teachers can do to lessen the probability of the problem occurring.

Problems associated with ...	Solutions
1 characteristics of the message	Prepare students; activate schemata and predict content. Give content information in another format or genre (e.g. pictures or an article) before listening to the same content. Pre-teach key words.
2 characteristics of the delivery	Allow a **tune-in period** (students listen for a few seconds to get used to the voices, speed, tone, etc). Chunk the text. Pause after difficult phrases, while the sounds are still in the students' short-term memory, and elicit what they heard. Use the transcript. Empower students by encouraging them to participate – they can ask for clarification, take charge of machinery, etc.
3 characteristics of the listener	See listening as an opportunity, not a test. Get students to invest something of themselves in the task, e.g. give opinions. Personalise: ask students to listen for something relevant to themselves. Do the listening in the language laboratory, if you have one, so students can work at their own pace. Vary the task; use TPR, maps and drawings.
4 characteristics of the environment	These characteristics may be out of your control. A few solutions: close doors and windows. Check equipment before class. Investigate the opportunities for swapping rooms or machinery with another class, or going to a language laboratory. Ensure that the volume is appropriate for students in all corners of the room (check beforehand or ask them).

Another potential problem is that the students are of mixed ability. Perhaps some of them find listening easy and find comprehension questions trite, while others struggle to piece together connected speech. What can the teacher do? One answer may lie in combining some of the ideas contained in the section 'Choosing and adapting published materials' earlier in this chapter (see page 113). Other solutions involve collaboration: faster students can help slower students, or in groups they compare what they understood. A very well-prepared teacher may consider setting different tasks, one basic and another more advanced, and asking the students to do as much as they can. Teachers can also give listeners the option, after hearing a passage a couple of times, to read the transcript while listening a third time. Stronger students may not feel the need, while less able students will.

A final point about anticipating problems in class: teachers need a positive outlook. We need to see 'problems' as opportunities for teaching and learning. Here are some examples of 'teachable moments':

A Brazilian student keeps saying that her breakfast consists of 'cough with cream'; a Thai claims he went to 'primate school'; a German woman studying for a listening exam asks if we can turn off the 'ear conditioning'. The teacher recognises the pronunciation problems and does some phoneme discrimination exercises by way of remedial work. The teacher also models the different mouth positions involved, and for the German woman's class (just four students) brings a number of small mirrors to the next lesson. The students make the sounds in front of the mirrors, checking their mouth position. Not all of them succeed, but in terms of awareness-raising, the activity has been worthwhile for all.

Other aspects of a positive outlook: praise students for making good guesses, because guessing is an important skill. Focus on what students understood as well as what they didn't understand. You can do this by getting students to write notes on the board or asking them to pool their ideas to reconstruct a text. Encourage students to go beyond the superficiality of right or wrong answers; ask them how they arrived at their answers. This is sometimes called a **process-based** approach, as opposed to a **product-based** approach. Being able to justify their hypotheses will give them confidence. Ask further questions: *What can we tell about the speaker's character or mood? What is the speakers' relationship? Why might the speaker have said this?* By creating a positive atmosphere of inquiry, and by getting students to share what they understood, listening becomes less associated with problems (and therefore dread) than with achievement (and therefore pleasure).

Young learners

When it comes to anticipating problems, the type of students in the class is clearly a major issue. The differences between planning listening lessons for adults and those for children are enormous. Firstly, we need to say what is meant by young learners. The term can be used to describe children from any age between four and eighteen. Breaking it down, we can divide young learners into three groups: very young (four to seven), preteens (eight to twelve) and teenagers. Many of the differences between planning listening lessons for young learners and for adults exist because of general factors such as their interests, their respective vocabularies and the way they learn, and we need to consider briefly some of the developmental differences and stages that they go through. After this, we will look at a number of practical steps that teachers need to take in light of these stages.

First, we will consider very young learners. Children aged four to seven go through a process of developing motor skills such as writing and drawing, and also basic literacy in their first language. Literacy begins with comprehending signs: long before they can read and write, children see the golden arches of McDonald's and understand that a burger and fries is coming their way. Later, as they begin to write, they struggle to form letters, spell whole words and, finally, put together meaningful strings of words. Throughout these stages, they are growing familiar with the correlations between sound and written form.

In terms of cognitive skills, they have little or no sense of the abstract, and young children manipulate features of language with great difficulty. If you asked them for the past tense of the verb *to be*, you would get blank faces. Also, young learners' range of schemata is extremely limited. Although they may have vivid imaginations, their references comprise little that is outside their immediate world of family, food and routines at home and in school.

Even their understanding of school is far from complete. Very young learners will probably be experiencing their first moments in formal education, so language isn't the only thing they need to learn. They are getting used to patterns of behaviour – where to sit, what to do with the objects around them – and their role in the social whirl of the classroom. As well as this, they have very few study skills.

Children's attention spans are typically short. Generally, they cannot concentrate for more than a few minutes at a time, particularly on disembodied voices, although stories can be an exception, as we will discuss below. This inability to concentrate for long also affects the tasks we devise. Asking children to sit still and listen is unlikely to be successful in most cases. In addition to this, they are easily distracted, which is of enormous use for consoling crying children, but not so good in educational settings!

Moving on to preteens, as the child gets older, the features described above begin to become less pronounced. The children can concentrate for longer, their range of schemata broadens as they start to make sense of the world, and they develop the ability to see formal patterns in the sensory data that they encounter. As they see these patterns, they learn to theorise, which in turn allows them to make deductions.

Their cognitive development means that, as listeners, they are able to hold more information in their minds, make reference to things that happened in the past or may happen in the future, and conceptualise objects or phenomena that are not present. This means that the input can be richer; while still embedded in a context they can recognise, it can come from more sources and encompass cultural issues that would not be comprehensible to very young learners. Preteens will usually have acquired at least some study skills, although they still cannot concentrate for long on disembodied voices, and visual stimuli are still useful.

By the teenage years, the cognitive abilities and motor skills are usually well developed, but there may be significant social and emotional issues that affect second language learning. Motivation is a particularly relevant issue. Teenagers, unlike most small children, tend to be less eager to please their teachers, and are often more critical, especially if they are unable to see the relevance of the activities they do in class. Furthermore, they have the language to voice their criticism. This is not necessarily a bad thing; it makes teaching teenagers challenging and often rewarding.

Another feature of adolescence is that it often coincides with a period of self-consciousness, so teenagers may be anxious about the impression they make on their peers. These are important issues in foreign language learning because, in a sense, all learners must go through a stage resembling early childhood in that they are unable to express themselves or make any sense of the new language. This is potentially embarrassing for sensitive students. It isn't really true to suggest that foreign language learners are as powerless as infants, but they do need to cope with situations in which they understand little and can express even less. Teenage listeners, when faced with incomprehensible 'noise' that does not seem relevant to their lives, are likely to react with hostility or boredom.

However, teenagers can also be extremely attentive, creative and dynamic ʲ topic they are interested in – something that is at the heart of teaching this aʓ also have the intellectual resources to find things out for themselves, and this, ʋ. one of the best ways to learn anything.

Teaching young learners to listen to English

The younger the learners are, the more teachers need to address the whole child. By this, I mean the child's cognitive, emotional and physical being. Listening activities with young learners are never just listening activities. There is so much else going on: growing familiarity with social interaction, objects surrounding the child, the structures of stories and games, writing, real-life situations involving the outside world, physical actions, and the child's relationship to nature and the community. Addressing the whole child requires a great deal of creativity on the part of the teacher. During a listening exercise, teachers must find a way to bring the input to life, getting the children to participate physically or conjuring up colourful images by using intonation and objects. In the best listening exercises for children, gym mats become magic carpets, water bottles hold rare potions, and pumpkins really do become royal coaches.

Besides creativity, good classroom management is extremely important. Very young children are unfamiliar with classroom routines, so when it comes to giving instructions, everything needs to be demonstrated, and the teacher usually does the first few activities with the students. Providing them with a model to follow gives children security, and initially they learn a lot by observing and copying. This brings the danger that the child will simply copy without understanding, but good teachers, by scaffolding and providing steady support, tend to know when to take the scaffold away – to let the child act independently to achieve a task.

One common mode of scaffolding, used with very young learners, is for the teacher to talk while pointing to relevant pictures. This allows the children to see connections. The teacher may also stop regularly to ask what is happening, and elicit information. This type of interactivity, involving reading, listening, speaking and looking at pictures is essential for the child's development. In terms of oral input, the teacher's voice is what the children mostly listen to, as he or she gives instructions, reads stories, and uses language for social purposes. Repetition is common, and routines make the children feel secure. They will happily sing the same songs and hear the same stories throughout the term.

This is not the case with teenagers, who generally dislike the feeling that they are repeating material. Older children can listen to a wider range of input: longer, more complex stories, recordings that involve other cultures and other voices, recordings that draw on other subjects, and faster speech. They can also predict more accurately.

Having spent longer in educational settings, teenagers are, in a sense, institutionalised. They know the procedures and need less scaffolding. In fact, when it comes to teaching listening to teenagers and adults, many of the principles are the same: the schemata need to be activated, the students need a reason to listen, there should be follow-up activities, and there should be diagnostic work to see where problems occurred and how they can be dealt with. The main difference may be that, with their horizons more limited than those of adults, teenagers might not perceive the need to understand English. In these circumstances, enjoyment of either the material or the task is vital to keep students motivated. It is hoped that earlier chapters of this book can provide ideas for both.

Tasks for young learners

For all of the reasons mentioned above, young children learning to listen to English need an activity-based approach. More than any other types of student, young learners benefit from 'listen and do' activities (see Chapter 5, page 94). These are mainly non-verbal responses, such as miming, dancing, pointing to illustrations, colouring pictures, sticking cards onto surfaces, etc. Teachers who employ a range of tasks that use several of the senses will have an advantage in keeping the students' attention. Gestures and visual input are vital.

Another aspect of while-listening task selection is that the task must be embedded in the child's present and his or her immediate surroundings. Very young children can barely conceptualise other places or time frames. Also, they need to focus on real things: objects or people in their sight. The exception to this, as we will see in the next section, is when they listen to stories. Even young children are capable of using their imaginations to become engrossed in the fantasy world of stories, but these need to contain elements of the familiar.

Children learn through play. For this reason, tasks with a game-like element can be highly effective. The younger the children, the less self-conscious they are, so they will be happy to participate in many types of game, drama and movement. Unlike many teenagers, young children usually like to be picked, and their enthusiasm needs to be used by teachers in order to convert listening input into some kind of output, whether it be acting out a story with puppets or using mime, recital or some other way to reflect the listening material.

Above all, the tasks must be do-able. Children, as much as adults, like to succeed, and the teacher needs to provide constant encouragement and approval.

Listening material for young learners

For young learners, stories are useful as teaching tools because they comprise complete imaginary worlds in which listeners can get immersed. Stories often have typical structures with common features. They usually contain a formulaic opening sequence (the words *Once upon a time* are so powerful that they still activate the schemata of adults who long ago stopped believing in fairy tales). Following this, the characters and setting are introduced. Then some kind of conflict or difficulty arises that needs to be overcome, and a series of events, usually told chronologically, leads to a resolution. This is rounded up with a formulaic closing line – in fairy tales, *And they all lived happily ever after* – and perhaps a moral.

Besides the recognisability of the structure, there are other features. Many stories use **parallelism**, repeated patterns, such as *What big eyes you have! What big ears you have! What a big nose you have!* (from the story *Little Red Riding Hood*), which reinforce the language. Another feature is the richness of the vocabulary. Adjectives come thick and fast to describe the characters, and interesting verbs are used to bring events to life. In fairy tales, the names of the characters are also unusual – Rapunzel, Cinderella, Aladdin – offering children a glimpse of the delights of language. Children's stories also often contain humour, suspense and magic: animals that talk, dinosaurs that watch TV, wizards that wave wands and reduce witches to dust. What's more, the moral (usually the good live happily and the bad die horribly) may be useful as a way to introduce values.

In terms of language used, there is an element of play to the prose style of many children's writers: they use features such as alliteration (Little Red Riding Hood, the big, bad wolf), puns and other wordplay. Even in a second or foreign language, these features may be perceived by children at some stage.

Besides stories, music plays a large role in children's experiences with listening. We have already discussed the benefits of music in Chapter 3, and in this chapter we looked at activities to use with songs.

Summary

Overall, these things need to be taken into consideration when we think about teaching listening to young learners:

- Compared to those used with adults, the listening texts need to be shorter, simpler and must usually involve the students doing things with their bodies or manipulating objects.

- Repetition is valid for reinforcement and young children are unlikely to get bored with the same songs. Young children have vivid imaginations and can be entranced by stories, so listening that uses stories and scaffolding is especially effective.

- With teenagers perhaps the key is to find topics that interest them, and then combine enjoyable activities with the rigorousness that their developing intellects require.

English for specific purposes (ESP)

As with teaching children, ESP classes require a different approach to that of general English for adults. ESP is one of a whole plethora of abbreviations that range almost literally from A to Z, though this writer has yet to see a course in English for zoologists. Among the alphabet soup, some of the more common include EAP (English for academic purposes), EOP (occupational), and EST (science and technology).

Before discussing listening in ESP, we should identify some of the features that characterise ESP classes.

Firstly, a brief comment on the origins of ESP. As linguists began to study language more closely in the 1950s and 1960s, and as developments in methodology began to emphasise the importance of the learner, we came to realise that the language used for diplomacy or for science and technology is very different from that used in, say, advertising or the tourist industry, and that the best starting point for a language class might be what the student wishes to do with the language being learnt.

Underpinning the whole idea of ESP is the importance of meeting the students' needs. Unlike general English, ESP classes tend not to follow generalised grammatical and topical syllabuses. Instead, the lessons are framed around the particular disciplines, occupations and activities relevant to the students. In this sense, ESP courses are goal-oriented; by the end of the course the students should be able to do something in English that is essential for their career or their studies.

We can identify a few other characteristics typical of ESP courses: they tend to be for adults who already have a level at least equivalent to intermediate in general English, and a basic knowledge of grammar and competence in the skills is assumed. Being goal-oriented, the courses also tend to be of limited duration.

The advantages of ESP courses are that they are often very motivating and they tend not to waste any time. Everything – from the material used to the tasks set – is relevant to the students.

Teachers, materials and methodology in ESP

Teachers do not need to be experts in their students' fields. We cannot be expected to know every nuance of international law just because we are teaching English to a class of lawyers. However, we must understand enough about the content to act as a sort of language consultant or advisor while the student plans how to achieve any specific task in English. This being the case, ESP lessons are often more collaborative than other types of English class: the students know more about the content, while the teacher's field of expertise is the English language. Compared to general English classes, ESP lessons tend to be based more on tasks. The teacher evaluates how successfully the students achieve the task and advises them on how to improve.

In terms of materials used, again, relevance is vital. Authentic material is the norm. Dialogues invented solely to carry grammar points are a rarity. If it is not always possible to provide up-to-date material concerning the students' subject or occupation, there must be what Harding calls a 'transfer' stage in which the content can be related directly to the students' jobs or fields of study.

The same is true of tasks. ESP is very practical. The students are there because they need to do things with the language (rather than know about the language). The tasks, therefore, must reflect the students' needs.

Many ESP teachers produce their own materials to fit the class. In fact, in many areas of ESP there are no existing coursebooks that fit the students' specific needs. **In-house materials** (made in the school by the teachers) are useful in that they are tailored to the specific teaching situation. One drawback is that the teachers may have no skill or expertise in producing such materials. There is no easy fix for this, but a good place to start is to look at published materials, read the teacher's guides, and try to see the pedagogical principles behind every activity while also looking at the whole sequence and how it fits together. The rest is practice, and constant critical evaluation of the materials in action.

ESP teachers who want to improve their students' listening may well need to find appropriate passages and also devise pedagogical sequences for them. This requires nothing different from the advice given elsewhere in this book about planning with authentic materials, but the ESP teacher is more limited in choice. As much as possible, teachers need to collaborate, and share and store texts, worksheets and recordings so that there is a bank of material that can be relied on: a bank of bankers for the bankers!

Six essentials for planning listening lessons

We close this chapter with a checklist that summarises some of the basics of planning listening lessons.

1 Check the recording, if you are using one. Don't rely on reading the transcript. Scripts tell us nothing of speed, accent or clarity.

2 Check the machine, if you are using one. If it is a tape recorder, make sure that the tape is cued to the beginning of the correct recording. If the tape recorder has a counter, set it to zero so that you can rewind and know exactly where the recording will start.

3 Calculate how long the whole listening sequence will take.

4 Anticipate 'trouble spots' that will be difficult for students, and consider how you will deal with these.

5 Prepare different tasks for first, second and third listenings, i.e. a *sequence* of tasks that builds on what students understand. Make this sequence success-oriented so that the majority of students will be able to complete these tasks. If the task is too easy, you run the risk of boring the students. If it's too difficult, students become demotivated.

6 Be ready to abandon your plan at any moment. Abandoned plans allow for reactive, responsive teaching, a sure sign that the teacher is engaged in what is happening here and now in the classroom. But be warned: too many abandoned plans mean that the teacher is planning badly!

Conclusions | *In this chapter we have:*

- discussed the roles of the teacher as planner – both long-term and short-term – such as moment-by-moment decision-maker and provider of material.
- looked at listening in the syllabus and the need to provide variety.
- talked about how to choose and adapt published materials.
- discussed planning the lesson with authentic materials and in particular the materials now available on the Internet.
- suggested the importance of anticipating problems while planning, and offered some solutions.
- discussed the special challenges of teaching young learners and how to plan listening lessons for them.
- discussed ESP courses and how to plan listening lessons for them.
- named six essentials for planning listening lessons.

8 | Listening in the wider context

Most of the successful people I've known are the ones who do more listening than talking. (Bernard Baruch)

- **Integrated listening**
- **How to assess listening**
- **Encouraging students to listen outside the classroom**

- **Self-access and listening in the language lab**
- **Teacher autonomy; becoming a better teacher of listening**

Integrated listening

As we have seen in previous chapters, the four skills – reading, writing, speaking and listening – rarely take place in isolation. What would writers be without readers? Even private diaries are read, perhaps years later, by their own writers. What would speakers be without listeners? Here's one answer to that question: when Britain's Prince Charles admitted that he spoke regularly to his plants, some British newspapers concluded, not altogether seriously, that he was mad.

The majority of EFL and ESL lessons, certainly in general English classes, incorporate all four of the skills, plus grammar, vocabulary and pronunciation, in varying patterns and ratios. Classes may take the form of speak–listen–speak or speak–read–write–speak or read–vocabulary–speak or, in some cases, grammar–grammar–grammar. Sometimes the lesson may focus almost exclusively on one skill or aspect of the language. For example, if you are preparing a class for a written exam, it may be valid to have the students writing for a large chunk of the lesson. Furthermore, there are programmes – in many intensive English courses in US universities, for instance – which separate the skills into listening classes, speaking classes, writing classes, and so on. Here we will argue that a balance of skills is desirable for any one lesson, and that the teaching of listening is more effective when integrated with other skills.

The strongest arguments for an integrated skills approach are that it prepares us best for what we will encounter outside the classroom, and it allows more variety as a way of approaching language learning. You can't learn to write without reading, and you can't learn to speak without listening. If you want to take an exam in listening, you will almost certainly have to *read* some questions, *write* the answers, and maybe even *speak* about the passage you heard.

Even in non-exam situations, the tasks we ask our students to perform in class often require more than one skill. All of the activities proposed in Chapters 4, 5 and 6 are based on listening, but the emphasis varies; in some, the students may spend more time speaking or writing than listening. The only listening activity in which other skills tend not to be used is extended listening, something we will discuss later in this chapter.

In considering the integration of the skills, we need to examine the difference between 'the listening lesson' and 'listening in the lesson'. The former aims to improve the students' listening only. It incorporates strategy training, whether overtly or covertly, and will probably contain an element of troubleshooting – examining those problematical areas where listening becomes difficult. Any other benefits – acquired vocabulary and grammar, for example – are incidental. In other words, the focus is purely on the listening skill.

'Listening in the lesson' entails using a recording or listening to the teacher or other speakers to elaborate on a given topic; it may serve as a context for the target grammar or vocabulary; or as a model for speaking. What it will not do is focus *in depth* on the skill of listening.

Having outlined the differences between these types of lesson, we should be aware that the boundaries between them are often blurred, and even non-listening lessons will inevitably benefit our students' listening. Learning new grammar and vocabulary improves listening because it allows the students to broaden the range of input that is comprehensible to them. Improved reading also benefits listeners, as the inner voice 'pronounces' the words and the students develop their vocabulary and awareness of discourse patterns.

Of all the skills that complement listening, pronunciation has arguably the closest link. Every focus on every aspect of pronunciation is also a focus on listening. Students need to know the way sounds change in connected speech – elision, assimilation (see Chapter 1) – in order to improve their listening as well as their speaking. Sensitivity to rhythm and stress patterns – traditionally seen as aspects of pronunciation – is vital for listeners. Approximately 80 per cent of multisyllable content words in English are stressed on the first syllable. Native listeners use this knowledge subconsciously to perceive word boundaries – where words begin and end. This perception may not be available to non-native listeners unless they have a strong affinity with the rhythms of English. From before we are born, we hear, and possibly feel, the rhythms of our native language. Thereafter, we often subconsciously assume that this rhythm fits all languages. It doesn't. In English, the stressed syllables are up to three times as long as the unstressed syllables. In Italian and Spanish, the stressed syllables are only 1.5 times as long as the unstressed. For this reason, much early teaching of listening and pronunciation needs to be concerned with getting students used to the rhythm of English by highlighting stress. Many of the difficulties that native speakers experience in understanding speakers whose first language is not English lie less in the production of individual sounds than in the fact that the latter have not mastered the language's rhythm.

In addition to these two points – rhythm, and the way sounds change in connected speech – intonation is also a listening issue. It affects the meaning of an utterance. For example, intonation alerts us to the mood or attitude of the speaker, and also tells us, via a falling pitch, when the speaker has finished.

In summary, the many facets of pronunciation affect our ability to listen and comprehend. It follows logically that the teaching of pronunciation and listening needs to be integrated.

In Chapter 1 we mentioned Multiple Intelligences theory and the importance of balancing the skills. By using a variety of skills in the classroom, we increase the likelihood of our lessons catering to all of our students with their diverse intelligences. The shy, silent student who completes grammar exercises faultlessly (logical-mathematical intelligence) will learn best during the stage in which the class focuses on grammar rules. Students with interpersonal intelligence, who tend to be fluent but inaccurate, will benefit particularly from the speaking stages of the lesson because they learn by interacting. If we cater for only one skill, boredom will set in for many students, but if we use a variety, everyone will be interested at least some of the time. Teachers are well-advised to investigate, in the light of Multiple Intelligences theory, how their students like to learn. This can be done through questionnaires or simple observation of the students during different activities.

The integration of skills is a subject that surfaces when we try to assess our students' listening ability.

How to assess listening

Different types of assessment include **placement tests**, **progress tests**, **achievement tests** (testing what has been learned over a period of time) and **proficiency tests** (measuring overall ability). It is likely that, at some stage of their career, teachers will be involved in preparing students for at least some of these.

In any discussion of assessment, we need to make a distinction: on the one hand there is the type of assessment that is ongoing and takes place informally every time students engage in listening. This is sometimes called **formative assessment**. It is process-oriented, and designed as a diagnostic tool to help the students to improve. On the other hand, there is **summative assessment**, which is the type required by schools, colleges and governments. It is formal and results-oriented in that the students always receive a grade. In a rather useful analogy, one article states that: 'When the cook tastes the soup, that's formative assessment; when the customer tastes the soup, that's summative assessment.' Here, for clarity, we will refer to the more formal type as testing, and the ongoing type as assessment. Let us deal with testing first.

It is very difficult to test listening without bringing other skills into play. If we ask our students to discuss a listening passage, their errors may reflect lack of speaking proficiency rather than a failure to comprehend. It is then unfair to assign low grades for a listening test when the student's problem lies in a different skill. This is an issue related to a test's **validity**.

Validity concerns the use and interpretation of the test. Imagine asking our students to listen to a ten-second radio advertisement and then telling them to write a three-page essay on advertising. If we then grade the essay and use the score to place our students *in a listening class*, this is not valid because the students only listened for ten seconds. Validity, then, is concerned with whether the exam really tests what it is supposed to test.

The other important factor in testing is **reliability**, the certainty that the test will produce consistent results no matter who is marking it or what mood they are in.

Testing is an extremely complex process. There are many variables which make it so, and validity and reliability are far from easy to achieve. The factors that can make listening difficult, which we discussed in Chapter 1 – the message, the delivery, the listener and the environment – may, in some cases, be described as the factors that make listening tests *unfair*. Take cultural issues included in the message, for example. If the listening passage discusses topics which the students know nothing about, the problem is not listening but background knowledge. Or a student may understand the passage well enough but not the questions that accompany it. Is this a listening problem or a reading problem?

Furthermore, there is almost always a delicate balance between testing listening ability and testing memory. Imagine you attended a lecture on the winners of the Nobel Prize for Literature, and were asked afterwards to name their birthplaces (mentioned by the lecturer), you would probably fail. Does this mean you didn't understand the lecture? No. It means you couldn't remember such details. Tests need to focus on what is relevant rather than asking students to recall incidental facts.

The nature of the task is, of course, crucial. As explained in Chapter 5, nonverbal responses, such as true/false questions and multiple choice, take less time for students to complete and ensure little distraction from actual listening. This type of task also allows large numbers of items, a factor which increases the reliability of the test. The drawback is that, with true/false items, the students might guess and get lucky. In fact, they have a 50 per cent chance of this! With multiple-choice questions, there is less chance of this as there are usually three **distractors** (wrong options). The problem with this, however, is that multiple-choice questions require the students to hold four possibilities in their heads while listening. As such, the distractors need to be kept as short as possible.

With productive responses, the likelihood of a lucky guess is smaller, but the task demands ability in two skills, not one. There is also a heavier load on memory when students need to produce something related to the passage. A further problem concerns the grading of productive responses: it is more difficult for teachers/testers because there are other criteria involved apart from correct or incorrect answers. These criteria include accuracy in terms of grammar and vocabulary, use of the conventions of spelling and punctuation, and possibly the use of the students' imagination. All of these need to be taken into consideration when the teacher/marker is grading the response, and none is strictly a listening phenomenon. There are also partially correct answers to consider, as well as the thoroughness and extent of the response. What one tester regards as 'a full answer', another might describe as 'waffle' – saying or writing too much that is of too little consequence.

Between these poles – multiple choice and written response – lies what is possibly the best listening task for a test: a very short written answer. Sentence completion can also be effective, particularly if the answer consists of no more than a few words.

Most teachers do not have to write listening tests. There are a number of exam boards, such as those administering the CAMBRIDGE, IELTS, TOEFL and TOEIC exams, which do this for us. But during our careers there is every likelihood that we will have to teach exam classes. For this reason we will now look at some ways to prepare students for listening tests.

The first thing we need to consider is the fact that listening tests are regarded with trepidation and sometimes outright fear by students (Jeremy Harmer describes summative tests as 'sudden death' events). We have already discussed at length the reasons for this: lack of control over input, lack of interaction due to the unavailability of the speaker, and the real-time speed of listening which, unlike reading, allows no opportunity to go back and check. Tests also prohibit collaboration with other students, and usually the listeners are allowed to hear the passage only once or twice.

The strategies and skills that we teach our students for general listening are also applicable to these issues in exam contexts. However, because of the psychological factor and the specific nature of test formats, we need to prepare our students in a number of ways that would not be necessary in a general English class. Here are a few ideas for teachers and students.

Things teachers should do

- Make sure the students know exactly what is in the test: the number of passages they will listen to and the approximate length, the type of questions they will answer, and how many times the recording will be played.
- Prepare the students for the types of topics that occur and make sure they have mastered the basic vocabulary pertaining to these topics.
- Make sure the students know administrative issues such as where they will write their answers and how long the whole test will last.
- Do several practice tests, preferably in the same room in which the real test will take place. If possible, set up the room as it will be for the test.
- Include an easy initial question to increase confidence and allow the students to 'tune in' to the speakers.
- Go over the answers in the practice test in order to demystify the exam. Get students to justify their answers, including their correct ones.

Strategies for students to use in listening tests

Strategy	Explanation
Read and predict.	Read the questions before listening. Predict answers based on world knowledge (What animals will a South African hunter speak about?) and linguistic knowledge (What type of word will go here – noun or verb?).
Get ready.	Have the pen or pencil poised above the page before the recording starts.
Answer immediately.	As soon as you hear the answer, write it down. Do not rely on your memory to 'serve up' the answer later.
Be word-wise.	Listen for the words in the questions and synonyms of these words. They will alert you to the fact that the answer is coming.
Focus your listening.	Don't listen generally; target your listening so that you only focus on the information necessary to answer the questions.
Don't give up.	If you get lost, keep listening; you may not have missed any important information and you may be able to get back on track.
Listen for pauses.	Pauses always *mean* something. They may tell us that there is a change of topic or a transition point, or that the speaker is building up to an important moment.
Notes first.	If you have to write at the same time as listening, write notes first. Write full sentences from your notes once the recording is over.
Guess.	If you missed the answer, make a guess using the context.

The question remains: how can I teach the strategies listed above? One way is to 'take a recording for a walk'. This follows a process used by researchers called a **think-aloud**

protocol (during the activity, the participants talk about how they are solving a task). The version suggested here involves pausing a recording at certain points and talking about how you are dealing with it in relation to the exam questions. Here are some of the things you might say: *The speaker mentioned cowboys. What country might she be talking about? Maybe the US. Let's hear a bit more. She said guns. That word has a similar meaning to a word in the question. What word is that? Ah, yes, weapons. The speaker just said 'on the one hand'. She's going to give an opinion and then what will she say? She'll say 'on the other hand'. What comes after 'on the other hand'? A contrasting opinion.* Rather than 'thinking aloud', some teachers may prefer to elicit answers and ways to deal with the passage from the students themselves.

Taking a recording for a walk is a way of showing the students strategies in action. It requires practice and a fair amount of confidence, but the benefits can be long-lasting if the students get into the habit of asking similar questions. Another tip for teaching strategies is to name them, using a maximum of three words. On occasions when a particular strategy is necessary, remind the students, using the name. For example, if the practice test is about to begin and one student is busy combing his hair, pen resting on desk, we might say *Get ready!*

We began our discussion of assessment by describing two types: formal testing and ongoing assessment. Let's move on to the latter.

One useful tool for ongoing assessment comes courtesy of the Common European Framework, a brainchild of the Council of Europe. The Council is an intergovernmental body concerned with describing and standardising the proficiency levels of learners of foreign languages. The Common European Framework's 'Can do' statements are a checklist of abilities connected with the skills. These statements describe exactly what students at six different levels of proficiency should be able to do in terms of the foreign language. By differentiating the **sub-skills**, the statements allow a more precise assessment of a student's listening skills, rather than simply a general listening grade. For example, under the heading *Overall Listening Comprehension, level A1* (the lowest) is the following descriptor:

> *Can follow speech which is very slow and carefully articulated, with long pauses for him/her to assimilate meaning.*

At B1 level (intermediate), the student:

> *can understand straightforward factual information about common everyday or job-related topics, identifying both general messages and specific details, provided speech is clearly articulated in a generally familiar accent.*

and:

> *can understand the main points of clear standard speech on familiar matters regularly encountered in work, school, leisure, etc, including short narratives.*

At C2, the highest level, a student:

> *has no difficulty in understanding any kind of spoken language, whether live or broadcast, delivered at fast native speed.*

Using these descriptors can provide clear goals and show students their progress. Using them, however, is far from straightforward. Training is required. Student and teacher need to discuss and negotiate levels of achievement as there are many grey areas in which it may not be clear what the student can do. Things we can do in the controlled environment of the classroom are often not so simple outside the classroom when we are under pressure and lacking the frameworks that language learning pedagogy provides (the pre-listening activity, the transcript, the sympathetic teacher).

Another tool in our assessment box is the portfolio. The language student's portfolio comprises a record of his or her work in the target language, including examples such as essays and projects, which are kept in a folder or file. How can listeners keep records of their achievements? They can put the following in their portfolio: recordings, transcripts of conversations involving the students, lists and summaries of programmes and films watched, transcripts of songs learned.

Portfolios are best used as a spur to discussion. The teacher and student should look through the portfolio together at least once a term and talk about the student's progress. While the teacher may be aware of the student's in-class development, the portfolio should give a broader view. It also presents a chance to compare the student's work now and in the past, a valuable asset particularly for long-term students.

Long-term assessment of listening abilities is difficult because of all the variables: our students' listening may be good one day and poor the next simply because of their mood or the topic or the weather (or those builders next door). Besides formal testing, how can we tell if our students are progressing? Perhaps it will be helpful to consider a number of stages that students go through in their listening development. Because listening happens in the mind, it is usually very difficult to detect when students pass from one stage to another. Many teachers, however, will recognise the criteria, the tendencies and even some of the comments described below.

Skill	Before, students said ...	Now they say ...
Persevere during moments of incomprehension	'It was too difficult. I gave up.'	'I got lost, but when she said XXX, I was able to understand.'
Listen to faster passages	'They speak too fast!'	'I didn't catch everything, but I understood the main point.'
Listen to longer passages	'I couldn't concentrate. The recording was too long.'	'I was able to follow the whole thing.'
Listen to passages with more low-frequency vocabulary	'There were a lot of words I didn't understand.'	'I didn't "go blank" when I didn't understand the words.'
Listen to passages with higher-density and more complex structures	'It was too difficult.'	'It sounded like *real English*.'
Understand a wider range of text types	'This isn't what I did with my last teacher. We listened to her stories.'	'It's good to listen to stories, but I like listening to discussions, songs and lectures, too.'

Isolate problem areas rather than consider the whole passage too difficult	'I don't understand any of this.'	'I don't understand *this part*.'
Move beyond the set task to interact personally with the passage	'I got the answers right.'	'I liked the bit when she said ...'
Be a worldly listener and link the passage to other texts, ideas or stories	'We did the listening on page 122 of the coursebook.'	'We listened to a passage about a famous hotel. It reminded me of a story I heard ...'
Become aware of **metalinguistic** issues (how a speaker says something)	'I understood everything.'	'Why did she express it like that? Why didn't she say ...?'
Question the completeness of your understanding	'I understood everything.'	'I understood the words, but there is something missing in my interpretation.'
Become aware that not every part of the input is of equal value	'I want to understand every word.'	'That bit didn't seem too important, but I listened carefully to the other bit.'
Recognise playful uses of language, such as puns, wordplay and jokes.	'?'	'Ha ha!'

Many of the features in this list were mentioned in Chapter 3 when we discussed the characteristics of effective listening. How can teachers use such a list? It is not a question of ticking boxes or trying to provide a syllabus that contains all of these ideas. It is more a case of being aware of the students' changing responses to input during the course. Teachers may also try to encourage some of the responses in the column on the right, using techniques such as eliciting during the post-listening stage and journal writing (students write about their studies and feelings towards language learning).

Self-assessment

In the long term, one of the most important types of assessment is self-assessment. This will allow the learner to work independently and make progress outside the classroom environment.

There are three basic elements that need to be assessed: 1) goals – what the student ultimately needs to achieve; 2) current level of ability in relation to these goals – what the student can do now; and 3) the options, techniques and strategies available to bridge the gap between 1) and 2).

The idea of self-assessment is problematic. Firstly, there is the question of capability: whether the students are able to assess themselves with a degree of validity and reliability. To answer this, we will look at research findings. Blanche and Merino, from a survey of twenty-one self-assessment studies, claim that: 'The emerging pattern is one of consistent overall agreement between self-assessments and ratings based on a variety of external criteria. The accuracy of most students' self-estimates often varies depending on the language skills and materials involved in the evaluation ... but these estimates are generally *good* or *very good*.' This suggests that reasonably accurate self-assessment is possible. In truth, accuracy is not the major issue; what we really want is to get our students reflecting on their progress. In most cases concerning language learners, a little self-delusion will not do much harm.

There is a second issue, which relates to culture: in rigidly hierarchical societies or contexts in which the teacher is the sole arbiter of grades, the very idea of self-assessment may be rejected. For this issue, informal self-assessment, of the type in which students simply self-monitor but do not assign grades, is one answer.

Encouraging students to listen outside the classroom

Self-assessment is closely linked with learner independence. If students become more autonomous, they can measure their own development and take the necessary steps to improve. Four hours of English lessons per week (the average in many contexts) is not enough, particularly when it comes to the difficulties of listening.

Recent technological developments, such as webquests – structured projects using listening texts and downloads on the Internet – allow students access to listening material, but they may need training in what to do with it. To this end, students might benefit from frameworks or generic tasks. These might include writing down words they understood, writing a summary or completing a Who/Where/What/When chart (see page 120). There might also be a link to critical thinking; you could ask the students to listen/watch and rate the content, something that is done already on www.youtube.com, one of the world's most popular websites. YouTube is a useful resource in that it allows anyone to post their video clips. As a result, there is an enormous choice, and many are accessible.

In fact, the choice on the net may be bewildering. One solution is to do some 'flood listening'. Flood listening consists of students choosing one topic and listening to everything they can find about it (they get a flood of input). Naturally, the students will choose either something they are interested in or a topic they need to research for academic purposes. An incidental benefit of flood listening is that certain words and expressions will keep recurring – an excellent aid to vocabulary acquisition.

Clips and downloads from the Internet tend to be short. Of greater benefit in the long term is the habit of listening to extended texts such as stories. Extensive listening is a highly effective way to develop listening skills outside the classroom. There are a number of characteristics which mark it off from other listening exercises and make it so valuable. These include authenticity, pleasure and choice. A good story is a good story in any language, and there are many readers (books graded by linguistic difficulty) available on the market with an audio component. While these recordings are excellent starting points for extensive listening as their content is tailored for specific levels, radio plays are a potentially rich source of input for more advanced students. Another aspect of the authenticity of extensive listening lies in the listener's task. Generally speaking, there isn't one. The listener listens for pleasure.

Listening proficiency comes about largely because some of the processes have become automatised – in other words, the students have begun to use the same listening skills and strategies as L1 listeners do: ignoring irrelevant details, not worrying about understanding every word, anticipating with the aid of context, etc. These developments tend to happen very gradually for anyone above the age of eleven or twelve. Young children in the process of acquiring a second language through immersion (by being surrounded by L2 speakers), as opposed to learning a language (only taking lessons in L2), go through a silent period before suddenly being able to speak and listen, often as proficiently as native speakers.

For most adults, whether immersed in L2 or not, the process is different. There is no Eureka moment. Listening development moves at a similar pace to that of the other skills and the acquisition of grammar and vocabulary. Where children have an advantage is in the long silent period in which they are not pushed to respond, and in their exposure to massive quantities of input. This is where extensive listening plays its part; it is input to which the listener does not have to respond productively.

Self-access and listening in the language lab

For students who wish to practise their listening independently, one of the best places to start is the self-access centre of their school or university. According to Gardner and Miller, 'Self-access language learning is an approach to learning language, not an approach to teaching language'. This describes one of the most important features of self-access – it is learner-centred.

A good self-access centre should contain most or all of the following listening materials: a bank of graded recordings plus transcripts and photocopied worksheets with answer keys; daily radio news accompanied by worksheets and transcripts; extensive listening in the form of recordings of stories, perhaps from graded readers; exam material; a wide variety of recordings from authentic sources such as the BBC; and a real live human being at least some of the time! The latter may be there to advise, point students towards suitable materials, and provide some real-life listening practice.

Language laboratories have traditionally been places where students practise language drills. *Drill* has two meanings; the first is repeated practice, the second is a tool used for boring. The language lab has been a venue for both over the years! However, with the current emphasis on student autonomy and independent learning, the lab has great potential for L2 listeners. One of its great benefits is that it allows students to work at their own pace and to repeat recordings as often as necessary.

The standard procedure in the lab is no different from that of classroom listening. However, the fact that the students are working alone presents certain opportunities. The students who finish the task quickly can do a number of things with the recording, such as transcribing, shadow reading and marking the stress on a transcript. In addition to the many activities in earlier chapters of the book that work well in the language laboratory, here are two more ideas:

 Story swap: the students record themselves telling a story or anecdote from their lives on one console. A sheet of paper is placed at every console, and the students are put in groups of four. They listen to each other's stories by moving to different consoles. While listening, the students think of two follow-up questions to ask the storyteller, and write them on the paper, which is not removed from the console. They change consoles again, listen to another story and add two more questions (different from those already on the sheet) about this second story. The procedure continues until all four students in each group have listened to the four stories and written their questions. They then get in their groups and answer the questions about their story.

Listen and read aloud: the students are given a transcript of the recording. They simply read aloud at the same pace, with the same pauses, as the speaker. After several attempts they can record themselves over the original speaker. This task is excellent for practising the rhythm and speed of English, but it is harder than one imagines! Normal, natural speed for a native speaker is extremely fast for a student, even if the student knows the passage and understands it perfectly. The exercise teaches students to process language in terms of 'thought groups' or units of information rather than individual words. Thought groups are usually chunked – said without pauses – so the students also have to speed up in order to keep up. Another benefit is that the exercise alerts students to many pronunciation features such as contractions and elision.

A final comment about self-access and the language lab: students and teachers will probably need an induction to both. They need to know what is available, when it's available and how to use it. This should happen as early as possible in the course.

Teacher autonomy; becoming a better teacher of listening

Becoming a better teacher of listening isn't very different from becoming a better doer of anything. One needs at least some of the following: practice, help from experts, reflection, experimentation and perseverance. Here are some ideas.

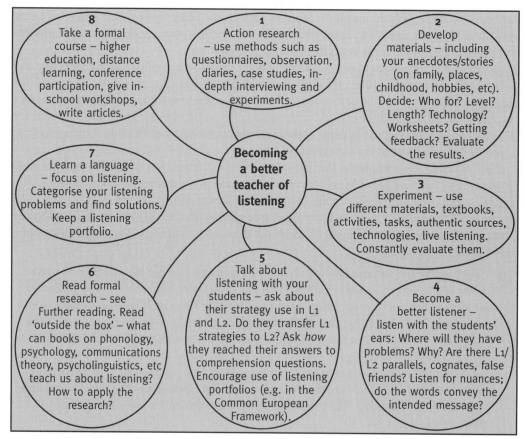

It should be stressed that many of the ideas contained in the diagram can easily be applied to general development and not only to teaching listening. Clearly, one is unlikely to develop abilities in teaching one skill in isolation while not improving as a teacher of other skills. As we become more experienced, we tend to develop in all areas. For example, as we become more aware of pronunciation problems, we naturally develop our awareness of students' problems in listening and spelling. As we learn more about motivation, our classroom management, ability to pace a lesson and techniques for giving feedback also improve.

Suggestions 1–7 are largely self-directed development. Nothing is timetabled and the teacher works at his or her own pace, which is one of the hallmarks of teacher development as opposed to teacher education. There is no curriculum or syllabus suggested here either; the teacher explores his or her own interests, free to abandon false trails or dead ends.

The ideas, of course, are only a starting point. If you really want to know how effective your speaking style is and what students perceive when they listen to you, you will record or film yourself – something that requires considerable commitment. Materials development, too, especially for digital immigrants (see page 52), can be very time-consuming. An **action research** project – which follows the basic pattern of 1) recognise a problem in class, 2) make a plan to deal with the problem, 3) try it out, 4) reflect on the results, and 5) plan the next step – may take anything between three lessons and three years.

Experimentation demands courage. One teacher reports that he did an experiment while teaching a pronunciation course, getting his students to stretch rubber bands to mark long vowel sounds. The first time he tried it, the students looked at him as if he was mad. But he didn't give up. By the third week they were bringing their own rubber bands. These became as accepted and uncontroversial as pens and pencils in class, and every time a rubber band broke, the class would erupt with laughter.

Conclusions | *In this chapter we have:*

- discussed integrated listening, and the difference between listening in the lesson and the listening lesson. We proposed an integrated model as this reflects real-world use of the skill and keeps students motivated.

- talked about how to assess listening, looking at formal tests and ongoing assessment. We discussed some of the difficulties of test-writing, the advantages of using portfolios and some ideas to help teachers and students prepare for a listening exam.

- discussed ways of encouraging students to listen outside the classroom, looking particularly at the possibilities offered by the Internet and the benefits of extensive listening.

- talked about self-access and the language lab, commenting on the learner-centred nature of these facilities and looking at a few activities to put into practice.

- highlighted the importance of teacher autonomy and discussed how to become a better teacher of listening, stating that teachers need to explore their own practices and actively seek out new ideas in order to keep developing.

Chapter 1: Listening in the world and in language learning

A The why and how of listening – motivation and mechanics (pages 9–10)

Complete these statements in any way you choose.

We listen when …
We don't listen when …
Listening is difficult when …
Listening is easy when …
A good listener is someone who …
The best listener I know …

B The characteristics of spoken English (pages 10–12)

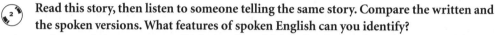 **Read this story, then listen to someone telling the same story. Compare the written and the spoken versions. What features of spoken English can you identify?**

A scorpion needed to cross a small lake but it couldn't swim. It went into the water and began to drown. A holy man standing near the water saw the scorpion drowning. He reached in and picked up the scorpion and it bit him. The holy man went to the doctor and was saved.

The following day the same scorpion needed to cross the lake. It went into the water and again began to drown. The same holy man passing by saw the scorpion and rescued it again. And again it bit him.

Every day for a week the holy man was bitten by the same scorpion and every day he went to the doctor to be saved.

Eventually the doctor asked, 'Why does the scorpion keep biting you when you rescue it?' 'It is the scorpion's nature,' replied the holy man. And the doctor asked, 'Why then do you keep picking up the scorpion instead of leaving it to drown?' The holy man replied, 'Because that is my nature.'

C Why listening is difficult (pages 12–15)

Read the sentences/passages. What problems might students have when they listen to them?

1 Whatchya doin'?
2 The world of art theft is not, as one might presume, populated with stylish aesthetes masterminding their operations from tax-free hideouts.
3 Are you crazy? You can't just mosey on in here two hours late for work! Who do you think you are? You're just taking the mickey.
4 It's the first Test to be played here at the MCG and I think the Wallabies will be keen to get a W.

 Now listen to a linguist commenting on the difficulties.

D Why students should listen to English (pages 16–17)

 Listen to some students explaining their motives for studying English. Why do these students need to *listen* to English?

	Why should he/she listen to English?
Speaker 1	
Speaker 2	
Speaker 3	
Speaker 4	
Speaker 5	

What type of input would be useful for them? Choose from the list and explain your choices.

academic lectures   TV documentaries   TV news   films and film extracts   advertisements
teachers' anecdotes   face-to-face conversations with other students   guest speakers
radio news   recordings of dialogues and monologues from general English coursebooks
recordings of presentations   recordings from business English coursebooks   songs

E The place of listening in language teaching (pages 17–19)

Match the name of the methodology to some of the ways in which listening was/is used.
a Audiolingualism
b The Natural Approach
c Total Physical Response
d Suggestopedia
e Communicative Language Teaching

1 ☐: The teacher gives commands which the students act out. When they are ready, the students take the role of command-giver.

2 ☐: The students are given a pre-listening activity to get them attuned to the topic, and a while-listening task. The emphasis is on the passage as a piece of communication with real meaning. After listening, the students discuss what they heard. The passage may be used either as a container of target language – usually grammar or vocabulary – or to practise the listening skill itself.

3 ☐: The teacher acts as a provider of oral input. The students listen but are not forced to respond until they are ready.

4 ☐: The students sit in language laboratories. They listen to and repeat phrases. They also do drills which manipulate grammatical patterns.

5 ☐: The students are helped to relax through the provision of a comfortable environment, perhaps with music. The teacher reads a text at natural speed, which the students follow. The teacher reads the text a second time more slowly and calmly.

Chapter 2: Listening texts and listening strategies

A What makes a good listening text? (pages 25–30)

 Read and listen to four coursebook passages on the same topic: food. What are the differences in level, speed, complexity, density, vocabulary and authenticity?

1

In the 16th century, a famous Spanish explorer, Hernan Cortes, brought chocolate back from the Americas to Spain. Drinking chocolate soon became very popular in Europe. Three hundred years later, a scientist in Holland learned how to make chocolate into candy. Today chocolate is one of the most popular and best-loved foods in the world.

(from Abbs, B, Barker, C, Freebairn, I and Wilson, J (2008) *Postcards 2* (2nd edn), Teacher's Edition, Pearson Education, page 14)

2

MALE: How much rice do you buy each week?
FEMALE: I usually buy two kilos of rice.
MALE: And how many tomatoes do you eat?
FEMALE: About six.
MALE: How much coffee do you buy?
FEMALE: I buy about 250 grammes of coffee.
MALE: How many pineapples do you get?
FEMALE: Oh, only one.

(from Foley, M and Hall, D (2005) *Total English Elementary*, Pearson Education, page 152)

3

Q: Is it true, Lisa, that you always have bacon and eggs for breakfast?
LISA: Well, it used to be true, but it isn't true any more. People often have toast and cereal, jam, yoghurt, things like that, but not many have time to cook bacon and eggs. It's only in hotels when you get bacon and eggs – what we call a cooked breakfast or an English breakfast.

(from Greenall, S (1997) *Reward Elementary*, Heinemann, page 117)

4

I: Michael, you've had the opportunity to taste some of the more unusual dishes from around the world. Can you tell us something about them, and in particular, what they taste like?
M: Yes, well, I've just come back from Thailand and in the winter, sackloads of grasshoppers and locusts are brought into Bangkok from the countryside because the Thais love them. They make a really crisp and tasty snack. In fact, fried grasshoppers are tasty to most people, provided they don't know what they're eating. They eat crickets in parts of North America, and they taste just the same.
I: Hmm. I'm not sure I'd like to eat insects.

(from Kay, S and Jones, V (2000) *Inside Out Intermediate*, Macmillan Heinemann, page 156)

B Authentic versus pedagogic (pages 30–33)

1 Look at the list of features. Which are typical of scripted dialogues and which are usually found in authentic speech?

a No background noise

b Overlaps and interruptions between speakers

c Loosely packed information, padded out with fillers like *um* and *er*

d Structured language, more like written English

e Normal rate of speech delivery

f Complete sentences

g Relatively unstructured language

h Background noise and voices

i Little overlap between speakers

j Slower (maybe monotonous) delivery

k Densely packed information

l Incomplete sentences, with false starts and hesitation

2 Listen to five passages. Which are authentic? Which are scripted? What features tell us this?

	Authentic or scripted?	Features
Passage 1		
Passage 2		
Passage 3		
Passage 4		
Passage 5		

C Strategies good listeners use (pages 34–38)

Read three situations in which students have problems listening. What strategies would you suggest?

1

A Brazilian economist on a lecture tour in the UK thought he needed to learn a lot more English, and came for one-to-one lessons. My first reaction was: 'I can't improve this man's English in a dozen lessons over two months. Why does he want lessons?'

A brief interview revealed that his set-piece lectures went fine. The trouble came at question time. He felt he did not understand the questions. I gave him a cassette recorder to tape his next post-lecture question session.

At our next meeting he played back the cassette: it was clear to both of us that he was not letting the questioner finish the question. He leapt in with the answer, regularly cutting the questioner short. He then admitted to me that he had a card-index in his mind of about 40 economic or political categories into which questions neatly fitted. If he heard a question he thought was coming from category 28, he immediately came in with stock answer 28. Working in English, he would often miscategorise, and so give a brilliant answer to the wrong question and the wrong mindset. In so doing, he would frequently antagonise the questioner.

(from Davis, P, Garside, B and Rinvolucri , M (1998) *Ways of Doing*, Cambridge University Press, page 125)

2

A student in a private language school wanted to understand news broadcasts in English, which he accessed from the Internet. He was a high-level student, and very motivated, but the broadcasts were just too difficult. He found that the newsreaders spoke very fast and he couldn't keep up. Also, the changes of topic as the newsreader went from one news story to the next were difficult because suddenly you 'needed to activate a whole new vocabulary'. He asked me what he could do.

3

I was training a student for a general proficiency exam. In all other respects she was at the right level for the exam – her speaking, writing, vocabulary and grammar were OK – but she kept failing the practice tests we did for the listening part of the exam. We looked closely at where she was failing and found that she would always get the first questions correct but then her performance would tail off. By the time she got round to the final questions for each passage, she barely wrote any answers.

 Listen for the solutions.

Chapter 3: Listening sources, listening tasks

A Different sources of listening (pages 41–54)

1 Think of six types of listening you have done this week. Make notes in the chart.

Content (What was it about?)	Mode of delivery (live/radio/phone, etc)	Teaching potential (interest? level?)
1		
2		
3		
4		
5		
6		

2 You are designing a number of listening courses. Here are the four titles you have chosen for these courses.

Contemporary life in the UK and the US
Songs in English
News and views from around the world
Real conversations

Choose two and write as many sources of listening input as possible.

Answer these questions.

a How will you obtain this input?
b What will you do with it?
c What other features will your course have?

B Teacher talk (pages 41–45)

What are the following and what is their relevance to teacher talk?

signposting   macro-markers   linear sequence   redundancy   colloquialisms
analogies   interaction   paralinguistic features   monitoring

C Textbook recordings (pages 47–48)

Read and listen to the extracts from transcripts of coursebook recordings and answer these questions.

a What level are they?
b What are the difficulties?
c Would you use these in class? For what type of student? Give reasons.

1

Excuse me. Can you help me?
Do you know the way?
I want to go to North Street
And find the blue café.

Sure I can. It's easy.
Take the second turning right.
The café's on the corner.
It's painted blue and white.

Excuse me. Can you help me?
I'm looking for a school.
It's Belmont school in King Street.
It's near a swimming pool.

Sure I can. It's easy.
You don't need to go by car.
You take the second turning left
It isn't very far!

2

AK: We'd like to get away for a little bit, you know … last-minute holiday, you know, just a quick break.
TA: OK. So if I can just ask a few questions …
AK: OK.
TA: … just to find out the kind of thing you're looking for and then I can feed in your details into our database and see what we can offer you …

3

Despite the recent fall in share price, the company remains confident that its strategy is absolutely correct in the current trading environment and that it will be well-placed to take full advantage of any economic upturn.

4

In Thailand, taxis are called tuk-tuks. The tuk-tuk drivers come speeding up to you in the street, shouting 'tuk-tuk, tuk-tuk!' The taxis are quite low to the ground, and the top is covered, but the sides are open to let in some air, and you really need it, because it's so hot that you practically stick to the plastic seats, dripping in your own sweat. But the tuk-tuks are pretty cheap and I suppose they're quite convenient.

D Television, video, DVD and radio (pages 48–49)

What are the benefits of the following genres and what type of linguistic features do they contain?

- television or radio news and weather reports
- film clips
- film trailers
- television advertisements
- television documentaries
- episodes in a comedy series
- animation

- television or radio talk shows/interviews
- television or radio game shows/quiz shows

E Types of comprehension exercise (pages 54–57)

 Read and listen to a recording of the transcript below.

A: Did you read that story in the Sunday papers about the Harlem hero?

B: Who?

A: The Harlem hero.

B: No. What happened?

A: A nineteen-year-old student – I think he was nineteen – fell onto the subway tracks.

B: What, here in New York?

A: Yeah. And this guy, they're calling him the Harlem hero, this guy rescued him. He jumped down and held the guy flat on the tracks.

B: No way!

A: And the subway train passed over them.

B: Is that for real?

A: The papers are all full of it. I can't believe you didn't see it.

B: Didn't read it.

A: Now the guy's a hero, he was given some medal by Bloomberg, and Donald Trump gave him ten thousand bucks or something. And get this: he got a free trip to DisneyWorld.

B: Man!

Here are four exercises students can do while listening. Write appropriate statements for 1, questions for 2, incomplete notes for 3 and events in the wrong order for 4.

1 Are the statements true or false?

   Example: The story was in a Saturday newspaper. (False)

2 Listen and answer the questions.

3 Listen and complete the notes.

4 Listen and put the events in order.

Chapter 4: Pre-listening skills and activities

A What a listener needs to know before listening (pages 63–64)

You are a teacher planning to use this passage with a class of elementary general English students. What will they need to know before they hear this? Build a group of pre-listening activities to use with the passage. Which vocabulary will you pre-teach, if any?

W = woman, **M** = man

W1: OK, that's the end of my talk. So, any questions?

M1: Yes, I want to ask about meetings. When should we arrive?

W1: Good question. For business appointments, you should definitely arrive on time or possibly five minutes early.

W2: Should we bow when we meet people?

W1: Well, greeting people in the UK or the US is a little different. It's not important if you're young or old … you should shake hands with everyone. Also, you shouldn't use first names. Wait until they call you by your first name and then you can do the same.

M2: What about invitations? What should we do when we visit someone's house?

W1: I'm glad you asked that question. When you go to someone's house for dinner, you should take a bottle of wine or a small present. But there's one big difference from Japan … you shouldn't take your shoes off. I did that on my first visit and I was the only person in the room with no shoes.

W3: So what should we wear?

W1: For formal business meetings, you should wear a suit. For social occasions, you can ask your host. They're usually very friendly … I know, I married one.

(from Le Maistre, S and Lewis, C (2002) *Language to Go Elementary*, Pearson Education, page 123)

B Activating schemata/predicting (pages 64–75)

1 Look at the diagram, which shows ways to activate the schemata about the topic of work.

2 Think of ways to activate the schemata for the following topics:

travel food education shopping sport film/TV

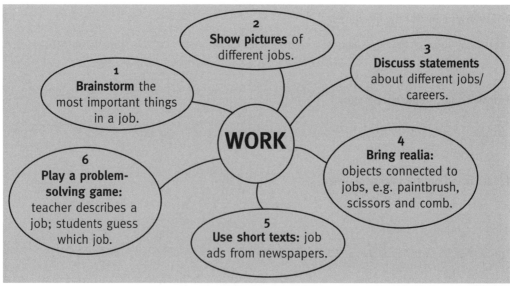

3 Choose one of the topics in Exercise 2 and make a diagram like the one on page 154.

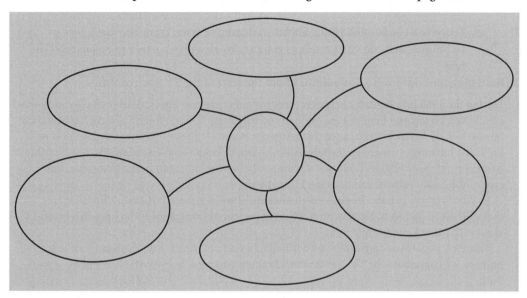

C Things to avoid during the pre-listening stage (page 79)

 Read the transcript of a recording the students are going to hear. Listen to the three ways that teachers introduce the passage. What are the strengths and weaknesses of each introduction? Which is the most appropriate? Why?

To feel motivated, workers have four kinds of needs called the four Cs. The first C is connection. To feel connected to the company, people need to understand their role and feel that they are helping to achieve the company goals. The second C is contentment. Workers need to enjoy the job in order to get satisfaction from it. The third C is context: the company's systems and organisation. This can include the IT network, machine maintenance or the pay system. If things don't work smoothly – because the computer system is out-of-date, for example – workers will soon become demotivated because they can't do a good job. The final C is climate, or company culture. It depends on the relationships between management and staff. In order to create a good climate, managers need to listen to the staff and respond to their suggestions. They should encourage staff to have ideas and use their initiative, and support their team when they need help. Employees may feel angry or stressed if the climate is poor. So it's very important to create a good climate. Companies should pay close attention to these factors so that their staff will be more productive.

	Strengths	Weaknesses
Introduction 1		
Introduction 2		
Introduction 3		

Chapter 5: While-listening skills and activities

1   **Listen to a teacher describing a while-listening activity. Using the dictogloss technique, write down as much as you can. Work with a partner to reconstruct the text.**

2 **Read the transcript from a programme about the start of the TV age in politics.**

During the 1960 presidential campaign there was an organised political debate between the two candidates, Nixon and Kennedy. Nixon had recently been ill, and with his swarthy appearance he also looked somewhat unshaven. He refused to wear TV make-up for the debate, and with the lights burning overhead in the television studio, he began to sweat. Kennedy, on the other hand, was far more telegenic. He was a younger, better-looking man in the first place, but crucially, he didn't sweat, and he wore TV make-up.

So who won the debate? In polls taken after the show, it turned out that radio listeners thought Nixon had won. He was, after all, an experienced campaigner who knew his brief. TV viewers thought Kennedy had won.

The 1960 debate has come to be recognised as a seminal moment in the history of US politics. It inaugurated the TV age in which looking good was as important as anything you said.

Which of the while-listening activities/exercises below would be appropriate for this passage? Why?

- Listening for gist
- Listening for detail
- Inferring
- Participating actively
- Note-taking
- Dictation
- Listen and do

3 **Read the dialogue below and design three while-listening tasks.**

R: Good morning, Western House.
A: Hi, I'd like to book a single room for two nights, please.
R: Certainly, madam. For which dates?
A: I'm arriving on the 14th of April and I'm leaving on the 16th.
R: OK. I'm just checking on the computer. OK. That's fine. How are you going to pay?
A: Is American Express OK?
R: Yes, of course. The full course is 100 pounds. Can I take your number?
A: Yes, sure. It's 0489-6666-1072-3465.
R: And the expiry date?
A: 04-09.
R: And your name as it appears on the card?
A: Mrs A Jones.
R: Great. Thank you, Mrs Jones. That's one single room for April the 14th and 15th. We look forward to seeing you then.
A: Great. Thank you. Bye.

(from Dellar, H and Walkley, A (2005) *Innovations Elementary*, Thomson Heinle, page 127)

4 Match the activities to transcripts 1–5. Evaluate the activities in terms of purposefulness, authenticity and suitability. ✐

Activities

a Listen and do **b** Guess the subject **c** Label the photos **d** Make notes **e** Draw a map

Transcripts

1

SARAH: This is my mother in our garden at home.

GUY: Let's see. Is that your father?

SARAH: No, it's Martin, her partner. My mum's divorced.

GUY: Does your mother work?

SARAH: Yes, she's a nurse. And Martin's a doctor at the same hospital. I don't like him very much. This is my sister Lisa and her husband Philip. And their daughter, Sophie.

GUY: Ah – she's really sweet. How old is she?

SARAH: She's three.

GUY: Do you have any more nieces or nephews?

SARAH: No, just Sophie for the moment.

GUY: Is that you?

SARAH: Don't laugh! Yes, that's from last Christmas, at my grandparents' house.

GUY: Who's that?

SARAH: That's my cousin Adam. Adam and I are really good friends. He's a singer in a band. They play in local pubs and clubs …

(from Oxenden, C, Latham-Koenig, C and Seligson, P (2004) *New English File Elementary*, Oxford University Press, page 115)

2

A: It's a small town, and very easy to get around.

B: Right.

A: The main road runs parallel to the river, and … um … everything you need is basically on this road. Most of the university buildings are here.

B: OK, that's easy. What about the library? Is that …

A: If you keep going straight here, you'll find the library on your left. Opposite the library there's a very good restaurant called Gritos where a lot of students have lunch.

B: Oh, yeah, I've heard of it.

A: Next to Gritos, there's Davies Hall, which is a hall of residence where a lot of students live.

B: Davies Hall. OK.

3

He's not especially tall but he's very athletic. He's quite good-looking, with dark hair and a small nose. He's famous all over the world but especially in Switzerland, where he comes from. He probably trains twice a day, practising his shots and getting very fit because his job involves a lot of running and hitting a ball.

4

Hi, it's Chris here. Just wanted to see if you're still going to the party. I could give you a lift. I'm going to be leaving at about 9.30. Call me back when you get this message. The number is 987 2769.

5

So, then you add the chopped parsley and the ginger. You may also want to add a little bit of salt, like this. You place it on a baking tray – there we go – and leave it in the oven for thirty-five minutes on medium heat.

Think of three other while-listening activities the students could do with each of these passages.

1 **Listen to the passage and read the transcript of a listening text from an intermediate coursebook. Look at five post-listening tasks with different aims. Which are appropriate/inappropriate for the passage? Why?**

The person I admire most in the world is Nelson Mandela. He was the President of South Africa during the 1990s, but before that he spent more than twenty-five years, I think, in prison. He was put in prison because of his political beliefs. He wanted to get equal rights for black people in South Africa, and the government put him in prison because of his political views ... um ... he was a lawyer before he went to prison and he represented himself at his trial. Some of the things he said during his trial were amazing. They're still famous speeches, I think.

The reason that I admire him is that in spite of the fact that he spent such a long time in prison he never changed his views. It would've been quite easy for him to perhaps stop campaigning for the rights of black people, but he never did that. Right until the end of his time in prison, he was still campaigning. When I went to South Africa, I met somebody who was in prison with him and it was amazing to hear about how they were ... they found it so easy to forgive the government and the people who'd put them in prison, they weren't bitter or angry about it.

I think he's really influenced the way people think about how they can make changes, political changes, by standing by what they believe in and stating their beliefs very clearly.

(from Cunningham, S and Moor, P (2005) *New Cutting Edge Intermediate*, Pearson Education, page 164)

A Work with a partner and discuss the following questions.
  • Do you agree with the speaker that Mandela is admirable?
  • Do you think Mandela is an interesting choice as 'the person I admire most'?
  • If you could choose a person that you admire, who would you choose? Why?

B Imagine you could interview Nelson Mandela. Prepare a set of questions to ask him about his life. One student will act as Mandela. Conduct the interview.

C Discuss the following: how much do you think the speaker knows about:
  • Nelson Mandela?
  • the political history of South Africa?
  • 'how they [political prisoners] were'?
  • what Mandela said at his trial?
  Give reasons for your answers.

D 'He <u>was</u> the President of South Africa during the 1990s, but before that he <u>spent</u> more than twenty-five years, I think, in prison.'
  'Was' and 'spent' are irregular verbs. Underline all the other irregular past tenses of verbs in the passage.

E Work in pairs. Look at the key words from the listening passage:

  admire prison political beliefs rights trial campaigning forgive angry influenced changes
  Retell the passage you heard, using the key words. Do not write.

Label the post-listening tasks with these headings:
• Reconstructing
• Discussion
• Critical response

- Deconstructing
- Creative response

2 **Listen to an anecdote, a joke and a ghost story. Construct post-listening tasks to: 1) check comprehension, 2) allow personal response, 3) enable the students to reconstruct the text, and 4) make the listening a model for the students to follow. Which post-listening task is the most/least suitable for each extract? Why?**

	Post-listening task: check comprehension	Post-listening task: allow personal response	Post-listening task: get students to reconstruct the passage	Post-listening task: make the passage a model for the students to follow
Anecdote				
Joke				
Ghost story				

3 **Read what some teachers say about using transcripts/tapescripts. Write 1) – it's a very good idea; or 2) – it's an OK idea but it has some problems; or 3) – the idea isn't especially good; or 4) – it's a terrible idea.**

a 'I let my students read the transcript for homework before listening in class. It helps them if they know what's coming.' ☐

b 'I avoid using tapescripts. If I used them, my students, who are teenagers, would want to use them all the time and they would never learn to listen.' ☐

c 'After listening to a difficult passage from the book, we sometimes read through the transcript. It's a way for the students to see the written version of the difficult words and ask about them.' ☐

d 'I get my students to listen and read at the same time and highlight where the stresses fall on each sentence. Then they act out the dialogues or monologues with the script in front of them.' ☐

e 'I give them the transcript cut up into strips. In groups, they put the strips in the right order. This gets them thinking about the structure of the conversation.' ☐

f 'I choose ten important words from the recording and write them on the board. Then the students have to piece together what was said, using the ten words. After this they check by listening again and reading the tapescript.' ☐

Chapter 7: Preparation and planning

A Listening in the syllabus (page 113)

Put these stages of a listening lesson in the order in which you might do them in class.

a Students check their answers to 'listen for detail' questions in pairs or groups. ☐

b Teacher pre-teaches vocabulary. ☐

c Whole class checks detailed information. ☐

d Students are given a speaking task involving a personal response to the passage. ☐

e Students listen for gist. ☐

f Students listen for detail. ☐

g Students are given a more challenging task that asks for more detailed information. ☐

h Teacher checks answers to comprehension questions. ☐

i Teacher activates students' schemata (e.g. by showing pictures about the subject). ☐

j Students ask about any areas of particular difficulty. ☐

k Teacher sets comprehension questions. ☐

Now match the stage (above) to its purpose (below). Write the letter of the stage in the box.

Stage ☐: Make sure the students know the key words that will help them understand the main message.

Stage ☐: Give the students a reason to listen again but for more detailed information.

Stage ☐: The students listen to the passage and understand the main idea.

Stage ☐: Check that the students understood the main idea of the passage.

Stage ☐: Bring the class together to go through the answers.

Stage ☐: Give the students a reason to listen.

Stage ☐: The students listen to the passage again.

Stage ☐: Give the students a chance to respond to the content of the passage, voicing their own views about what was said.

Stage ☐: Get the students interested in the topic and help them predict the content of the passage. Get them thinking about what vocabulary they may hear.

Stage ☐: Give the students a chance to say what they found difficult or where misunderstanding occurred. Try to work out why the problem occurred and what can be done about it in future.

Stage ☐: Give the students a chance to compare their answers, work out any areas of contention or misunderstanding, and give them confidence in what they could understand.

Answer these questions.

a Are the stages essential or optional?

b What does it depend on?

c When and why might you change the order of the stages?

B Choosing and adapting published materials
(pages 113–119)

Look at the listening sequence from a coursebook. Think of ways to adapt it …

a to make it easier.

b to make it more challenging.

c to make it more personalised.

d to make it longer.

e to make it shorter.

f to focus on grammar.

C Anticipating problems
(pages 125–127)

You are going to teach separate listening courses to all four of the classes described below. Answer these questions.

a What are the different types of problems they might have with listening?

b What would you do about these problems?

c What different types of listening input and tasks would you use?

d Which class would you prefer? Why?

Class A consists of fifteen children aged between seven and ten. They are happy, bright and interested, but they like to run around a lot and cannot concentrate for long.

Class B consists of five business students from the same engineering company. They are very serious and studious when they are in class, but they are also very busy. Some of them tend to arrive late for class – or not at all if something important crops up at work.

Class C consists of twelve adults who all want to learn general English. Some of them want English in order to travel overseas; others are just interested in the language. Some are very serious and prefer not to play games or listen to songs in class. Others are there to have fun as well as to learn English.

Class D consists of twenty-five fourteen year olds in a secondary school. Many of them feel that learning English is a waste of time. A few are keen and quite good at languages, but pressure from the others prevents them from taking an active part in lessons.

Module 2

4 His Or Hers?

Before you start

1 What jobs do you do at home? Use the Key Words and the Mini-dictionary to help you.

KEY WORDS: Housework
clear the table, do the cleaning, do the cooking, do DIY, do the gardening, do the ironing, do the shopping, do the vacuuming, do the washing, do the washing-up, lay the table, look after the children, look after the pets, make the beds, tidy my room

2 Listen to a radio programme and complete the table with the results from a UK national survey.

Job	National survey	
	women	men
cooking and washing-up		
cleaning and tidying up		
gardening/looking after pets		
DIY and repairs		
looking after children		
washing and ironing		

3 Your Culture What do you think the times are for men and women in your country?

18

Chapter 8: Listening in the wider context

A How to assess listening (pages 136–142)

1 How do you know your students are getting better at listening in the long term? Complete the sentences with some ideas.

a They are able to listen to …

b They are able to recognise …

c They begin to interact with …

d They persevere even when …

e They can understand a wider range of …

f They question the completeness of …

2 Look at the extracts from a variety of listening tests. What are the advantages and disadvantages of these test types?

a Multiple choice

Choose the correct option.
1 Robert says he likes
  A horror films
  B all kinds of films
  C cowboy films
  D Hollywood films
2 Jenny hates
  A happy endings
  B sad endings
  C bad acting
  D car chases

b True or false?

1 The weather in San Francisco is going to be hot.
2 Thunderstorms are expected in California.
3 The weather is hotter now than it was this time last year.

c Answer the questions

1 How many brothers does Mohamed have?
2 Where does Mohamed go to school?

d Listen and write a reply

Listen to the phone call. You are the supplier. Write a follow-up letter confirming the delivery of the goods.

e Complete the notes

1 Sharks can detect other fish's _____ .
2 Lemon sharks grow a new set of teeth every _____ .
3 Sharks navigate by sensing changes in the Earth's _____ .
4 Some sharks can detect one part of blood in _____ .

Wilson *How to Teach Listening* © Pearson Education Limited 2008
PHOTOCOPIABLE

B Encouraging students to listen outside the classroom (pages 142–143)

1 Think of advantages and potential difficulties of these ways for students to listen to English outside the classroom. ✏

a Use a self-access centre.

b Keep a portfolio of your experiences of listening to English.

c Look regularly at websites such as www.youtube.com to hear people talking about things you are interested in.

d Listen to audio books for a certain amount of time a day.

e Do homework, e.g. write a report on something you watched/listened to, that involves listening to the radio or watching television programmes.

f Interview people in the community who speak English as their L1 or who are highly proficient speakers.

g Have an evening in which the whole class gets together and watches a film in English.

2 (14) Listen to four teachers discussing ideas for students to practise listening beyond the classroom. Make notes on the ideas as you listen. Which of the ideas are possible in your current/future teaching situation? Which ideas could you experiment with? Why?

	Ideas
Teacher 1	
Teacher 2	
Teacher 3	
Teacher 4	

C Self-access and listening in the language lab (pages 143–144)

Read a case study of a failing self-access centre/language laboratory.

We have had a self-access centre with a language lab since the seventies. It contains a lot of cassettes, most of which have been there since the beginning. They are organised alphabetically according to the title, and not graded. Some of the recordings are very difficult, containing radio programmes for native speakers. There used to be worksheets to go with the cassettes, but now there are hardly any left because students used the master copies.

We have about twenty videos, but they are quite old and the picture and sound quality isn't very good. There are two televisions in the centre, but the headphones don't work.

Classes at the school finish at 4 p.m. and the self-access centre/lab is open until 5 p.m. Many students know there is a self-access centre, but they don't know how to use it or what material there is. Some of the teachers who have been at the school a long time know what is in the self-access centre, but the newer teachers never go there.

Answer the questions.

a Identify as many problems with the self-access centre/language lab as you can.

b You have been given $1,000 to improve the centre in the short term. What would you do with the money?

c Think of a long-term plan of action to improve the centre.

D Teacher autonomy; becoming a better teacher of listening (pages 144–145)

Here are five projects that teachers can do to become better teachers of listening.

1 Devise a questionnaire for your students about what they like listening to.

2 Find a scene from a film or TV programme or a download from the Internet that can be used for teaching listening. Write an accompanying worksheet. Think about how to adapt the worksheet for a different level.

3 Invite a guest speaker to the class. Decide how to prepare the students, and devise pre-, while- and post-listening tasks.

4 Write a dialogue or plan a semi-scripted discussion. Record it with colleagues and prepare a sequence of activities for the students to do with the recording.

5 Make a poster of listening strategies. Put it on the classroom wall. Refer to it before and after the students listen in class and discuss their strategies.

Answer the questions.

a Which of the projects are possible in your (future) teaching situation?

b What benefits might there be?

c What difficulties might there be?

d Which would be the most useful and the least useful?

TASK FILE KEY

Chapter 1
B

Features of spoken English in the story include:

- hesitation: *um*
- interaction with listeners: *Now, as you know, what do you think happened next? Now, you remember the holy man who rescued the scorpion? And what do you think happened?*
- spoken discourse markers: *so, well, anyway*
- pronunciation and intonation features: pausing for emphasis, stressing important words

The story is … um … about a scorpion that needed to cross a small lake. Now, as you know, scorpions can't swim. So, the little scorpion went into the water and began to drown. Um … and as it was drowning … um … a holy man standing near the water saw the scorpion. He reached in and picked it up, and what do you think happened next? The scorpion bit him. Well, the holy man went to the doctor and was saved.

The following day the same scorpion needed to cross the lake. So it went into the water and again began to drown. Now, you remember the holy man who rescued the scorpion? Well, this same holy man was passing by. And he saw the scorpion and rescued it again. And what do you think happened? It bit him again.

Now … um … every day for a whole week the holy man rescued the scorpion and every day the scorpion bit the holy man.

Anyway, eventually the doctor asked, 'Why does the scorpion keep biting you when you rescue it?' And the holy man replied, 'It's the scorpion's nature.' And then the doctor asked, 'So why do you keep picking the scorpion up instead of leaving it to drown?' And the holy man replied, 'Because that is my nature.'

C

1 The question *Whatchya doin'?* in standard form is *What are you doing?* and the pronunciation of *whatchya doin'* involves significant changes in the sounds. The word *are* more or less disappears from the question and the *t* of *what* becomes a *ch* sound. I think the problem here, for students, is recognising the words in the stream of sound. *Whatchya doin'?* sounds completely different from the standard written form and also the standard spoken form: *What are you doing?*

2 *The world of art theft is not, as one might presume, populated with stylish aesthetes masterminding their operations from tax-free hideouts.*
This is a very densely packed, complex sentence. It contains an embedded clause, namely *as one might presume*. But it's the lexical density that makes it difficult for students. Firstly, they have to understand the subject, which is art theft. Then they have to get past the embedded clause. Then they have to understand what a *stylish aesthete* is. Now, even if they know what an *aesthete* is, recognising the word in written form and recognising it in fluent speech are two very different things. Finally, of course, you have the difficulties of the verb *to mastermind* and then *tax-free hideouts*. *Hideout* isn't a common word. Overall, I think, only the most advanced student would get this sentence.

3 *Are you crazy? You can't just mosey on in here two hours late for work! Who do you think you are? You're just taking the mickey.*
This is difficult because of the slang. There are two very idiomatic expressions here: *mosey on in*, which means walk in casually, and *taking the mickey*, which means tease someone, show no respect. Interestingly, the first idiom is American, while the second is British English, so this speaker is obviously quite international! But I don't think these two idioms are in any language syllabus so they would be very hard for students to understand.

4 *It's the first Test to be played here at the MCG and I think the Wallabies will be keen to get a W.*
The problem here is the context, as well as abbreviations and acronyms. The language isn't particularly difficult, but unless the students have spent time in Australia they are unlikely to know that the MCG is the Melbourne Cricket Ground. They can probably guess that some kind of sport is involved but there's no way they can tell who or what the Wallabies are. They're the Australian rugby team, by the way, which is playing a game at the cricket ground. Finally, what does *getting a W* mean? It means getting a win, winning the game.

D

	Why should he/she listen to English?
Speaker 1	Because he wants to communicate with his grandchildren and will need to be able to understand what they are saying. Useful input: teachers' anecdotes, face-to-face conversations with other students, recordings of dialogues and monologues from general English coursebooks
Speaker 2	Because the speaker plans to live in the UK and will also need to understand academic lectures and tutorials. Useful input: academic lectures, TV documentaries (on the topic of study), face-to-face conversations with other students, guest speakers, recordings of presentations, recordings of dialogues and monologues from general English coursebooks
Speaker 3	Because the speaker wants to be able to understand fast, colloquial speech in American TV programmes and music. Useful input: TV documentaries, TV news, films and film extracts, advertisements, songs
Speaker 4	Because the speaker wishes to use English as a lingua franca while travelling and will need to understand different accents. Useful input: teachers' anecdotes, face-to-face conversations with other students, guest speakers, recordings of dialogues and monologues from general English coursebooks
Speaker 5	Because the speaker will need to survive in the US and also use English for work purposes – in meetings and discussions with colleagues. Useful input: face-to-face conversations with other students, guest speakers, recordings of presentations, recordings of dialogues and monologues from general English coursebooks, recordings from business English coursebooks

1 I need English because I can't communicate with my grandchildren any more. They only speak English.

2 I need the English because I want go to UK to do doctoral degree.

3 I want to watch American TV programmes and be able to understand. I also want to understand their music. Sometimes I sing and I don't know what I am singing!

4 I want to communicate with people from different countries when I travel, and English seems to be the language everybody is learning.

5 I need English because I am going to work in the US for six months and I will go to meetings with colleagues and discuss work issues.

E

1 c 2 e 3 b 4 a 5 d

Chapter 2
A

Passage 1 is from *Postcards 2*, a pre-intermediate level coursebook for teenagers. The sentences are fairly short and simple. They are written for a pedagogical purpose rather than being authentic. The use of several names gives the passage some density. The vocabulary load is not too heavy although there are a number of adjectives. The story is told sequentially, which helps students, but there are three time periods being talked about in a short passage, which does make it slightly complex for listeners to follow.

Passage 2 is from *Total English Elementary*. It is written for a pedagogical purpose (to teach the grammar of *how much* versus *how many*) and is not authentic. The scripted nature of it is clear as there are no repetitions, misunderstandings, hesitations or other features of authentic speech. The passage is very simple as there is little variety in the structures used and the sentences are very short. The vocabulary is also very controlled; it is designed to review types of food.

Passage 3 is from *Reward Elementary*. It is probably more authentic-sounding than passage 2, as the communicative context is more realistic, but it still sounds scripted as the speakers talk in perfect sentences. There are a few grammatical features (*used to*, the construction *Is it true that …?*) that suggest the dialogue is not so tightly controlled that it avoids everything above elementary level, and Lisa's sentences are longer and more complex than anything in passage 2. The vocabulary load is again not too heavy and it is based on reviewing items of food.

Passage 4 is from *Inside Out Intermediate*. The sentences are longer than in the other passages and more complex, containing structures such as the present perfect tense (*you've had, I've just come back*), some tricky vocabulary (*sackloads, crisp, locusts, crickets*) and some link words and discourse markers that would be difficult for low-level students (*in particular, provided*). The delivery is fairly fast, and the passage is quite dense – Michael's monologue contains a lot of information and several place names. This passage is probably the most authentic-sounding of the four, although the perfectly formed sentences suggest that it is scripted.

B

1
Scripted: a, d, f, i, j, k
Authentic: b, c, e, g, h, l

2

	Authentic or scripted?	Features
Passage 1	authentic	Conversation – the speakers talk at normal speed. They use fillers (*um*), vague language (*sort of, he just kind of watched*), slang (*bog standard*) and incomplete sentences with false starts and hesitation (*people who … vegans or … 'cos they can just choose, right*). There is overlap between the speakers (Woman 2: *I said* ‖ Woman 1: *Did he not eat anything?*) and background noise.
Passage 2	scripted	Lecture – the speaker talks in perfect sentences with no hesitations. The talk is very structured and organised. There are several very formal phrases (*with regard to, in order to*).
Passage 3	authentic	Service encounter – the speakers talk at normal speed. They use fillers (*um, er*), unstructured language (*Er, no, no*) and repetition (*cheese sandwich* is repeated four times, *Thanks, Thank you, Thanks a lot, Thanks*). There is background noise.
Passage 4	scripted	Dialogue – they talk in perfect sentences with no hesitations or interruptions. No background noise.
Passage 5	authentic	Teacher instructions – the teacher uses unstructured language (*er … settle down, no, sit over there. Yes, right now*) and repetition (*get into pairs*). There is background noise and other voices.

1

WOMAN 1: Your, um, your tapas meal … was it with sort of Spanish friends – is that why you went for tapas or was it just for …

WOMAN 2: Um, we were in Camden – it was one of those moments where you think where shall we go, what shall we do? And I've just got this thing about tapas.

WOMAN 1: I just wondered because I know that Amy sometimes goes for sort of special, you know, sort of Argentinian things … with her Arg … she gets a group of people who've got Argentinian connections – who either come from there or studied there and and they go for Argentinian meals, so …

WOMAN 2: Well, I just always go for tapas and my friend who I was with, he doesn't actually like tapas …

WOMAN 1: So you just made him eat it! Oh, so nice!

WOMAN 2: And he just kind of watched, but, you know, I said …

WOMAN 1: Did he not eat anything?

WOMAN 2: Hmm, meatballs … and that's all. And I was like getting in there, really enjoying it. I just love the fact that you go in, you look at a menu, and you can choose so many different things … rather than making one decision …

WOMAN 1: And it's OK if there are vegetarians with you or people who … vegans or … 'cos they can just choose, right …

WOMAN 2: Exactly.

WOMAN 1: But how can you not like tapas? That's like not liking Italian food or something … it's just.

WOMAN 2: I know. It's like bog standard, basic food …

2

With regard to professional development for teachers, we often talk about the three Cs. The first of these is courses. In order to get qualified to become a teacher, we usually need to take a course of study. These vary in length and type. Some may last a week; others take place over several years.

The second C is conferences. Attending conferences is a great way to hear about new developments in the profession and meet colleagues. Presenting at conferences is another good way to develop your knowledge of the field and to share your ideas.

The third C is perhaps the most important: colleagues. Unlike conferences and courses, our relationships with colleagues last for the whole of our working life. We can learn so much by talking, observing and being observed by them.

These are the three topics I will be discussing today.

3

MAN: Hiya.

WAITRESS: Hiya.

MAN: Could I have, um, a a cup of tea and, um, er, a slice of cake?

WAITRESS: Yes.

MAN: Oh, er, no could I have, er, a coffee … and, er, a cheese sandwich?

WAITRESS: Cheese sandwich. So you want coffee, tea and cheese sandwich, yeah?

MAN: Um, yeah, er, a coffee, a tea, a cheese sandwich and a slice of cake.

WAITRESS: Could I have one tea and one coffee, please? Anything else?

MAN: Um … Oh, I don't know. Er, no, no, I think that's it. Yeah.

WAITRESS: That's £3.50 altogether, please.

MAN: Thanks.

WAITRESS: Thank you. Your change.

MAN: Thanks a lot.

WAITRESS: Thanks.

MAN: Cheers.

4

A: Excuse me, can you tell me the way to the nearest post office?

B: Yes, it's not too far. You need to go left here.

A: OK, go left.

B: Then go to the end of the street.

A: OK.

B: And you'll find it on the right, opposite the bank. You can't miss it.

A: OK, so I need to go left, go to the end of the street and it's opposite the bank.

B: That's right.

A: Thank you very much.

B: You're welcome.

5

TEACHER: OK, listen up, everybody. I'd like you to open your books at page 52, get into pairs and we're going to be looking at three questions, and I want you to look at each of these questions and discuss it with your partners and, er ... settle down, I haven't finished, settle down, now. Yes, I want you to get into pairs ... no, sit over there. Yes, right now, what have I just said?

C

1 I suggested that he simply count slowly to three after hearing the end of the question. He tried this and our work together was over.

2 I suggested he prepare himself very thoroughly before listening. I told him to read the stories in his own language first, which was Italian. This way, he would already know the content and the names of the people involved. I also told him to read the story in English before listening. This would give him a good idea about what vocabulary he could expect to hear. Finally, I told him to simplify his expectations. Instead of thinking about what he couldn't understand, I tried to get him to think about everything he did understand.

3 I observed her doing a practice test, and realised she was writing full sentences to answer the early questions. This meant she was missing the rest of the passage because she couldn't write and listen at the same time. I taught her to write notes for the answers and to concentrate on listening rather than writing. In the end, she passed her exam.

Chapter 3
B

signposting: telling the students which direction the talk is headed in. For example, the teacher might say *Now we will move on to ...* . Signposting makes teacher talk more interactive and helps the students to follow the twists and turns of any extended piece of speech. It also allows students to monitor their comprehension.

macro-markers: full expressions or phrases used to organise the content of what we are saying. For example, *Before moving on to our next point, let's summarise ...* , *Now we are going on to discuss the implications.* Macro-markers provide signposts (see above) to allow our students to follow extended speech.

linear sequence: telling a story chronologically (literally, in a line). This is easier for students to follow as they do not need mentally to jump around in different time periods.

redundancy: a feature of authentic speech in which words or phrases are used despite being unnecessary. Some use of redundancy can be helpful as it means students do not have to concentrate on every word.

colloquialisms: words and expressions that are only used in very informal circumstances among a specialised or local population. Colloquialisms are used in spoken language (street talk) more than written. Teachers should avoid most colloquialisms because students usually cannot understand them and won't need them.

analogies: making reference to something (e.g. a cultural product, an object, a person) in order to describe something else. Many analogies are culture specific and even if the students understand the words, they may not see the point being made by the use of the analogy. Teachers should monitor their use of analogies carefully.

interaction: two-way involvement in an activity or talk so that all can participate. Teacher talk is often better when made interactive through allowing students to ask questions.

paralinguistic features: things that speakers do that help to communicate the message, but which do not involve language use (e.g. gestures and facial expressions). Teachers should use these to help communicate their message.

monitoring: checking that everything is going to plan. Teachers need to monitor while speaking; they can do this by watching the faces of the students, asking questions or asking students to summarise or recap.

C

Extract 1
Level and type of student: level 2 (between elementary and pre-intermediate), children
Difficulties: getting the rhythm right.

Extract 2
Level and type of student: pre-intermediate, adult
Difficulties: some colloquial English (*get away, last-minute*) and other difficult vocabulary (*feed in, database*); quite long, complex sentences.

Extract 3
Level and type of student: intermediate, business English
Difficulties: vocabulary (*share price, strategy, current trading environment, well-placed, take full advantage, economic upturn*), sentence length (very long), density (a lot of information for one sentence, with a high percentage of noun phrases), and complexity (the student has to hold the opening *despite* phrase in mind in the first part of the sentence and understand what *it* refers to).

Extract 4
Level and type of student: upper intermediate, adult
Difficulties: the third sentence is long, has a lot of description which may be difficult for students to visualise, and has some tricky vocabulary (*dripping in your own sweat*).

D
See table in Chapter 3, page 51.

Chapter 4
A

Need to know: the context – a woman has given a talk about cultural differences between Japan and the US or the UK.

Vocabulary to pre-teach: you could pre-teach *bow, shake hands* and *host* as these are topic-specific, important for the content of the listening passage and quite high-level for elementary students.

C

	Strengths	Weaknesses
Introduction 1	By introducing the key words, the teacher ensures that the students won't be hearing them for the first time on the recording. Speaks in short, clear sentences.	Gives far too much information so the students already know the content and are effectively 'doing the listening' twice.

Introduction 2	Personalises the content and gets the students involved by asking them to raise their hands. Shows enthusiasm for the topic.	Doesn't let the students as a whole make their own suggestions; only picks one student. Completely dominates the conversation, cutting Hassan off to correct his English without giving him a chance to extend his statement.
Introduction 3	Personalises the topic by getting the students to come up with their own ideas. Gives the students time to prepare their thoughts. Checks instructions.	Could have given a gentler lead into the topic; the students may be stuck for ideas without any concrete examples provided.

1

We're going to listen to a monologue about motivation. The speaker's going to talk about a number of factors that motivate people at work. He's going to mention something called the four Cs. These stand for connection, contentment, context and climate. The first one, connection, means feeling connected to the company. The second one, contentment, is whether the worker actually enjoys what he or she is doing. Context is about the company's systems and organisation. The last C, climate, is about the company culture and managers listening to staff and appreciating their input.

2

T: OK, put your hands up if these things motivate you at work. Money! Who's motivated by a good salary? Lots of you! What about recognition? Do you like to be recognised for your abilities? What about responsibility? Hands up if you like to be responsible for things at work? Lots of you again! Hassan, tell us what you are responsible for in your company.

S: I responsible for …

T: I'm responsible for …

S: I'm responsible for write contracts.

T: For writing contracts. Great. And that motivates you?

S: Yes.

3

T: OK, we're going to listen to someone speaking about motivation. First, can you take a pen and paper and spend three minutes writing down what motivates you at work. Just write a list; you don't need to write full sentences. Do this on your own, then you'll share your ideas in groups. OK? So what are we going to write?

S: A list of things that motivate us at work.

T: That's right. OK, three minutes.

Chapter 5

The activity involves a number of eggs and a prize, which is usually something like a big bar of chocolate. The students work in pairs. One of them is blindfolded. I usually use a tie or a piece of cloth as the blindfold. The student that isn't blindfolded has to give directions to their partner, who walks around the classroom trying to reach the prize. The students aren't allowed to guide each other by touching; only by speaking English.

The twist is that the prize keeps moving. Well, to be more specific, the teacher keeps moving the prize. The second twist is that there are a number of eggs placed on the floor. Obviously, the

students don't want to step on these, so the student giving instructions has to ॑
blindfolded student doesn't go too close to the eggs.
The activity is good for giving directions and instructions, and it's fun.

1

All of the while-listening activities would be appropriate except:

- Participating actively – it is difficult to see how the students could do this with such a high-level, high-content passage.
- Dictation – this is possible, but the passage as a whole, being very dense and complex, does not lend itself well to dictation. With such a difficult recording, comprehension would be the main goal.
- Listen and do – the passage is very high-level, and aimed at adults. They would probably want to focus their full attention on the content without having to do too much.

4

a 5   **b** 3   **c** 1   **d** 4   **e** 2

1 Label the photos

This is a purposeful activity. It is quite motivating and uses a visual stimulus. The context is authentic in that we often talk about photos while showing them, although we would not expect the listener to guess who is who. The activity is suitable for the input.

2 Draw a map

This is purposeful. It is potentially engaging for the students and involves integration of skills: drawing at the same time as listening. It is quite authentic; people sometimes do this in real life. It is suitable for the input, which is about places.

3 Guess the subject

This is purposeful. As a type of guessing game, it is engaging, and it gives the students a reason to listen carefully. As a genre, it is completely authentic in its own 'game-playing' terms. It is a suitable activity for the input.

4 Make notes

This is quite purposeful as it provides practice in something many students will need to do. The activity is authentic – we often make notes while listening to phone messages. The activity is suitable for the input.

5 Listen and do

This is potentially purposeful in that there is a tangible result if they follow the instructions: a meal. It is authentic in the genre of the cooking programme. It is not suitable, however, in the context of a language class: the students are unlikely to have the required ingredients and kitchen accessories to hand! It could work in certain contexts, however, if the students took the recording home and tried to follow the instructions. A more suitable classroom activity might be making notes or ordering pictures of the actions described.

Chapter 6

1

A (Discussion)

This seems appropriate as it gets the students discussing the subject of the passage. They then go on to personalise the task by choosing someone they admire. This is an effective exercise as they can use the model to help them prepare. It is also quite a realistic task that can be tailored to students with different interests and of different ages.

B (Creative response)

This is an appropriate task for a worldly, adult class with an interest in political figures such as Mandela. The task requires a lot of background knowledge and some imagination. A class with little world knowledge or interest in political figures would probably not be very motivated by the task.

C (Critical response)

This is perhaps not the most appropriate task because it focuses on the speaker and what the speaker knows, whereas the focus should be on Mandela's life. Also, the students have had no chance to react personally to the content. The task is quite difficult in that it requires a lot of inferring. It asks the students to give reasons for their answers, which is a good idea as it forces them to listen carefully for details that they can use to justify their answers.

D (Deconstructing)

This seems rather inappropriate if it is the first post-listening task. There should be at least some focus on the content of the passage before beginning detailed language analysis. The students have had no chance to react personally to the content.

E (Reconstructing)

This seems like an appropriate task as a way to check understanding, and it is communicative. However, it doesn't allow for any personal reaction to the text and might be very challenging for an intermediate class as the passage is quite long.

2

1 An anecdote

After a ten-hour journey from London I was really happy to have arrived at my host family's house in Colombia. They were extremely friendly even though I spoke only a little Spanish, and they plied me with lemonade and made me feel comfortable. After a while, the mother asked me: 'Estas casado?' I thought she was asking me if I was tired, so I said: 'Si, un poco,' which means, 'yes, a little'. Suddenly everyone laughed. Later I found out that 'casado' means 'married', and 'cansado' means 'tired'. So she'd asked me if I was married and I'd said: 'Oh, a little'!

(from Clare, A and Wilson, J (2007) *Total English Advanced Workbook*, Pearson Education, page 12)

2 A joke

A couple owned a cat, but the man hated it. So one day he decided to get rid of it. He drove ten blocks and threw the cat out of the car window. But when he got home, there the cat was, lying on the doormat. So the next day he drove twenty blocks and threw the cat into a river. But, on entering his driveway, the cat was there again, fast asleep by the door. So the next day he drove fifteen blocks, took a left, took a right, went down the motorway, crossed a couple of bridges and threw the cat into a large hole in the ground. After driving a while, he called his wife. 'Is the cat there?' he asked. 'Yes,' she said. 'Why do you ask?' 'OK, put the cat on the phone. I'm lost and I need directions home.'

(from Clare, A and Wilson, J (2007) *Total English Advanced Workbook*, Pearson Education, page 24)

3 A ghost story

The two boys were swimming when a girl in a blue dress appeared at the bank of the river. She called out to them, 'Don't swim there! It's dangerous!' The boys were strong swimmers and didn't believe her. 'What are you talking about?' one of them shouted. 'There's a whirlpool further ahead. Get out now!' The boys still didn't really believe her, but there was something about the urgency in her voice that made them listen. Reluctantly, they swam to the bank of the river and got out. They walked along the river and sure enough there was a huge whirlpool fifty feet from where they had been swimming. They put their clothes on and walked into the tiny town. The roads were blocked.

'What's going on?' they asked a stranger. He indicated a huge poster hung u; too street. The picture showed a little girl in a blue dress. 'Maggie Doyle's funeral. She was just t years old. Died two days ago. Drowned in the whirlpool.' The boys looked at each other. It was the same girl who had warned them twenty minutes before.

Chapter 7

A

a 8   b 2   c 9   d 11   e 4   f 7   g 6   h 5   i 1   j 10   k 3

Order of stages: 2, 6, 4, 5, 9, 3, 7, 11, 1, 10, 8

Chapter 8

A

2

a   Multiple choice

Advantages: takes little time for students to complete (no need to write); allows large number of items; easy to mark.

Disadvantages: students can guess and get lucky; students need to hold multiple choices in their head while listening; a lot of reading.

b   True or false?

Advantages: takes little time for students to complete (no need to write); allows large number of items; easy to mark.

Disadvantages: students can guess and get lucky.

c   Answer the questions

Advantages: flexible exercise type for any listening; can get to the heart of the content.

Disadvantages: answers may be partially correct; less reliable because individual teachers may prefer shorter/longer answers or accept different interpretations; often unclear whether spelling and grammar count towards the grade; often tests memory not comprehension.

d   Listen and write a reply

Advantages: potentially realistic.

Disadvantages: tests writing ability as well as listening; often unclear if spelling and grammar count; less reliable because individual teachers may prefer shorter/longer answers or have different criteria for grading.

e   Complete the notes

Advantages: short writing part so the students' attention should not be too divided; words on the page guide students through the passage so they can monitor their understanding.

Disadvantages: tests writing ability as well as listening – even if the student understands correctly, he or she may be unable to render the answer in written form; often unclear if grammar/word grammar and spelling count.

B

1

a   Use a self-access centre.

Advantages: it is learner-centred; there are probably a variety of materials to choose from; there may be worksheets so that the students can measure their progress; there may be opportunities to do extensive listening and use authentic materials such as the news.

Difficulties: students need a thorough induction in how to make the most of the self-access centre;

there may be difficulties with timing especially if the students also work – it is probably not always possible for them to go to the school/university when the self-access centre is open.

b Keep a portfolio of your experiences of listening to English.

Advantages: students build up a long-term record of achievement which acts as a tool to measure progress; portfolios can be discussed in class so that a community of learning is built up.

Difficulties: keeping students motivated to do this over the long term is not easy; the nature of listening makes it difficult to store physical evidence such as recordings, transcripts, cassettes or CDs.

c Look regularly at websites such as www.youtube.com to hear people talking about things you are interested in.

Advantages: students can choose their own listening material from a vast range; many students are Internet-savvy and used to working with the technology; most listening on the net is authentic; there is a variety of intensive and extensive listening, though mainly the former.

Difficulties: much of the listening on the net is ungraded and difficult for low-level students; there is so much on the net that students might need guidance on how to find what they are looking for.

d Listen to audio books for a certain amount of time a day.

Advantages: if the book is to the student's taste, this is very enjoyable and rewarding; the regularity of daily listening has long-term benefits.

Difficulties: finding the appropriate time, especially if the students are busy people; finding the appropriate audio book at the right level and of interest to the individual.

e Do homework, e.g. write a report on something you watched/listened to, that involves listening to the radio or watching television programmes.

Advantages: brings the outside world into the classroom; gets the students to watch with real purpose and reflect; develops good metacognitive strategies for learning the language.

Difficulties: finding programmes in English that are of the appropriate level and interest for the students.

f Interview people in the community who speak English as their L1 or who are highly proficient speakers.

Advantages: genuine communication will be involved and students will be able to practise listening and speaking in real time; the person interviewed may have interesting things to say from a cultural angle.

Difficulties: it may be hard to find highly proficient speakers in the community; it takes time and may involve travel, which isn't ideal for busy, working students.

g Have an evening in which the whole class gets together and watches a film in English.

Advantages: it's a great way for a class to socialise and learn some English; the content is authentic and may be very motivating; most students enjoy watching films.

Difficulties: this needs to be organised: booking a room or meeting at the cinema, choosing the right film, finding a time convenient for everybody, including the teacher; finding films for lower-level students is difficult so some pre-viewing preparation may be required.

2

1 I sometimes provide recorded correction of written work, using cassettes. The students submit a piece of writing which they did for homework. They number the lines. I read it once silently, then the second time I read it I record myself making comments. So I might say, 'in line 20 you've made a mistake with the verb tense' or 'I like the expression you used in line 6'. I give the students their own cassette which they listen to at home. Then they correct their writing. The benefit is that they've also had some authentic and motivating listening practice. It's a real dialogue between teacher and student.

2 At the language school we have a bank of cassettes and a self-access centre. What I do at the beginning of every course is get the students to choose a cassette that sounds interesting to them based on its title. They listen to it and take notes. Then, at the end, they tell each other about what they listened to. Sometimes I also get them to write a short review of the cassette for future students to refer to. It's a way to personalise the listening content of the course, and hopefully to encourage them to come and listen in their own time.

3 I've used English language guided tours at local tourist attractions for students to practise their listening. There are various tours in museums and galleries which are conducted in English, and it's a chance for the children to learn something about their own culture while also practising their listening.

4 I get my students to interview local English speakers. Here in Warsaw there are a lot of expatriate workers who are happy to give up a few minutes of their time. My students ask questions about this person's work, hobbies and opinions of Poland. The students record the interview and play it back for language analysis and to hear how native speakers pronounce words. It's very motivating.

CHAPTER NOTES AND FURTHER READING

Further reading

General: The following books are excellent general guides to the teaching of listening in EFL:

Anderson, A and Lynch, T (1988) *Listening*, Oxford University Press.

Brown, G (1990) *Listening to Spoken English* (2nd edn) Longman.

Flowerdew, J and Miller, L (2005) *Second Language Listening: Theory and Practice*, Cambridge University Press.

Rixon, S (1986) *Developing Listening Skills*, ELTS.

Rost, M (1990) *Listening in Language Learning*, Longman.

Rost, M (1991) *Listening in Action*, Prentice Hall.

Rost, M (2002) *Teaching and Researching Listening*, Pearson Education.

Underwood, M (1989) *Teaching Listening*, Longman.

Ur, P (1984) *Teaching Listening Comprehension*, Cambridge University Press.

White, G (1998) *Listening*, Oxford University Press.

Chapter 1

9 The facts about animals and listening come from Hartley, K, Macro, C and Taylor, P (2000) *Hearing in Living Things*, Heinemann.

10 Harmer, J (2004) *How to Teach Writing*, Pearson Education.

11 Pinker, S (1994) *The Language Instinct*, William Morrow and Company.

11 Kelly, G (2000) *How to Teach Pronunciation*, Pearson Education.

12 Nunberg, G (2001) *The Way we Talk Now: Commentaries on Language and Culture*, Houghton Mifflin Reference Books.

12 The information about question tags comes from Biber, D, Conrad, S and Leech, G (2002) *Longman Student Grammar of Spoken and Written English*, Longman.

13 Altman, R (1989) *The Video Connection*, Houghton Mifflin Company.

14 Multiple Intelligences theory was proposed by Gardner, H (1983) *Frames of Mind – The Theory of Multiple Intelligences*, Basic Books.

14 Richards, J (1983) 'Listening comprehension: approach, design, procedure' *TESOL Quarterly* 17(2): 219–240.

15 Harada, T (1998) *CATESOL Journal* 10 (1): 51–70, cited in Celce-Murcia, M and Olshtain, E (2000) *Discourse and Context in Language Teaching: A Guide for Language Teachers*, Cambridge University Press.

15 Rost, M (1990) *Listening in Language Learning*, Longman.

17 Nunan, D (1997) 'Listening in language learning' *The Language Teacher* www.jalt-publications.org/tlt/files/97/sep/nunan.html.

18 Chomsky, N (1957) *Syntactic Structures*, Mouton.

18 Krashen, S (1982) *Principles and Practice in Second Language Acquisition*, Pergamon.

18 Krashen, S and Terrell, T (1983) *The Natural Approach: Language Acquisition in the Classroom*, Alemany Press.

18 Asher, J, Kusudo, J and de la Torre, R (1974) 'Learning a second language through commands: the second field test' *Modern Language Journal* 58: 24–32.

19 The passage about Belgium is from the author's data.

20 The example is from Wilson, J with Clare, A (2007) *Total English Advanced Student's Book*, Pearson Education.

21 The quotations from students concerning listening are from the author's data.

22 Ganong (1980) cited by Aitchison, J in Brown, G et al (eds) (1994) *Language and Understanding*, Oxford University Press.

24 Helgesen, M (1998) 'Top-down, bottom-up listening and context: a response to Richard Cauldwell' *The Language Teacher* www.jalt-publications.org/tlt/files/98/oct/helgesen.html.

Further reading

Spoken English: See Thornbury, S (2005) *How to Teach Speaking*, Pearson Education. For useful discussions of the characteristics of spoken English, see Brown, G (1990) *Listening to Spoken English* (2nd edn) Longman; Brown, G and Yule, G (1983) *Teaching the Spoken Language*, Cambridge University Press. For a focus on pronunciation, see Kelly, G (2000) *How to Teach Pronunciation*, Longman; Underhill, A (1994) *Sound Foundations*, Macmillan; Jenkins, J (2000) *The Phonology of English as an International Language*, Oxford University Press.

English as a global language: See Crystal, D (1997) *English as a Global Language*, Cambridge University Press; Cooper, R (1982) *Language Spread*, Centre for Applied Linguistics; Tunstall, J and Machin, D (1999) *The Anglo-American Media Connection*, Oxford University Press; Jenkins, J (2007) *English as a Lingua Franca*, Oxford University Press.

Multiple Intelligences: Gardner, H (1983) *Frames of Mind – The Theory of Multiple Intelligences*, Basic Books; for practical applications of the theory, see Puchta, H and Rinvolucri, M (2005) *Multiple Intelligences in EFL: Exercises for Secondary and Adult Students*, Helbling Languages.

History of ELT: Howatt, A with Widdowson, H G (2004) *A History of English Language Teaching* (2nd edn) Oxford University Press.

Chapter 2

25 The quotation at the top of the page is from Sweden Graphics, quoted in Fiell, C and Fiell, P (eds) (2003) *Graphic Design for the 21st Century*, Taschen.

28 The passage about Bush is from BBC News at 6.00, 17 November 2005.

30 Widdowson, H (1985) 'Against dogma: a reply to Michael Swan' *ELT Journal* 39(3): 158–161.

30 Carter, R (1998) 'Orders of reality: CANCODE, communication, and culture' *ELT Journal* 52(1): 43–56.

30 The table is based on Underwood, M (1989) *Teaching Listening*, Longman.

33 Bell, J and Gower, R quoted in Tomlinson, B (ed) (1998) *Materials Development in Language Teaching*, Cambridge University Press.

34 Nisbet, J and Shucksmith, J (1986) *Learning Strategies*, Routledge and Kegan Paul.

34 Oxford, R (1990) *Language Learning Strategies: What Every Teacher Should Know*, Newbury House.

34 Chamot, A and O'Malley, M (1990) *Learning Strategies in Second Language Acquisition*, Cambridge University Press.

38 Cotton, D, Falvey, D and Kent, S (2001) *Market Leader Upper-intermediate Student's Book*, Pearson Education.

Further reading

Strategies: see Oxford, R (1990) *Language Learning Strategies: What Every Teacher Should Know*, Newbury House; Chamot, A and O'Malley, M (1990) *Learning Strategies in Second Language Acquisition*, Cambridge University Press; Chamot, A, Barnhardt, S, El-Dinary, P B and Robbins, J (1999) *The Learning Strategies Handbook*, Pearson Education.

Chapter 3

40 The Conklin quotation can be found at http://en.thinkexist.com/quotes/robert_conklin.

41 The Swiss saying appears in Woodward, T (1992) *Ways of Training*, Pilgrims Longman.

42 *The Joe Show* is referred to in Nunan, D and Miller, L (eds) (1995) *New Ways in Teaching Listening*, TESOL.

42 Davies, A (2002) 'Using teacher-generated biography as input material' *ELT Journal* 56: 359–367.

44 Jackson, J and Bilton, L (1994) quoted in Jordan, R (1997) *English for Academic Purposes*, Cambridge University Press.

47 The 'Teaching Unplugged' website is http://groups.yahoo.com/group/dogme.

47 Kay, S, Jones, V and Kerr, P (2002) *Inside Out Pre-intermediate Student's Book*, Macmillan.

48 Sherman, J (2003) *Using Authentic Video in the Language Classroom*, Cambridge University Press.

49 This statement is commonly attributed to the architect Frank Lloyd Wright.

50 Falla, T (1994) *Headway Elementary Video Activity Book*, Oxford University Press.

52 Prensky, M (2005/2006) *Educational Leadership*, 63(4): 8–13.

53 Abbs, B, Barker, C, Freebairn, I and Wilson, J (2007) *Postcards* (2nd edn), Pearson.

54 White, G (1998) *Listening*, Oxford University Press.

54 Cunningham, S and Moor, P (2005) *New Cutting Edge*, Pearson.

54 Soars, J and Soars, L (1996) *New Headway*, Oxford University Press.

54 Kay, S and Jones, V (2003) *Inside Out*, Macmillan.

54 Clare, A and Wilson, J (2006) *Total English*, Pearson.

56 The reference to the use of airline masks is from Nick Dawson (personal correspondence).

56 Soars, J and Soars, L (1996) *New Headway Intermediate*, Oxford University Press.

Further reading

Teacher talk: For an excellent discussion of how to grade language for poor L2 listeners, see Echevarria, J and Graves, A (1998) *Sheltered Content Instruction*, Pearson. For advice on how to deliver more effective lectures to students whose L1 is not English, see Lynch, T in Flowerdew, J (ed) (1994) *Academic Listening*, Cambridge University Press; Evans Nachi, H and Kinoshita, C (2006) 'Lecturing in miniature' *English Teaching Professional* 43: 28–30; see also Maley, A (2000) *The Language Teacher's Voice*, Macmillan.

Tasks: see Willis, J (1996) *A Framework for Task-Based Learning*, Longman; Nunan, D (1989) *Designing Tasks for the Communicative Classroom*, Cambridge University Press; Ellis, R (2003) *Task-based Language Learning and Teaching*, Oxford University Press. For useful lists specifically of tasks for listening, see Morley, J in Celce-Murcia, M (ed) (2001) *Teaching English as a Second or Foreign Language*, Heinle and Heinle.

Chapter 4

60 The quotation at the beginning of the chapter is from Gary Buck, in Mendelsohn, D and Rubin, J (eds) (1995) *A Guide for the Teaching of Second Language Listening*, Dominie Press.

61 The table summarising the sequence is based on Rixon, S (1986) *Developing Listening Skills*, ELTS.

63 The research was from Cole, R, Jakimik, J and Cooper, W (1980) 'Segmenting speech into words' *The Journal of the Acoustical Society of America* 67(4): 1323–1332.

66 Cunningham, S and Moor, P (2005) *New Cutting Edge Intermediate* (page 19, 1a), Pearson Education.

67 Soars, J and Soars, L (1993) *Headway Elementary* (page 56), Oxford University Press.

70 Yuko Torimitsu described these exercises in personal correspondence with the author.

70 Eric Clapton (1977) 'Wonderful Tonight' from *Slowhand*, Polydor/Umgd.

71 Cunningham, S and Moor, P (2003) *Cutting Edge Advanced* (page 98: The Unicorn in the Garden by James Thurber), Pearson Education.

71 Jeffries, A (2001) *Clockwise Advanced* (page 40, Listening Exercise 1), Oxford University Press.

72 This story comes from Middleton, N (2003) *Going to Extremes: Mud, Sweat and Frozen Tears*, Pan Books.

76 White, J and Lightbown, P (1984) 'Asking and answering in ESL classes' *Canadian Modern Language Review* 40: 228–244.

76 Long, M H and Sato, C (1983) 'Classroom foreigner talk discourse: forms and functions of teachers' questions' in Seliger, H and Long, M H (eds) *Classroom Orientated Research in Second Language Acquisition*, Newbury House, quoted in Lee, Y (2006) *TESOL Quarterly* 40(4): 691–713.

76 The teacher–student exchange is from Mehan, H (1985) quoted in Weissberg, R (2006) *Connecting Speaking and Writing in Second Language Writing Instruction* (page 126), The University of Michigan Press.

77 Chang, A and Read, J (2006) 'The effects of listening support on the listening performance of EFL learners' *TESOL Quarterly* 40(2): 375–397.

77 The quotation about pre-listening is from www.onestopenglish.com.

78 Bell, J and Gower, R (1999) *Advanced Matters* (page 38, Exercises 1 and 2), Pearson Education.

78 Kay, S and Jones, V (2003) *Inside Out Elementary* (page 14, Exercises 1 and 2), Macmillan.

79 The quotation is from Nuttall, C (1996) *Teaching Reading Skills in a Foreign Language*, Heinemann.

Chapter 5

84 The monologue about artwork is from Soars, J and Soars, L (2003) *New Headway Advanced* (page 139), Oxford University Press.

84 Colin Cherry's research is from Cherry, C (1953) 'Some experiments on the recognition of speech, with one and with two ears' *The Journal of Acoustical Society of America* 25(5): 975–979.

86 The story is from Clare, A and Wilson, J (2007) *Total English Advanced Workbook* (page 22), Pearson Education.

90 Ten reasons for using dictation appear in the opening chapter of Davis, P and Rinvolucri, M (1988) *Dictation*, Cambridge University Press.

95 The 'Grab the word' activity can be seen in the games section of Harmer, J (2007) *How to Teach English* DVD, Pearson Education.

Further reading

Dictation: see Davis, P and Rinvolucri, M (1988) *Dictation*, Cambridge University Press; there is also an excellent section on dictation in Woodward, T (1991) *Models and Metaphors in Language Teacher Training*, Cambridge University Press.

Note-taking: see Mendelsohn, D and Rubin, J (1995) *A Guide for the Teaching of Second Language Listening*, Dominie Press.

Chapter 6

100 The post-listening discussion activity is from Clare, A and Wilson, J (2006) *Total English Intermediate* (page 12), Pearson Education.

101 The comments are from Carter, R (2004) *Language and Creativity*, Routledge.

104 The Gary Buck quote is from Mendelsohn, D and Rubin, J (1995) *A Guide for the Teaching of Second Language Listening*, Dominie Press.

105 The comments about the exchange of information are from Pennycook, A, quoted in McKenzie, J and Bryce Davies, H (1990) *Filling the Tool Box, Classroom Strategies to Engender Student Questioning*, FNO.ORG.

107 Gairns, R and Redman, S (2005) *Natural English Pre-intermediate Listening Booklet* (page 24), Oxford University Press.

Chapter 7

111 The questions teachers ask about their short-term role are adapted from Richards, J and Lockhart, C (1994) *Reflective Teaching in Second Language Classrooms*, Cambridge University Press.

114 The cigar story is from Acklam, R and Crace, A (2006) *Total English Upper Intermediate* (page 174), Pearson Education.

115 The extract is from Abbs, B and Freebairn, I (2005) *Sky 2* (page 46), Longman.

116 The extract is from Johnson, C (2006) *Intelligent Business Pre-intermediate* (page 128, What motivates you to work harder?), Pearson Education.

117 Penny Ur's comment is from Ur, P (1996) *A Course in Language Teaching*, Cambridge University Press.

118 The top extract is from Dellar, H and Walkley, A (2005) *Innovations Elementary* (page 135), Thomson Heinle.

118 The bottom extract is from Jeffries, A (2001) *Clockwise Advanced* (page 11), Oxford University Press.

125 The description of the project is from Kern, R (2000) *Literacy and Language Teaching*, Oxford University Press.

132 Harding, K (2007) *English for Specific Purposes*, Oxford University Press.

Further reading

Planning: for a general discussion of planning, see Woodward, T (2001) *Planning Lessons and Courses*, Cambridge University Press.

Film: see Stempleski, S and Tomalin, B (2001) *Film*, Oxford University Press.

Technology/Authentic materials: Dudeney, G and Hockly, N (2007) *How to Teach English with Technology*, Pearson Education.

Young learners: see Vale, D and Feunteun, A (1995) *Teaching Children English*, Cambridge University Press; Cameron, L (2001) *Teaching Languages to Young Learners*, Cambridge University Press; Moon, J (2000) *Children Learning English*, Macmillan.

ESP: see Dudley-Evans, T and St John, M (1998) *Developments in ESP – A multi-disciplinary approach*, Cambridge University Press; Hutchinson, T and Waters, A (1987) *English for Specific Purposes*, Cambridge University Press; Harding, K (2007) *English for Specific Purposes*, Oxford University Press; Flowerdew, J (ed) (1994) *Academic Listening*, Cambridge University Press; Jordan, R (1997) *English for Academic Purposes*, Cambridge University Press.

Chapter 8

136 The analogy is from Black, P and Wiliam, D (1998) 'Assessment and classroom learning' *Assessment in Education* 5(1): 7–74.

137 Harmer, J (2007) *How to Teach English*, Pearson Education.

139 The 'Can do' statements come from the Council of Europe, *Common European Framework of Reference for Languages: Learning, teaching, assessment* (2001), Cambridge University Press.

141 The three basic elements that need to be assessed are from Tudor, I (1996) *Learner-centredness as Language Education*, Cambridge University Press.

141 The 21 self-assessment studies are from Blanche, P and Merino, B (1989) 'Self-assessment of foreign language skills: implications for teachers and researchers' *Language Learning* 39:313–340.

143 The comments on self-access are from Gardner, D and Miller, L (eds) (1999) *Establishing Self-Access: From theory to practice*, Cambridge University Press.

Further reading

Assessment: Buck, G (2001) *Assessing Listening*, Cambridge University Press; Bachman, L (1990) *Fundamental Considerations in Language Testing*, Oxford University Press; Genesee, F and Upshur, J (1996) *Classroom-Based Evaluation in Second Language Education*, Cambridge University Press; Hughes, A (2002) *Testing for Language Teachers* (2nd edn), Cambridge University Press; for a general discussion of exams, see Burgess, S and Head, K (2005) *How to Teach for Exams*, Longman.
Extensive listening: Prowse, P 'Extensive listening', www.cambridge.org/elt/readers; Dawson, N (2005) *Penguin Readers Listening*, Pearson Education.
Action Research: Wallace, M (1998) *Action Research for Language Teachers*, Cambridge University Press.
Self-Access: Gardner, D and Miller, L (1999) *Establishing Self-Access: From theory to practice*, Cambridge University Press.

Useful website addresses for listening

Websites have a habit of changing or disappearing altogether, and websites that were once free may now charge a fee for their use. At the time of writing, the lists below represent some of the best the web can offer for listening.

News/current affairs-based

www.bbc.co.uk
www.bbc.co.uk/bbcfour/audiointerviews
www.voanews.com/english/portal.cfm
www.cnn.com
www.cbsnews.com
www.euronews.net
www.britfm.com

ELT/ESL-based

www.esl-lab.com   Free. Has easy, medium and difficult levels – very useful grading. Includes pre-, while- and post-listening exercises. Rather obviously scripted material, but a very good selection. American English.
www.EnglishListening.com   A pay site, but has a guest area with around thirty free recordings. Authentic and fast. Comes with questions, answers and a transcript. American English.
www.cdlponline.org   Free and very extensive range of subjects suitable for working adults. It consists of people reading news stories, often at very slow speed. Some videos. American English.
www.esl.about.com/homework/esl/cs/listeningresource/index.html   Good selection, but mainly quizzes. Scripted. Variety of accents.
www.eviews.net/accentsinenglish.html   A pay site. Comes with worksheets, comprehension questions and transcripts. Extended authentic listening for intermediate to advanced students. Many different accents.
www.bbc.co.uk/worldservice/learningenglish   Check the 'Watch and Listen' section. Free, authentic (though quite UK-centric) and regularly updated. Includes scripts and definitions of key vocabulary.

For teachers to make recordings

http://audacity.sourceforge.net

GLOSSARY

This glossary contains entries for all the terms printed in **bold** in *How to Teach Listening*.

achievement tests – tests that are designed to measure what has been learned over an extended period, for example a whole course of study or a whole term.

action research – a type of research in which the researcher (in this case, a teacher) takes a role as a participant, looking at the effects of his or her own practice on the students' performance in class. The goal is to implement change through a cycle of observation and experimentation.

adjacency pairs – utterances and responses that normally come in pairs (e.g. *How are you? Fine, thank you. Have a good weekend. Same to you.*). Question and answer is the most common form of adjacency pair.

appropriacy – choosing language that is not just correct but also appropriate to the situation, in terms of who we are talking to and how formal or informal we want to be.

assimilation – the way in which sounds modify each other when they meet, usually across word boundaries. For example, *thin boy* sounds like *thimboy* in connected speech; *I'm right behind you* sounds like *I'm ripe behind you*; *good king* sounds like *goog king*.

Audiolingualism – a methodology popular in the 1940s–1970s, which relied on avoidance of error and used repeated and extensive drilling. The theory behind Audiolingualism stems from behaviourism, which posits the idea that language learning is the formation of good 'habits' through repetition.

authentic – a term used to describe texts or language usually produced for native or highly proficient speakers of a language (i.e. with no concessions for a foreign language speaker). An alternative definition suggests that it is the purpose of the text that gives it its authenticity: if the text or language is not originally written in order to teach language, but to communicate genuine messages, then it is authentic.

authentic-based – a term used to describe texts that are written to contain the features of authentic language, such as hesitation, repetition and false starts, and are used for teaching purposes.

automaticity – the phenomenon of being able to function (in a foreign language) without needing to stop and think about the language.

It occurs when the learner has reached a stage of comfort in and with the language.

awareness-raising – a term used to describe the process of getting students to notice features of language such as grammar or pronunciation. It is usually achieved by pointing out an example of the feature and letting the students work independently to find other examples.

backchannel devices – sounds or expressions used to show that we are listening, for example *uh-huh, mhm, right*, etc.

behaviourism – the idea that behaviour can be conditioned through the use of Stimulus–Response–Reinforcement procedures so that people will learn good habits through constant reinforcement.

blog – a diary (or weblog) which can be accessed via the Internet.

bottom-up – an approach to understanding texts that is based on perception of sounds and words. It is a text-based approach as it focuses on building up the message word by word rather than on the students' background knowledge of the situation, topic or theme. (See *top-down*.)

chunk – a group of words that often appear together and may be pronounced as if they are one word. Some examples are: *see you later, How do you do? Have you ever … ? a dream come true, paid on commission.*

cognitive strategies – techniques that we use to tackle tasks and/or language learning materials; for example, guessing the meaning of unknown words from the context or taking notes during a lecture.

collocations – two or more words that often occur together (**collocate**). For example: *a cup of tea, an early riser, have breakfast, happy birthday, catch a plane.*

communicative competence – the ability to activate language to communicate real meaning, rather than just practising language in a controlled environment.

Communicative Language Teaching (CLT) – a methodological approach which began in the 1970s. It encourages students to communicate real meaning as a way of learning, and it emphasises authentic texts and contexts. It also has a strong humanistic slant, using the students' personal experiences to inform the content. Various offshoots include Suggestopedia and Total Physical Response.

compensation strategies – ways to make up for a skill deficit, or lack of grammar and vocabulary, in L2. For example, if a student doesn't know the correct word, he or she can try to explain it by using a synonym, miming, drawing a picture, etc.

comprehensible input – a term used to describe language which the students see or hear and which they more or less understand, even if it is slightly above their own language level.

concept questions – questions that teachers ask students in order to check that they understand the concept being presented. For example, after presenting the word *giant*, a teacher might ask *Is it big or small?*

consonant clusters – groups of consonants found together in words, for example, the *thr* in *throw* and *tch* in *catch*.

content – the information in, and meaning of, a text/task.

context – the environment (topic and linguistic) in which a word or phrase occurs.

delivery – the way in which input – particularly speech – is delivered (e.g. fast, slow, loud).

density – refers to the number of high content words which carry meaning, such as *machine*, *pretty* or *run* (rather than function words like *of* and *to*) in a passage. Some texts can be very dense – they contain a lot of information in few words.

dictogloss – a technique where students try to write down exactly what they have heard (delivered at a faster speed than a dictation) and then compare their versions with the original in order to see how they differ.

discourse analysis – the close evaluation of any text (written or spoken) bigger than a sentence or, usually, paragraph or utterance.

discourse markers – words and expressions that show the relationship between what went before and what comes after. For example: *to tell you the truth, as I was saying, as far as I'm concerned, mind you, as a matter of fact.*

discourse structures – the underlying organisational patterns in texts. Some examples include: *question – response, phenomenon – example, cause – effect.*

display questions – questions designed to elicit a pre-ordained response, usually a target grammatical feature.

distractors – incorrect options in any test which uses multiple-choice or true/false questions.

download – an audio or video file that can be transferred from a website to other technological devices (e.g. to an iPod, MP3 player or laptop).

elision – a phenomenon of pronunciation in connected speech, when one word slides into another and a sound is omitted. For example, in the sentence *I helped him*, the *h* in *him* is not pronounced, so it sounds like *I help Tim.*

emoticons – signs or characters used in texts, particularly emails and text messages, which show the underlying feelings behind the messages. Emoticons are often made using a combination of punctuation marks so that they resemble a face. A smiley face ':-)' means the writer is happy; a winking face ';-)' means the writer is being ironic. The word *emoticon* derives from a mix of *emotion* and *icon*.

ESP – English for specific purposes, a course of study. Included in 'specific purposes' are English for business, science and technology, nursing, academic purposes and others. ESP is characterised by a focus on the students' vocational or academic needs rather than a syllabus imposed by a book or institution. Other common features of ESP include specialised vocabulary and a task-oriented methodology.

exophoric – describes references that we make to phenomena, facts or things from outside the immediate context and which are not described explicitly. Exophoric references imply shared knowledge between speaker and listener or writer and reader. This means it is not necessary to describe them. For example, a news broadcast might open with, *Bush goes to China.* There is no need to explain who *Bush* is because the newsreader assumes this is common knowledge.

extensive – material which is longer than most classroom texts. Students might engage in extensive listening for pleasure rather than to answer comprehension questions or do tasks.

finely-tuned input – a passage of speech (e.g. teacher talk or a coursebook recording) which is pitched specifically at the level of the students. It may use very limited vocabulary or grammatical structures, and is designed to be easily comprehensible to the target audience.

formative assessment – evaluation of what a student knows or can do in the target language, in order to help formulate future planning of the course.

gap-fill – a text with a number of words omitted. The students' task is to complete the text with the correct words. Gap-fills are a common way to practise or test language. They are sometimes called 'fill in the blanks'.

gist – the general idea of a text.

Grammar-translation – a methodology that involved translating texts from L1 to L2 and vice versa. It also emphasised rote learning of vocabulary and verb tables. The methodology lost popularity with the arrival of more humanistic approaches in the 70s but is still used in many countries.

graphophonic – a term that describes the relationship between the way something is written and the way it sounds.

higher-order questions – questions that demand inferences and interpretation of the text rather than solely asking for the bald facts. An example of a higher-order question would be *Why is Jay Gatsby a tragic figure?* A lower-order question would be *How old was Jay Gatsby when he died?* (See *lower-order questions*.)

incidental vocabulary learning – when students learn vocabulary by listening or reading, even when the vocabulary is not the focus of the lesson or is not overtly taught. Incidental vocabulary learning sometimes occurs when students are doing some extensive skills work such as reading a novel, and a word keeps recurring. Although not 'taught', the word is 'learned' by the student.

information gap – a type of classroom exercise in which two students each have some information that their partner needs in order to complete a task. They share their information, using the target language, and close the gap together.

in-house materials – language-learning materials that are produced by people who work in the language school or institution where the materials will be used. These are commonly used in specialised classes (see *ESP*) for which no coursebook exists.

inner voice – words, phrases and sentences sounded out in the head but not uttered out loud.

input hypothesis – Stephen Krashen's theory that the only way we can learn foreign languages is by receiving comprehensible input that contains some features slightly above our current level.

intensive – pertaining to a short unit of work (e.g. a text or a course) that is very challenging and demands full concentration.

interactional – when materials or lessons encourage student participation.

interactive model – a model that recognises the simultaneous activation of bottom-up and top-down skills when we listen.

interactive whiteboards (IWBs) – boards which are connected to a computer so that any computer images can appear on them, using a data projector. IWBs can also be written on, and the contents of the board can be printed out or saved. IWBs can be used as classroom resources in place of traditional blackboards or whiteboards.

interlanguage – words and phrases as used by a speaker who is at a transitional stage of learning the language. Typically, there are errors in grammar and vocabulary because the speaker has not yet acquired the standard form.

international English – a slightly simplified form of English that is not associated with any particular region or nationality, but used by the people of many nations as a way to communicate when they don't know each other's language.

intonation – a feature of speech, when pitch changes to convey meaning or functionality.

intrusion – a feature of speech, when sounds that do not belong in a word are added (usually between vowels) to enable the speaker to say the phrase more easily. For example, the intrusive *w* after *to* in *I'd like to analyse* and the intrusive *r* after *spa* in *the spa is wonderful*.

lingua franca – a common language used to facilitate communication between two groups that don't speak each other's language. English is often used as a lingua franca.

listening sequences – whole units of work organised to practise the skill of listening. For example, pre-, while- and post-listening activities constitute a listening sequence.

lower-order questions – questions that ask the students to supply factual information from a text, and require no interpretation or inferring on the part of the student. (See *higher-order questions*.)

low surrender value – a way to describe words or phrases that are not perceived as useful, usually because they are not very common or they cannot be used immediately in a communicative context. In contrast, words of high surrender value can be applied easily to communicative contexts, and are perceived as useful.

macro-markers – full expressions used to organise the content of what we are saying. For example, *One of the biggest drawbacks of this solution was ...* is a macro-marker used to introduce a problem; compare with *however* (see *micro-markers*). *The last thing I'm going to talk about today* is a macro-marker used to introduce a final point; compare with *finally*.

metacognitive strategies – techniques that comprise general study habits, such as buying a dictionary, keeping a vocabulary notebook, looking for opportunities to practise, etc.

metalinguistic – a term which refers to how someone uses language in relation to other factors such as their culture or behaviour. Metalinguistic knowledge allows listeners to interpret what someone says by considering the way they have said it.

micro-markers – words or short expressions used to organise the content of what we are saying. For example, *so* is a micro-marker used to indicate a deduction; compare this with *as a result of this phenomenon* (see *macro-markers*). *Then* is a micro-marker used to indicate the passage of time; compare with *after a number of years*.

Multiple Intelligences theory – a theory proposed by Howard Gardner (see Chapter notes) that recognises different types of intelligence. In Gardner's original work, there were seven types: bodily-kinaesthetic, interpersonal, intrapersonal, linguistic, logical-mathematical, musical and spatial. Various others have been added since.

nonreciprocal – a situation in which the listener cannot interact with the speaker, e.g. when the listener is watching a speaker on television or listening to a recording. This type of listening may occur because of the medium used to transmit speech (e.g. radio) or because of social reasons (the listener does not have the power to interact with the speaker). (See *reciprocal*.)

noticing – the act of paying conscious attention to a feature of language.

opinion gap – a type of speaking exercise in which a student does not know what his or her partner thinks of an issue. They discuss the issue to find out.

overload – a phenomenon that takes place when listeners are given too much information for them to retain. The result is that they may switch off and stop listening altogether.

paralinguistic features – things that speakers do that help to communicate the message, but which do not involve language use. For example, speakers often use their hands, gestures and facial expressions while talking.

parallelism – patterns or frameworks of language that are repeated regularly, often with small variations. These typically occur in children's stories, fairy tales and nursery rhymes.

placement tests – tests that are used to assign a student to a class appropriate for his or her level. Placement tests are usually conducted at the beginning of a course.

planned input – passages of speech which are not spontaneous, but either scripted or worked out in detail beforehand in the mind of the speaker. Some planned input takes on the features of written language, e.g. formal speeches.

podcast – an audio file that subscribers can access automatically from the Internet and which goes straight to their MP3 players or iPods. The files often contain programmes similar to radio broadcasts. Once the subscriber has received the 'feed', they can listen to it whenever they wish.

pragmatics – the study of how language users produce and comprehend speech acts in real contexts. The field is concerned with the gap between the meaning of the words used and the meaning intended by the speaker. The ability to communicate intended meaning is known as *pragmatic competence* and it includes aspects such as knowledge of which register to use in the context, cultural factors including politeness, and knowledge of how to form the utterance.

process-based – an approach to a task that emphasises the stages leading to the outcome. It is primarily concerned with the students' development and the ways they go about tackling a task rather than the outcome.

product-based – an approach to a task that emphasises the outcome of a task rather than the way it is achieved.

proficiency tests – tests that measure overall ability. These are often used in order to categorise students. For example, if we want to know which exam is suitable for a student, we give them a proficiency test.

progress tests – tests that measure how much a student has improved over a given period of time or number of hours' study.

realia – real objects that are brought into the classroom and used for various pedagogical reasons, e.g. to illustrate vocabulary, provide stimulus for a task, etc.

reciprocal – a situation in which the listener can interact with the speaker, e.g. any face-to-face conversation, such as a customer talking to a shop assistant. (See *nonreciprocal.*)

redundancy – a feature of authentic speech in which words or phrases are used despite being unnecessary. Typically, we say more than necessary to convey meaning, often repeating information or saying *er* and *um* when we can't think of the correct word. Redundancy may help listeners as it means we do not have to focus on every word but can listen 'with half an ear'.

register – the formality or informality of a piece of language. *Hi* is a greeting in an informal register. *Pleased to meet you* is in a more formal register.

reliability – a feature of tests, when they give consistent results regardless of who is marking them.

repair strategies – used when a speaker makes an error which disrupts the flow of the conversation, or there is a miscommunication. In these cases we need to 'repair' the conversation by offering an alternative or explaining what we meant.

response elicitors – words or phrases used to get a response. For example: *See? Are you with me? Got it?*

roughly-tuned input – a passage of speech (e.g. teacher talk or a radio broadcast) which is not pitched specifically at the level of the students. It may include unknown vocabulary and other features that are slightly above the students'

level, but they should be able to understand the main idea without necessarily understanding every word. (See *finely-tuned input.*)

scaffold – support for the students, for example by asking questions which lead to a deeper understanding, providing frameworks for them to shape their responses or making suggestions to help them. The idea is to provide this support until the students are able to work more independently. Scaffolding was popularised by Vygotsky, a Russian educator working in the early to mid twentieth century.

schemata – underlying organisational patterns, structures or conceptual frameworks by which we perceive our experiences of the world.

scripts – routine situations as represented in our minds. For example, our script for doing the shopping may involve someone driving to a car park, walking around a supermarket, putting goods in a trolley, using a credit card to pay, etc. In different countries the script may be different because of cultural factors.

selective listening – listening for specific details and ignoring everything else.

semi-planned input – talks, anecdotes or other kinds of monologue (or sometimes dialogue) that the teacher has prepared to say to the students but without writing a script. There is an element of performance about semi-planned input but it is not spontaneous because the teacher is aware of an underlying structure and organisation.

semi-scripted – a way to tailor a recording to fit a certain level of student or contain a particular language point by providing guidance to the actors on what to say but not a full script. This facilitates the inclusion of some natural features of authentic speech while maintaining a degree of control over the content, and means that the recording can be used for a very specific teaching point and level.

signposting question – a question that leads students towards a better understanding of a piece of text or an issue. The question might suggest a new way of looking at an issue.

silent period – the months or years in which a person is internalising a language, usually by listening, but unable to produce it. We usually associate the silent period with children learning L1, but it can also apply to people learning L2. The silent period is typified by a sudden ending as the language learner rapidly develops his or her ability to speak.

socio-affective strategies – strategies that consist of students using social means to learn (e.g. by studying with a partner, talking regularly to more proficient speakers, etc). It also includes finding ways to increase self-motivation, such as rewarding oneself after success in a language task.

sociolinguistics – the study of how language and linguistic behaviour is influenced by social factors. It also looks at how language helps to maintain social roles in a community, and the features of language that occur under any given social conditions.

speech act – a way to describe the function of a piece of speech or its particular type. For example, explaining a rule, asking for help, telling a joke, etc, are all speech acts.

spontaneous input – when a teacher makes 'off-the-cuff', unplanned remarks in the target language. These provide authentic non-pedagogically-driven language input.

strategic – describes students who consciously use strategies to learn L2.

stress – the degree of emphasis that is given to different words or syllables. The stressed parts tend to be louder, longer and at a slightly higher pitch than the unstressed parts. We usually put the stress on the most important words in a sentence, which tend to be the nouns, main verbs and adjectives which carry information that is new to the listener.

student-centredness – a way of looking at the language lesson or course that places the students' needs, traits, characters and learning styles at the centre. The idea is sometimes used in opposition to teacher-centredness, which sees everything in the lesson from the viewpoint of what the teacher is doing.

sub-skills – the skills broken down into component parts. For example, reading is a skill; scanning a text for information is a sub-skill. Listening is a skill; listening for specific information is a sub-skill.

Suggestopedia – a methodological offshoot of Communicative Language Teaching (see above). The classes take place in a relaxing environment, perhaps with music. The input is through the teacher reading texts repeatedly, which the students follow.

summative assessment – evaluation of what a student has learned by the end of a period of study.

Task-Based Learning (TBL) – an approach where students have to learn language to complete tasks, rather than just learning language 'because it is there'.

think-aloud protocol – a method of research that involves participants/students speaking about how they are doing a task at the same time as doing it. This real-time commentary allows the researcher to measure and evaluate the students' strategy use.

top-down – an approach to texts which emphasises the listener's or reader's knowledge of the topic, theme or situation as much as the actual words heard (or read). It is a student-based approach because it relies on the students' schemata and background knowledge. (See *bottom-up*.)

topical – pertaining to issues that are currently relevant, e.g. in the news.

transactional – describes an encounter between people in which there is some kind of exchange (usually of information or perhaps goods for sale or services). Transactional dialogues are typified by short, formulaic sentences.

transcripts – the written script of a piece of speech. Transcripts are often found at the back of coursebooks.

tune-in period – when the students listen to a short section of a longer text in order to get used to the voice, speed, accent, etc of the speaker(s) before listening to the whole recording.

turns – passages spoken by an individual until he or she stops and the next person begins his or her turn. A turn may be as short as one word or as long as a speech.

utterance – spoken phrases, i.e. a word or group of words that form a unit before the next speaker says something.

validity – a feature of tests, when they do what they say they will do, and when they are a good measure of what they are testing.

visual aspect – something the students can see that reinforces the language they hear or read. For example, teachers may hold up pictures to reinforce vocabulary.

vocatives – ways of addressing someone. For example: *Dad, John, my darling, Sir.*